An Introduction To The Study Of Language

You are holding a reproduction of an original work that is in the public domain in the United States of America, and possibly other countries. You may freely copy and distribute this work as no entity (individual or corporate) has a copyright on the body of the work. This book may contain prior copyright references, and library stamps (as most of these works were scanned from library copies). These have been scanned and retained as part of the historical artifact.

This book may have occasional imperfections such as missing or blurred pages, poor pictures, errant marks, etc. that were either part of the original artifact, or were introduced by the scanning process. We believe this work is culturally important, and despite the imperfections, have elected to bring it back into print as part of our continuing commitment to the preservation of printed works worldwide. We appreciate your understanding of the imperfections in the preservation process, and hope you enjoy this valuable book.

700
B65

700
B65

AN INTRODUCTION TO THE STUDY OF LANGUAGE

BY

LEONARD BLOOMFIELD

Ph. D., Assistant Professor of Comparative Philology and German in the University of Illinois

NEW YORK
HENRY HOLT AND COMPANY
1914

TO
A. S. B.

PREFACE.

This little book is intended, as the title implies, for the general reader and for the student who is entering upon linguistic work. Its purpose is the same, accordingly, as that of Whitney's *Language and the Study of Language* and *The Life and Growth of Language*, books which fifty years ago represented the attainments of linguistic science and, owing to their author's clearness of view and conscientious discrimination between ascertained fact and mere surmise, contain little to which we cannot to-day subscribe. The great progress of our science in the last half-century is, I believe, nevertheless sufficient excuse for my attempt to give a summary of what is now known about language.

That the general reader needs such information as is here given was recognized by Whitney, who wrote, in the preface of his first-named book: 'It can hardly admit of question that at least so much knowledge of the nature, history, and classifications of language as is here presented ought to be included in every scheme of higher education.' While questions of a linguistic nature are everywhere a frequent subject of discussion, it is surprising how little even educated people are in touch with the scientific study of language. I hope that my book will furnish a simple aid for those who choose to make up this deficiency in our scheme of general education.

Students whose vocation demands linguistic knowledge are subjected in our universities to a detached course or two on details of the phonologic and morphologic history of such languages as Old English, Gothic, or Old French, — details which are meaningless and soon forgotten, if no instruction as to their concrete significance has preceded. To this method of presentation is due, I think, the dislike which so many workers in related fields bear toward linguistic study. I hope that this essay may help to introduce students of philosophy, psychology, ethnology, philology, and other related subjects to a juster acquaintance with matters of language.

In accordance with this twofold aim, I have limited myself to a presentation of the accepted doctrine, not even avoiding well-used standard examples. In a few places I have spoken of views that cannot claim more than probability, of hypotheses, and of problems yet to be solved, but I have done this explicitly and only because I think it fitting to indicate the direction in which our study is at present tending. Consequently the matter here presented is by no means my own, but rather the property of all students of language. It will be found in fuller form and with bibliographic support in the books mentioned in Chapter Ten, and these books I may therefore name as my more immediate sources.[1] It will be apparent, especially, that I depend for my psychology, general and linguistic, entirely on Wundt; I can only hope that I have not misrepresented his doctrine. The day is past when students of mental sciences could draw on their own fancy or on 'popular psychology' for their views of mental occurrence.

L. B.

---

[1] Of Sweet's *Primer of Phonetics* the first, and of Meillet's *Introduction* the second edition was used in compilation, but the later editions do not, I believe, differ materially as to anything here discussed.

CONTENTS.

CHAPTER I.
THE NATURE AND ORIGIN OF LANGUAGE.

		Page
1.	Expressive movements	1
2.	Gesture-language	4
3.	Writing	7
4.	Audible expressive movements	8
5.	Development of language in the child	10
6.	The origin of language	13
7.	Language constantly changing	16
8.	Social character of language	17

CHAPTER II.
THE PHYSICAL BASIS OF LANGUAGE.

1.	Unconsciousness of speech-movements	18
2.	Writing an imperfect analysis	19
3.	The vocal chords	24
4.	The velum	26
5.	Oral articulation	27
6.	Oral noise-articulations	28
7.	Musical oral articulations	33
8.	Infinite variety of possible sounds	38
9.	Glides and mixtures of articulation	40
10.	Syllables	41
11.	Stress	43
12.	Pitch	51
13.	Duration	52
14.	Limitation of articulations in each dialect	53
15.	Automatic variations	54

CONTENTS

CHAPTER III.
THE MENTAL BASIS OF LANGUAGE.

		Page
1.	The place of language in our mental life	56
2.	Total experiences	56
3.	The analysis of total experiences	59
4.	The naming of objects	63
5.	The development of abstract words	65
6.	Psychologic composition of the word	66
7.	Grammatical categories	67
8.	Psychologic character of the linguistic forms	69
9.	Psychologic motives of utterance	70
10.	Interpretation of the linguistic phenomena	71

CHAPTER IV.
THE FORMS OF LANGUAGE.

1.	The inarticulate outcry	73
2.	Primary interjections	73
3.	Secondary interjections	75
4.	The arbitrary value of non-interjectional utterances	77
5.	The classifying nature of linguistic expression	82
6.	Expression of the three types of utterance	90
7.	The parts of utterances	92
8.	The word: phonetic character	97
9.	The word: semantic character	103
10.	Word-classes	108
11.	The sentence	110

CHAPTER V
MORPHOLOGY.

1	The significance of morphologic phenomena	120
2.	Morphologic classification by syntactic use (Parts of speech)	12
3.	Classification by congruence	1?
4.	Phonetic-semantic classes	1£
5.	Classes on a partially phonetic basis	1£
6.	Difference between morphologic classification and non-linguistic association	13£
7.	Classes by composition	140

CONTENTS IX

Page
8. Derivation and inflection 140
9. The semantic nature of inflection: the commonest categories 141
10. The semantic nature of derivation 150
11. The phonetic character of the morphologic processes . 151
12. Word-composition: semantic value 159
13. Word-composition not a phonetic process. 162
14. Simple word: compound: phrase. 165

CHAPTER VI.
SYNTAX.

1. The field of syntax. 167
2. The discursive relations 168
3. The emotional relations. 170
4. Material relations. 171
5. Syntactic categories. 174
6. The expression of syntactic relations: modulation in the sentence 176
7. Cross-referring constructions. 178
8. Congruence 180
9. Government 182
10. Word-order 186
11. Set phrases: the transition from syntax to style. . . 188
12. The complex sentence 190

CHAPTER VII.
INTERNAL CHANGE IN LANGUAGE.

1. Language constantly changing. 195
2. Causes of the instability of language. 195
3. Change in articulation 202
4. Analogic change 221
5. Semantic change 237
6. The ultimate conditions of change in language . . . 251

CHAPTER VIII.
EXTERNAL CHANGE OF LANGUAGES.

1. Language never uniform 259
2. Increase of uniformity 262

CONTENTS

                                                                                     Page

3. Decrease of uniformity does not offset the increase . . . 263
4. Inferences from historic conditions 265
5. The process of differentiation 273
6. Deduction of internal history from related forms 274
7. Interaction of dialects and languages 280
8. Standard languages 288

CHAPTER IX.
THE TEACHING OF LANGUAGES.

1. The purpose of foreign-language instruction 292
2. Character of the instruction 293
3. Age of the pupil 295
4. Equipment of the teacher 297
5. Drill in pronunciation 299
6. Method of presenting semantic material 300
7. Grammatical information 302
8. Texts 304
9. References 305

CHAPTER X.
THE STUDY OF LANGUAGE.

1. The origin of linguistic science 307
2. How to study linguistics 313
3. Relation of linguistics to other sciences 319

INDICES.

1. Authors, etc. 326
2. Languages 327
3. Subjects 331

CHAPTER I.
THE NATURE AND ORIGIN OF LANGUAGE.

1. Expressive movements. In the animal world every mental process is accompanied by a corresponding physical process. Some of these physical processes are *expressive movements*. Investigation has shown that the expressive movements are most directly co-ordinated with the *emotional* element that is present in every mental process.

In man as well as in the lower animals it is primarily the *intensity* of the emotional element which appears in the expressive movements. Everyday observation recognizes the intensity of emotion of monkeys, dogs, or birds and even of such distant forms as the ant or the fly. In man and in the animals nearer to man a mild emotion is accompanied on the physical side by a hurrying of pulse-beat and respiration. If the emotion is more violent, the expressive movements extend, successively, to the facial muscles, then to the hands and arms, and finally to the legs and feet, embracing a set of actions well known to common observation. As the violence of the emotion increases, these movements also grow more energetic. When a certain extreme, however, is reached, the mental turmoil suddenly ceases and, in exact correspondence with this, there is a stopping of all the physical manifestations: the muscles grow slack, the legs often refusing support, and heart-beat and respiration may temporarily or even permanently stop.

While the expressive movements are thus chiefly dependent on the intensity of emotion, some of them, especially in the monkey and in man, have come secondarily to indicate also the *quality* of the emotion. The quality of the emotion shows itself in the play of the facial muscles. The various facial expressions are probably mechanized forms of what were once instinctive efforts at dealing with experiences of *taste*. The familiar 'sweet' or pleasurable expression brings any substance that may be in the mouth as much as possible into contact with the tip of the tongue, which is most sensitive to sweet tastes. Similarly, the 'bitter' or abhorrent expression withdraws the back of the tongue, which is most sensitive to a bitter taste. Sour tastes are most felt by the sides of the tongue: a pleasantly sour taste can be best perceived in the position which we know as a 'smile' and an over-sour one best avoided by the 'weeping' grimace. These responses have, in the history of the race, become purely reflex and hereditary, appearing even in new-born children.

Owing, moreover, to association between these movements and the emotional qualities in these taste-experiences, the movements have come to be constant attendants of all experiences, even other than of taste, which involve such qualities of emotion. That is, the 'sweet', 'bitter', 'smiling', and 'weeping' expressions are now the physical concomitants of any and all experiences whose emotional quality resembles that, respectively, of a sweet, bitter, sour, or over-sour taste. Thus any pleasure is accompanied by the first of these expressions and any abhorrence by the second; the uses of the smile and of the weeping grimace are too well known to need description. It is not known to what extent this associational extension of these movements is hereditary.

Beside these expressions we find tension, — pleasant or unpleasant anticipation, — expressed by the innervation of the cheek-muscles, and relaxation, — satiation or disappointment, — by their loosening. Perhaps these reflexes originated in the use of these muscles in eating.

Another specialized type of expressive movements are those which indicate the *perceptual* content of an experience. In every experience there is present, beside the emotional elements (with which the expressive movements, we must suppose, are most directly connected), a series of perceptual impressions, whether of outer sensation or of imagery. In fact, it is only by an abstraction that we can separate the emotional and the perceptual contents of our mental life. Just as certain expressive movements originally connected with experiences of taste have come to indicate the emotional quality of an experience, so certain other movements, especially of the hands and arms, have come to indicate its perceptual content.

Such a movement is that of pointing at things. When a child grasps at things which it cannot reach, its misjudgment of distance results, in each case, in a mere movement of the hand in the direction of the object desired. As the child grows in intelligence it performs this movement even when it knows it cannot reach things, and finally also uses the movement to indicate things which it does not want, — things which merely excite its curiosity or interest, the subjects of its discourse. This development of the *deictic* expressive movement, which occurs in every child, is peculiarly human; the monkey does not get beyond the first stage of sometimes grasping at things which it cannot reach.

Another type of expressive movement that indicates perceptual content is the *imitative* movement. Imitation is a term that can be applied to many phenomena of expressive movement throughout the animal kingdom. When we find numbers of ants or bees, for instance, congruently performing some one task, we must suppose that an instinctive action of some individuals called forth the same action in all the others. The explanation seems to be that the bodily movements have become so closely associated with the mental processes which they accompany, that the sight of a fellow-individual going through the former at once awakens the same mental state in the beholder. Thus a child, seeing another child weep, enters at once upon the state of anguish associated with this expression, and consequently weeps in sympathy, as we say, with the other child. In a grown civilized man these imitative actions are, however, usually suppressed and even the sympathetic emotion is reduced to a minimum. This subjection of the imitative movements to the will allows them to become expressive of perceptual contents. For we may now accompany any chosen perceptual element of our mental state by imitative gestures, — provided only that this element is sufficiently charged emotionally, for, after all, these movements are at bottom indicative of intensity of emotion. Especially in speaking of actions we accompany our picturing with imitative gestures. Also, anyone asked to define the qualities 'compact' or 'spiral' will resort to imitative movements. The prevalence of these varies greatly as a matter of communal habit or good form among different nations.

2. **Gesture-language.** Gestures are frequently used as the means of communication where vocal speech is impossible or undesirable. The systems of gesture-language thus used by different peoples are strikingly uniform. The gesture-language of certain of the American Indians, used where tribes of different language wished to communicate, is closely like that which has been current in

southern Italy since Roman times (and no one knows how much earlier), or like that used by the lower classes in Japan, or by the Cistercian monks under their vow of silence; and all these forms closely resemble that which a company of untaught deaf-mutes will, in the course of a few years, produce for themselves.

Gesture-language is so uniform because it consists everywhere chiefly of the universally human expressive movements voluntarily used for communication. The origin of the communicative use is psychologically intelligible. An individual sympathetically taking up another's emotion might yet reproduce an entirely different perceptual content. In so far as his expressive movements indicated the latter they would differ from those of the first individual. This already would be rudimentary communication. It would develope into more and more deliberate and explicit forms as the race attained to voluntary use of expressive movements for any chosen part of one's ideas, and as individuals, after repeated occurrence of the divergence of gesture, should foresee this divergence and make gestures in order to call forth divergent gestures from their fellow, — in other words, as the exchange of messages became a motive. We must suppose that all this took place in connection with vocal language, but even where gestures are used without vocal language they remain close to their character of expressive movements.

The deictic movement is of very limited use in gesture-language. Objects which, under circumstances, may be absent cease to be designated by pointing gestures even when they are present. The deictic gesture thus comes to be used only of certain constant relations: for expressing the 'I', the 'you', the 'here' or 'this', and the 'there' or 'that'.

The imitative movements, on the other hand, receive a wide development in the *depicting* gestures. These have been divided into three classes. The simplest kind are the *representative*, which depart but little from primitive imitative movements, — as, for instance, when 'joy' is expressed by a glad grimace or 'sleep' by closing the eyes and inclining the head to one side. Like all depicting gestures, representative gestures are either *graphic* as when one draws the outline of a 'house' in the air (gable-roof and side walls), or *plastic*, as in the above gestures for 'joy' and 'sleep' or when one joins first finger and thumb in the shape of a circle to indicate 'coin' or 'money'. *Suggestive* gestures depict not the thing intended but some part or accompaniment of it that brings it up by association. Graphic examples are the outlining of a beard under one's chin to express 'goat' or of a hat over one's head to express, among the Indians, 'white man'. The plastic type appears in the gesture for 'silence' in which the lips are compressed and a finger raised or in that for 'hunger' in which the cheeks are hollowed and two fingers, as if grasping a morsel, are held before the open mouth. *Symbolic* gestures, finally, arise when still further associational processes have removed the gesture from all resemblance to the thing intended or any part of it. Thus the deictic gestures for space may be used for time: one points backward for the past and forward for the future, or, as a plastic example, the suggestive gesture for 'hunger' may be used for 'wish' or 'desire', or the suggestive gesture for a 'bad smell', raising of the nostrils, may be used to express anything arousing disgust.

The transition from the immediately significant gestures, the deictic and the representative, to the suggestive and the symbolic is a process of association. The gesture is closely associated with a type of experience, and a new experience with the same dominant features calls forth the same gesture, without any consciousness of a transference on the part of the speaker. We shall meet similar inevitable transferences or rather extensions of meaning when we speak of vocal language. In gesture-language they are limited, however, by the immediate and apparent connection or identity of most gestures with the natural expressive reaction to the experience. Because most gestures are so immediately intelligible a gesture not immediately intelligible is but slowly adopted, and the number of such never becomes very great. The main stock of every system of gesture is made up of such original forms as the deictic and the graphic representative gestures, which are practically identical with natural expressive movements.

3. **Writing.** The expressive movements so far discussed have given rise not only to gesture-language but also to writing. Picture-writing is originally the tracing of an expressive movement on a permanent material. Its close kinship with gesture results in the transference of symbols from one to the other. We find not only delineations of objects (such as a house) made with exactly the same strokes as are used in representative gesture, but even symbolic gestures are indicated in the picture. Among the Indians a hand-movement upward from the head means 'big man' or 'chief': in picture-writing the same meaning is expressed by a line drawn upward from the head of the figure. Similarly, we find transference of pictorial symbols to gesture. The pictorial symbol for 'exchange' among the Indians consists of two crossed lines, — significant either of the act of exchange itself or of the crossing of paths at which barter between primitive communities usually takes place. In

gesture-language this symbol is used in the form of two crossed fingers.

The further development of writing takes place, as we shall see, entirely under the influence of vocal language.

4. Audible expressive movements. We have seen how the expressive movements have developed in man into a voluntarily used set of symbols by which even abstract meanings may be communicated. The principal development of expressive movements in this direction did not, however, take place in connection with the noiseless movements which we have so far considered. These are in several respects under a disadvantage. It is perhaps rash to say that they are not capable of sufficient variation to be fully adequate to our needs; perhaps, if vocal speech had been denied us, they would have shown themselves modifiable enough to serve for communication in all respects. There is no question, however, but that they are laborious and slow, demanding a great amount of muscular action on a large scale for even the briefest utterance. They appeal, moreover, to the sense of sight, which is not so powerful an arouser of the attention as hearing and must, indeed, be turned, often by movement of the entire body, to receive an impression from a new direction. Opposed to all this, the *sound-producing* expressive movements are performed by a delicate machinery requiring but little muscular effort and appeal to the attention by a channel that is nearly always open and requires no adjustment of the receiving apparatus.

Expressive movements producing sound occur widely in the animal kingdom. Such insects as crickets make noise by rubbing together parts of their bony covering; this type of audible expressive movement has nowhere reached a high development. The more familiar type, in which air expelled from the lungs meets with obstacles in the breath-passage, appears in amphibians, such as the frog, and especially, of course, in birds and mammals. The original form seems to be the cry of pain or rage. Under a violent unpleasurable emotion the breathing apparatus, and trachea are suddenly contracted. The breath, hereby forcibly expelled, sets into vibration certain elastic protuberances within the breath-passage, the *vocal chords*, and is further forced through the mouth and nose. The result is a penetrating noise.

Such animals as the mouse and the rabbit utter sound only under extreme emotion. The development from this primitive outcry seems to occur in two directions. Among gregarious animals the primitive outcry becomes an instinctively used call for help or for the presence of a fellow-individual. On the other hand, the cry of anger of the fighting males at mating-time develops into a general vocal expression of the emotions of this period. By a further transition this vocal expression accompanies any lively pleasant emotion, as in the male song-bird. The development in this direction brings it about that the vocal utterance is used not only under extreme stress, but also for lesser and for pleasurable emotions. Thus there comes about a differentiation between the utterance of highly unpleasant emotion on the one hand and that of lesser pleasant or unpleasant feelings on the other. The latter, less violent expressions tend to include some repeated movement of the mouth or some periodic change in the production of the voice-sound itself. No better example of this differentiation could be found than the squeak of a bird in extreme fright or pain and, under less emotional stress, its regular song. The less violent kind of utterance may be modulated predominantly as to pitch or as to the noise-quality of the sound. Pitch-modulation is, of course, characteristic of the song of birds, noise-modulation of the dog's bark or of human speech. In our song we combine the two; it has been thought that our unmelodious speech is a degeneration from an earlier singing habit of expression, but extended research has shown that this is not the case, human song having probably originated in the chant of rhythmic labor. The melodious quality of the bird's song is due to the position of its vocal chords at the very bottom of the trachea, which leaves a long sounding-tube for the pitch-modification of the sound; our speech, on the other hand, receives its great scope of variation as to noise-character from the extreme mobility of our tongue and other oral muscles. The various movements of these were, no doubt, in their origin, expressive movements like those of the 'sweet', 'bitter', and 'sour' or 'tense' and 'relaxed' types. The effect of the sound upon the producing individual and his fellows was, however, so forceful, as opposed to that of the mere movement and grimace, that the acoustic impression of the sound and not the movement itself became the basis for further associational development.

5. Development of language in the child. The different stages of vocal utterance appear very clearly during the growth of a child. The new-born child shrieks with wide-open mouth when in pain. By the end of the first month it yells also under other sensations of discomfort and soon afterwards it croons when it is contented. As these less violent emotions are accompanied by less violent muscular effort, there is already some differentiation in the sound produced. Gradually modifications of these less violent oral movements set in and are furthered not only by the growing practice of the mouth-muscles, but also by the appearance of the teeth, which makes articulation of tongue-tooth sounds possible. Up to about the end of the first year the child performs an increasing variety of articulatory movements, especially during pleasurable emotion. There can be no question that the tendency to this form of expressive movement, and especially to the great variety of these movements, is inherited from the past generations of speaking ancestry.

The element of mimicry — that is, of imitation of the speech of the surrounding adults — becomes more and more prominent toward the end of the first year, until the child finally succeeds in repeating, — with no consciousness of their meaning, to be sure, — syllables and words that are spoken to it.

At about the same time the child begins to understand gestures; that is, to associate people's gestures with emotional and even perceptual experiences. It begins by connecting facial expression with states of emotion, recognizing, as we say, an angry or a cheerful countenance. Then comes the association of deictic gestures with objects, the child's eyes following the direction in which one points. At last words begin to be understood: aided, at first, by pointing gestures, the child begins to associate such sound-sequences as the nursery words for 'mother', 'father', 'good', 'bad', 'bed', or 'sleep' with the corresponding experiences.

As yet, however, the child does not utter these sound-sequences to express the experiences. When it utters them at all, it does so purely in mimicry. Even in a normal child the end of the second year may arrive before the cross-association between the sounds which it imitatively utters and the significant sounds which it understands when others speak them, becomes lively enough to enable the child to repeat words with consciousness of their significant value. When this cross-association has been formed speech may be said to have begun. To be sure, the child's reproduction of what it hears is for a long time imperfect. It is no simple task to associate correctly a sound heard with the articulatory movements that will produce it, even though, in the case of some, such as the lip-closure sounds p, b, m, the eye aids the ear. The child is very much in the position of the adult who hears a foreign language; its perception is often wrong. Such mistakes as the confusion of t and k, of f and th are due to the unsureness of the perceptive habit: the child actually hears the wrong sound, so far as consciousness is concerned. Only after long practice do hearing and articulation become accurate and closely associated with each other.

The child's associating the sounds it hears with certain experiences is due, of course, to the fact that grown-ups are constantly producing the sounds in connection, and in as plain connection as possible, with the proper objects and actions. The association, for instance, between *mama* and the child's mother is presented entirely by the child's elders. In many cases the child will be led to form a wrong association, which is gradually corrected, as when it at first calls every man *papa*. In no case does the child itself invent a word, in the sense of spontaneously giving meaning to a sound-sequence. Mother or nurse, to be sure, will often connect some one of the child's meaningless sound-productions with some person, object, or other experience and then teach the child so to connect it: it is in this way that our nursery-words have arisen. They are sound-groups which are uttered by most children and have come to be traditionally connected by the adult speech-community with certain meanings; the child, however, learns to give them these meanings just as it learns the value of any other words. The connection between sound and sense is in no case originated by the child.

While we thus see in the child the development of sound-producing expressive movements from the unmodified yell of pain to the most manifold varieties of articulation, differentiated in general character to correspond to different emotional states, the spontaneous rise of the use of certain fixed sounds for certain fixed types of experience does not occur in the child. The significant use of sounds is, so to speak, prematurely forced upon the individual, who has no opportunity of arriving by his own powers at the goal of actual language. How the human species arrived at this significant use of sound-utterance is therefore not explained by the development of the individual under normal circumstances. There are some accounts, most famous among them that of Herodotus (*Histories*, II, 2), of children who, for the purpose of ascertaining the original development of language, were left to grow up without hearing anyone speak. The experiment is really impossible, for, to be significant, it would have to be made with a large group of people left to themselves for generations and even centuries, since the development of language in the race can not have been other than gradual and communal.

6. The origin of language. The question remains, then: How did man come to associate fixed sound-sequences with fixed types of experience? The older answer to this question was based on the individual's learning of language. According to earlier theories the place of the child's elders was filled, with regard to the race, by divine care: a divinity directly gave men the use of speech. A more materialistic but essentially identical notion was that man himself invented the trick of attaching significance to sounds; some genius of primitive times, for instance, may have conceived this brilliant idea. More tenable was the view that the speech-sounds were originally imitations of what they denoted (Stoics, Herder), or the view that they were originally the natural and inevitable emotional responses to the corresponding experiences (Epicureans, Rousseau).

The evolutionary point of view has shown the falsity of the first two explanations and growing psychologic insight has deprived the last two also of probability. Gesture-language is in this connection especially instructive. Gesture-language, as we have seen, is nothing but a higher development of the expressive movements common, in their basis, to many animals. Vocal language is not essentially different. It consists, at bottom, of expressive movements. In the case of gesture-language the expressive movements themselves remained the means of communication; consequently the connection between a gesture and the original expressive movement is nearly always apparent, as when the deictic gesture is plainly a weakened grasping movement and the depicting gestures scarcely differ from natural imitative movements. In the case of vocal speech, on the other hand, it was not the movement itself that attracted attention and became the starting-point for further development, but the sound which the movement produced. This sound is an effect which bears only in respect to emotional intensity any distinct and recognizable relation to the experience calling it forth. The 'sweet' face-gesture, for instance, accompanied by production of the voice-sound gives a sound in no way directly related to the experience of something sweet or otherwise pleasant. Now, so long as the face-gesture remained in use, the importance of the sound could always be secondary, the gesture actually conveying the message. The sounds themselves were neither directly significant of the experience, nor could they, in any conceivable way, have been imitative of most experiences: only the movements which produced the sounds were the expressive correspondents and, therefore, the indications of the experiences. After the sound, however, had entered into association with the gesture (and, thus, with the experience), it gradually usurped the more important place, owing to the advantages already set forth, and finally came into independent use, without the gesture. This use of the sound alone opened the road for unlimited transferences of meaning of the same kind as those which produce symbolic gestures. In the case of the latter the predominant direct connection between an experience and a gesture, — a connection obvious to all and constantly refreshed, — forbade too divergent a development. In vocal speech, however, where direct connection between experiences and sounds was never felt, the further development by means of associational shifts of meaning has been unlimited. The connection between sound and meaning, thus, which cannot even in its origin have been a direct one, is further destroyed by the freedom of transference due to the lack of any immediately felt connection between experience and utterance, such as prevents too free a development of symbolic gestures.

It is clear, therefore, that even if one could survey the whole evolution of sound-producing expressive movements from the single cry of pain to which some animals are limited, up to the present speech of man, there would be no point at which one could say: Here language begins. Expressive movements are the physical phase of mental processes: whatever the mental processes, the expressive movements correspond to them. Man's mind and his expressive activity have developed in indissoluble connection. In the animal world, as we know it, the evolution of one phase without the other is inconceivable. This, indeed, is why it is impossible to set up a strictly logical definition of language as opposed to expressive movement in general. Language is the form of expressive movement adequate to the mentality of man. This mentality is defined no less than man's language in the aphorism that 'Man is a speaking animal'.

7. Language constantly changing. The absence of immediate connection between sound and experience appears in the fact that, unlike gesture-language, vocal language differs vastly in different times and places, — a fact too familiar to need exposition.

The change of language in time is of interest in the present connection because its phases again illustrate the absence of any conservative relation between sound and sense. The sounds habitually uttered under a given type of experience are in an unceasing process of change: those which we utter today are not like those which speakers of English uttered a thousand or even a hundred years ago. On the other hand, the transference of meaning also is unlimited; the history of languages shows us innumerable associational changes of meaning, which in gesture, where some connection between expression and experience is upheld, would be impossible. It would be difficult to find an English word which, if it existed at all a thousand years ago, has not since then in some way changed its meaning. All this is due to the fact that there never was a stage in which a hearer could recognize any but an arbitrary connection between sound and sense.

The change of language is not a mere endless shifting of sounds and meanings: we find speech rising in the course of time to the power of more delicate and abstract expression and to greater brevity. This development is due to the assimilating effect, which we shall study in detail, of experience upon expression; in return the growing power of expression, as we shall see, reacts favorably upon the mental processes. Thus the freedom in which vocal language differs from that of gesture has made possible a much higher development.

8. Social character of language. We have seen that the greatest stimulus toward the development of expressive actions is their emergence into voluntary communicative use. Language has been developed in the interchange of messages, and every individual who has learned to use language has learned it through such interchange. The individual's language, consequently, is not his creation, but consists of habits adopted in his expressive intercourse with other members of the community. The result of this is the individual's inability to use language except in the form in which the community as a whole uses it: he must speak as the others do, or he will not be understood. As a matter of fact he does not, in normal cases, try to speak otherwise, but unquestioningly follows his and his fellow-speakers' habits. The change which occurs in language is thus never a conscious alteration by individuals, but an unconscious, gradual change in the habits of the entire community. The motives which cause it are not individual reflective considerations of the result, but new associative tendencies or new conditions of innervation due to some change in the circumstances of life affecting the community. As we examine more closely the different aspects of language, we shall again and again find the same characteristic: as the individual speaker receives his habits from the community, individual motives do not come into play, but only causes affecting the community as a whole. And as, moreover, the individual, from childhood, practises his speech until the details of it are mechanized and unconscious, he is rarely aware of the specific characteristics, such as the phonetic or the grammatical, which are involved in it.

CHAPTER II.
THE PHYSICAL BASIS OF LANGUAGE.

1. Unconsciousness of speech-movements. The individual's unconsciousness of the details of his speech-activity appears strikingly when we inquire into the movements by which speech-sounds are produced. While we know that we speak with the mouth, tongue, and larynx, the separate movements of these organs rarely or never enter our consciousness. If we are asked to describe them, we answer in vague, metaphoric expressions or say things that are altogether wrong. In fact, as to some of these movements not only the normal speaker but even the scientific observer is at a loss. For, in spite of the fact that all these muscles are ultimately at the command of the will, the innervations which control them have become mechanized; we consciously give the impulse for whole words and phrases, but the details of their utterance always proceed unconsciously. The impulse, moreover, is given in terms of sound, for, in the association of articulatory movements with sounds, which is formed very early in life (p. 11) and is, of course, constantly practised, the latter are entirely dominant, the former almost forgotten. It appears, then, that even as regards our own speech-movements of every day, some scientific examination of the facts is necessary.

It happens, moreover, that not only different languages but even different local variations of the same language use different sounds. When the normal speaker hears a foreign dialect or language, he encounters a twofold difficulty. His perceptive habits lead him to hear sounds that merely resemble those of his own speech as if they were identical with the latter; and where two or more of the strange sounds resemble one of his own, he may fail to distinguish between them. Thus a German who is picking up English will confuse our *v, w,* and *wh* sounds, our *d* and *th* (as in *then*), our *t* and *th* (as in *think*), and our *sh* and *s* (as in *azure*), for in his own language he has but one sound resembling each of these groups. The second difficulty lies in producing the foreign sounds even when their distinctive character is heard: thus our German may in time come to appreciate the distinctions we have mentioned, but will still be unable to produce the English sounds.

These difficulties usually prove fatal to the efforts of those who try to describe languages without adequate knowledge of *phonetics*. From nearly all the published material about American Indian languages, for instance, it is impossible to get any adequate conception of how these languages are pronounced. So great a Chinese scholar as Joseph Edkins was unable to describe some of the commonest Chinese sounds. It is for this reason that even teachers who have spoken a language from childhood are often unable to impart their information to others. No one can teach a foreigner his language, unless he can tell his pupil exactly what to do with his vocal organs to get the proper effect: and this, we have seen, he cannot do without a certain amount of scientific study.

2. Writing an imperfect analysis. There is one activity in the course of which nearly all civilized peoples have made some analysis of the sounds of their speech, and that is writing. This analysis has, however, been gradual and incomplete. In its most primitive form writing is simply the drawing, carving, or painting of the visible features of an experience or of symbolic elements representing it (p. 7). When this method of communication is frequently used, certain elements in the pictures come to be drawn always in a certain way and to have a fixed meaning. Gradually such elements may come to be used as symbols for corresponding words of the vocal language and to be arranged in the order that these words have in speech. As the association between written symbol and spoken word becomes fixed, the symbol may come to be drawn without reference to its original pictorial value, and to deviate from its older form, associating the word rather than, in a more direct sense, the experience. When this has happened, the association may grow to be simply one of written symbol and sound, regardless of the meaning borne by the sound, until, after a time, the symbols are used purely in their phonetic value. The number of symbols may then be lessened to the point where there is a single character for every syllable used in the language. Such 'syllabaries' are a very common form of writing; examples are the alphabets of India (derived from ancient syllabic forms of Semitic writing), and the national alphabets of the Japanese. It is a further simplification when these characters come to be used not for whole syllables but for single sounds of the language, as in the Greek, Latin, and derived alphabets, including our own.

All this development is, of course, gradual. There is, in most instances, at no time a deliberate and systematic examination of the sounds of the language and an assigning to each of a written symbol. Accordingly, we hardly ever find perfect consistency in the relation between sound and writing. There are two factors which lessen even such consistency as might otherwise develop. One of these is the use of foreign alphabets. When the English, for instance, took over the Latin alphabet, the sounds of English were so different from those of Latin that consistency was impossible, — a difficulty under which we labor even today, for our alphabet has not enough signs for our vowels, and none for our *th*-sounds, our *sh*, our *s* as in *azure*, our *wh*, or our *ng* as in *sing*, and, on the other hand, contains the superfluous characters *c, q, and x*. The second factor interferes even more seriously with the regularity of alphabetic writing: it is the necessary conservatism of orthography. Reading and writing would be very slow processes, if, every time we read or wrote, we actually stopped to analyze each word into its component sounds; moreover, according to emphasis, speed, personal habit, and so on, the spelling of each word would then be variable, — a condition which would further militate against ease. Such a state of affairs never continues long, for the spellings of whole words are of course remembered and become traditional. Opposed to this necessary conservatism of writing, there is the fact that all language at all times is in an unceasing process of change, — a process so gradual and subtle that no speaker, through all his life, is aware of it, yet so unceasing that the orthography of every language becomes in a few hundred years thoroughly antiquated even in those features which were formerly consistent.

This, of course, is a reason why writing, though involving to a certain extent an analysis of the physical phase of language, does not satisfy scientific requirements in this direction. Indeed, so far as the linguistically untrained person is concerned, writing is often misleading, for the individual movements of writing are so much more consciously performed than those of pronunciation, that the naive speaker will often think that he speaks as he writes, when this is not the case. He will think, for instance, that *passed* and *past* or *close* (verb) and *clothes* are pronounced differently, when actually he may never in his life have heard or made such distinctions.

There are other reasons, too, why writing cannot and need not accurately analyze the spoken sounds. Although the human vocal organ can produce an infinite number of different sounds, each language uses but a limited set. Given, therefore, an alphabet of a limited number of symbols, it could be used by all languages, though no two of them would give each symbol the same value. Now, within limits this is actually the case: thus letters like *p* and *t* are used by both English and French, but with different values, *v* and *s* by both English and Germans, but again with differing values in the two languages. This circumstance may be convenient, on occasion, to printers; it would be absurd, at any rate, for us to request the Germans and the French to give up their use of these letters because it does not agree with ours. Consequently there are differences between the pronunciations of different languages which do not appear in writing. The same is true, moreover, of the different local variations of the same language. The words of the English language are pronounced very differently, let us say, by a Chicagoan and by a Londoner. These dialectal differences of pronunciation may be so great that scarcely a word will be pronounced alike over all the territory in which a language is spoken. In the case of Chinese, in fact, distant dialects are mutually unintelligible, though the writing is the same. It would obviously be a great inconvenience and a source of much confusion, if such variations appeared in the writing: it would mean, for instance, that a Chicagoan could only with difficulty read a book printed in London. Thus we see that much of the value of writing is actually dependent on its not conveying the exact manner of pronunciation.

More than this, there are in the language even of one and the same person many subtle and complex variations, which do not demand notation for the practical purposes of reading and writing. Thus we pronounce our vowels longer before *d* than before *t*, — the *o* in *rode* longer, for instance, than that in *wrote*, — but it would be superfluous to indicate this difference, for every English-speaking person regularly and unconsciously speaks his vowels longer before *d* than before *t*. An orthography which actually indicated all the phonetic facts of speech would be a very cumbersome affair, difficult for even an expert phonetician to handle, and requiring, above all, close attention to every single utterance that one wanted to represent in writing.

It is obvious, then, that even a regular and consistent orthography for practical purposes would not contain a full analysis of the pronunciation of a language, such as is often needed by the scientific investigator and, in some degree, by the teacher of languages. For scientific use several such fully analytic alphabets have been devised; today the standard one is that of the International Phonetic Association, which shall be used in this book (phonetic characters being printed in square brackets). It is customary, however, even in scientific discussions, to avoid a constant complete analysis by describing, at the outset, the sounds and regular variations of a language and assigning a simple character of the phonetic alphabet to each typical sound. Such a simplified phonetic alphabet is of course best for teaching the pronunciation of a foreign language, and, if it can be made to fit all the local variations of pronunciation, would be the ideal practical alphabet.

3. The vocal chords. The human vocal organ is a wind instrument which produces sounds by interfering with the breathed air that is being driven from the lungs in expiration. The first interference which the expired breath meets is at the head of the trachea, in the larynx or Adams's apple. Within the larynx, to the right and left, are two muscular protuberances, the vocal chords, between which the breath must pass. In ordinary breathing the muscles of the vocal chords are relaxed and the breathed air passes freely through the aperture between them, which is called the *glottis*. When one holds one's breath with open mouth the vocal chords are stretched so as to close the glottis firmly. Owing to their delicate musculature, and to two movable cartilaginous hinges, the *arytenoids*, in which they terminate at the rear of the larynx, the vocal chords can be set also in a number of positions intermediate between that of breathing and that of firm closure.

Firm closure of the glottis, suddenly opened, occurs just before coughing or clearing the throat, also under any strain, as in lifting a heavy weight. As a speech-sound it is used in German initially in the pronunciation of words that in writing begin with a vowel. The sound so produced is called the *glottal stop*, and its phonetic symbol is [ʔ]; a German word like *arm* 'poor' is therefore pronounced [ʔarm]. The glottal stop occurs also in a great many other languages, such as Danish, where *hund* 'dog' is pronounced [huʔn], but *hun* 'she' [hun], Lettish, Hebrew ('aleph'), Arabic ('hamza'), and some Chinese dialects. Its frequent occurrence in such languages as

Danish produces in English ears the effect of constant interruption by little hiccoughs.

If the vocal chords are a little less firmly closed, the compression gives way, from instant to instant, to the pressure of the breath, so that a vibration productive of musical sound results. This musical sound we call *voice*. The *pitch* of the voice is modulated by changing the length of the chords, for this of course controls the rapidity of vibration. The loudness or *stress* of the voice depends on the violence of the vibration, and may therefore be regulated in two ways. In singing the regulation is (or ought to be) chiefly effected by varying the breath-pressure, that is, by expiring more or less rapidly; in ordinary speech the less cumbersome method prevails of slightly widening the glottis for a less loud sound and slightly narrowing it for a louder; for, as the narrowing of the glottis allows less breath to pass through, the accumulated breath underneath exercises pressure, against which the vocal chords vibrate under tension, producing a loud sound.

The voice is not heard in every sound of speech. In the glottal stop, for instance, it obviously is absent. Many of the other speech-sounds, also, are unaccompanied by the voice. If one places a finger on the Adam's apple or stops up one's ears, the voice will be felt as a buzz or trembling; if one now speaks, such sounds as *p, t, k, f, s* [p, t, k, f, s] will be found to lack this buzzing accompaniment, while such as *b, d, g, v, z* [b, d, g, v, z] have it: the former are *unvoiced* or *breathed*, the latter *voiced* sounds, as are also, for instance, our accented vowels.

If the vocal chords are so far separated that the voice no longer sounds pure, but is accompanied by a friction sound produced by the breath as it passes through the glottis, we get a *murmur*. Most of our unaccented vowels in English are spoken with murmur instead of voice. As an independent speech-sound the murmur is heard in the 'voiced *h*' of Čech and of Sanskrit, symbol [ɦ]. If the glottis is still farther opened, the voice ceases and only the friction-sound remains: this is the sound of our *h* [h].

Still another position of the vocal chords is represented by the *whisper*, in which only the cartilage-glottis, that is, the space between the arytenoids, is open, the vocal chords themselves being in contact. In what we ordinarily call whispering the whisper is substituted for the voice, the unvoiced sounds remaining unaltered.

Both in whispering and in ordinary speech the unvoiced sounds are pronounced with the glottis in its widest-open position, the muscles of the vocal chords being relaxed and the breath passing freely through the larynx: this, as we have seen, is also the position for regular breathing.

The remarkable delicacy and rapidity of adjustment of the vocal chords in passing from voice to breathing, from either of these to murmur, whisper, or *h*, and in changing the pitch and stress, requires no further comment. It is to be remembered, of course, that the details of all these movements, in spite of complete subjection to the will, are so mechanized as to be unconscious: anybody can speak an *h*, but it takes careful scientific observation to determine exactly how the sound is produced.

4. The velum. When the breath leaves the larynx it passes, in normal breathing, through the nose. During most of the sounds of speech it is, however, precluded from doing so by the raising of the *soft palate* or *velum*, which now cuts off the nasal passage from the throat and mouth. If one stands with open mouth before a mirror, breathing through both nose and mouth, and then suddenly pronounces a pure, long 'ah...' [ɑː], the raising of the velum can be easily seen, especially if one watches the uvula. Most speech-sounds are thus purely *oral*. In a few, such as *m* [m] or *n* [n], however, the breath escapes entirely through the nose, the velum being lowered: such sounds are called *nasals*. There are other sounds in which the breath escapes through both mouth and nose: these are called *nasalized* (symbol ˜), e. g. the vowel in the French *cent* [sã] 'a hundred'. Most speakers are, of course, quite unconscious of the movements of their velum; yet it is lowered and raised again every time they speak an *m* or *n*.

5. Oral articulation. The mouth performs a double function in speech. It serves, in the first place, as a resonance-chamber for the musical sound of the voice or for the whisper. By changing the shape of this resonance-chamber we vary the tone-color of the sound: thus by narrowing and flattening it we get the high tone-color of the vowel-sound in *fee*, by hollowing it, the low tone-color of the vowel in *foe*.

Secondly, by moving the tongue and the lower lip during the passage of the breath, we can produce noises. Most of these depend on the resistance of the breath-stream, but noises can also be produced by suction (symbol [*]), as in the sound with which we urge on a horse by 'snapping' the tongue against the palate [c*]. Such suction-noises occur as regular speech-sounds in the languages of the African Bushmen and the Hottentots. Where the noises are produced by means of the breath, voiced or unvoiced, there are two principal methods: either a complete closure is made and then explosively burst, as in our *p, b, t, d, k, g* [p, b, t, d, k, g], — *stops*, or *explosives*; or the closure is incomplete and the noise is produced by the friction of the breath passing through the aperture, as in our *f, v, th* as in *think, th* as in *then, s, z, sh, z* as in *azure* [f, v, Θ, ð, s, z, ʃ, ʒ], — *spirants* or *fricatives*. Both stops and spirants may be modified by lowering the velum; in the case of the former the breath escapes entirely through the nose and we hear the *nasals*, such as *m, n, ng* [m, n, ŋ]; in the case of the spirants it escapes through both mouth and nose, producing nasalized spirants.

6. Oral noise-articulations. The noise-articulations can be produced in various parts of the mouth.

a) *Labials*. Stops produced by closure of the two lips, — *bilabial* articulation, — are our unvoiced *p* [p] and voiced *b* [b]. The corresponding nasal is our voiced *m* [m]. Bilabial spirants are not common; a voiced one [v] occurs in Dutch (written *w*) and in Spanish (written *b, v*).

Our English unvoiced [f] and voiced [v] are *labiodental* spirants, in which the friction is produced between the lower lip and the upper teeth and accentuated by the collision of the escaping stream of breath with the upper lip.

b) *Dentals*. Most of the oral noise-articulations are made with the tongue. The tongue produces noises with either the tip or the back articulating against the teeth or the palate: articulation with the tip is called *coronal*, with the back, *dorsal*.

Coronal articulation against the upper teeth or the gums just behind them is called *dental;* it produces, of stops, the unvoiced [t] and the voiced [d]. These occur in several varieties, such as the interdental, against the lower edge of the upper teeth, the post-dental, against the back of the upper teeth (thus in Spanish and in many modern languages of India, and, in a different variety, in French), against the border of the upper teeth and gums (so in German), or a little farther back still (as in the English *t* and *d*), — the last two variants being specifically called *alveolar*. Such variations are indicated, where necessary, in phonetic writing by diacritical marks such as [˨] for articulation with the tongue drawn back, [˩] for articulation with the tongue advanced, [˔] for greater raising of the tongue, and [˕] for greater lowering; but these signs can usually be dispensed with by stating beforehand what varieties are current in a given language. The voiced nasal corresponding to these stops is our *n* [n], which often occurs unvoiced [n̥] in such words as *mint, snow*, where it is spoken just before or after unvoiced sounds. Dental spirants, more specifically interdental or post-dental, are our unvoiced [Θ] as in *think* and voiced [ð] as in *then*.

Dental articulation is used also in the *trills* or *r*-sounds of most languages. These sounds are produced by tightening the tongue-muscles so that they elastically resist the pressure of the breath from instant to instant; an example is the Slavic or Italian 'rolled' *r* [r], which is used also in the stage-pronunciations of French and German. The *r*-sound of American English [ɹ] is pronounced with the tongue relaxed, so that there is no trilling and even very little breath-friction; in consequence the acoustic value of the sound is as much musical as noise-like. An unvoiced [ɹ̥] with increased friction often occurs in such words as *try*. The friction element of a trilled [r] reaches a maximum, if the tongue is held close to the roof of the mouth, especially at the sides, where it touches the upper teeth; if the friction-noise is very great, we seem to hear a trilled [r] and, simultaneously, a spirant resembling the sound of *s* in *azure*: this strongly spirant trilled [ř] is heard in Čechish.

Another dental articulation is that of the *l*-sounds or *laterals*. In these also friction is so slight that it would be as well to class them with the musical sounds as with the noises. Their characteristic resonance is due to the fact that the breath escapes at the sides of the tongue, the tip of the tongue being pressed tightly against the upper teeth or gums. The tone-color of such an [l] can be varied by raising or lowering the back of the tongue, — that is, altering the shape of the resonance-chamber. Very high tone-color, due to raising of the tongue, is heard in the 'light' *l* of the Slavic languages; less high is that of German or French *l*, while that of English is especially dull, owing to the lowering of the middle of the tongue.

c) *Cerebrals.* Leaving the dental position, we come to another form of coronal articulation, the *cerebral*. In this the tip of the tongue is drawn up and back, so as to articulate against the highest point of the palate. Many languages of India possess these cerebrals [ṭ, ḍ, ṇ] by the side of the dentals, distinguishing between the two as sharply as they or we should distinguish between, say, *t* and *k*. Some of these languages have cerebral [ɹ] and [ḷ] which may also be heard in the English pronunciation of many Americans.

d) *Blade-sounds.* We come now to the dorsal tongue-articulations, in which parts of the upper surface of the tongue (as opposed to the tip in coronal articulation) are brought into contact with the teeth, gums, or palate. The dorsal articulations that are made farthest forward are produced, naturally, by the front of the upper surface of the tongue, which is called the *blade*. In these sounds the tongue is contracted so as to form a furrow along the median line: the breath passes along this furrow, which directs it against the edge of the upper front teeth. Here the narrow, strong stream of air produces a sharp, hissing noise, whence these sounds receive the name of *sibilants*: unvoiced [s], voiced [z]. They occur in several varieties: in French they are post-dental, the tip of the tongue touching the lower teeth, and the blade, except in the center, where the furrow is formed, touching the upper teeth. The English and German sibilants are alveolar; in Swedish there is even a cerebral variety.

The distinctness of the sibilant hiss is lessened, if the tongue is moved so as to displace the furrow from its proper relation to the upper teeth, for then the narrow stream of breath is not accurately directed against the edge of the teeth, but, instead, eddies round, producing a peculiar muffled hiss. These *abnormal sibilants* are usually produced by drawing the tongue back from the [s]-position: so in our English unvoiced [ʃ], as in *shall* and voiced [ʒ], as in *azure, vision*. The exact nature of the eddying current of the breath in these sounds is not known. The 'kettle' or 'gorge' of the eddy can be enlarged by protruding and rounding the lips [ʃ)], as in the German *sch*-sound. The French varieties lower the tip of the tongue and slightly raise the back.

The front articulations may be formed in more pronouncedly dorsal variations. Such are our [tʃʴ] and [dʒʴ] as in *cheap* and *jump*, the 'palatalized' Russian [tʴ], [dʴ], and [sʴ], the Russian and Polish [tʃʴ], the Polish 'palatalized' *s* [ʃʴ], the Norwegian [ʃʴ], and the German [ʃʴ] before consonants. These more dorsal varieties of dental and blade sounds are often conveniently indicated, both in practical and in phonetic writing, by placing an accent-mark over the letter, e. g. *t'* [t'], rather than by fully indicating the tongue-position, e. g. [tʴ⊥]. It is also sometimes convenient to express them by the signs of the series of sounds to be next spoken of, provided the conditions of the language do not make such expression misleading or ambiguous.

e) *Palatals*. Dorsal articulations against the hard palate are called *palatal*. As the hard palate is comparatively extensive, they occur in several varieties. The stops, unvoiced [c] and voiced [ɟ], are heard in French dialects, in Lithuanian, and in Hungarian, the nasal [ɲ] also in Spanish (written *ñ*), Italian (written *gn*), and French (*gn*), the French variety being pronounced farther back **than** the others. The spirants of this position are unvoiced [ç], as in the German *ich* [ʔiç] 'I' and voiced [j], as in many German pronunciations of such words as *ja* 'yes' and *legen* 'to lay'. Palatal trills cannot occur, for the back of the tongue has not enough elasticity to vibrate. A palatal lateral [ʎ] occurs, however, in southern French, Spanish (written *ll*), and Italian (written *gl*). Those who have not in their native language the habit of palatal articulation best learn it, if they produce the sounds with the tip of the tongue pressed against the lower teeth, but this is not necessary to the articulation.

f) *Velars.* Dorsal articulations against the soft palate again allow of a great deal of variation, owing to the extent of this region. The sounds here produced are called *velars*. In English the velar stops, *k* [k] and *g* [g], are produced farthest forward before the *i*-vowel heard in *kin* and *give*, farther back in *can* and *gap*, and farthest back before back vowels as in *coop, goose*; the same habit prevails in German. The velar nasal occurs in English, written *ng*, as in *sing*, symbol [ŋ])[1]. The spirants are: unvoiced [x], as in the German *Bach* [bax] 'brook', and voiced [g], which occurs in modern Greek and in many German pronunciations of such words as *sagen* 'to say'. A very open [xᵥ], with little friction, is heard in the Slavic languages. A velar trill is impossible, but a velar lateral [ł] is produced in Polish by raising the back of the tongue: while accurate median contact with lateral opening is here impossible, the general effect still resembles that of the tongue-tip [l], as well as that of an English *w*.

g) *Uvulars.* The hindmost of the dorsal articulations

---

[1] In such words as *finger*, however, the spelling *ng* represents two sounds, [ŋg].

is that of the rear upper surface of the tongue against the uvula, the little pendent part at the back of the soft palate. Of these *uvular* articulations the unvoiced stop [q] occurs in Arabic and in Greenlandish; the latter language uses also the voiced nasal [N]. In the trill [R] it is the uvula and not, as in the dental trill, the tongue, which vibrates. This uvular trill is the regular *r*-sound in Northumbrian English (the 'burr'), in Danish, and in the city pronunciations of French and German. In French and Danish it occurs also unvoiced [я]; in these languages it is often pronounced without the trill-vibration, as a uvular spirant, both unvoiced [я] and voiced [ʁ].

In connection with the oral noise-articulations we may again mention the *laryngeal*, produced by the vocal chords; of these the stop ['] and the spirants, unvoiced [h] and voiced [ɦ] have already been mentioned (p. 24, ff.). Two more laryngeal spirants can be produced by compression of the entire musculature of the larynx: the 'hoarse *h*' [H] and its voiced form, the 'ayin' [Q] of the Semitic languages.

7. Musical oral articulations. We may turn now to the musical articulations or 'vowels'. It is important to observe that there is no definite boundary between the noise-articulations and the musical articulations. Any spirant can be articulated with varying degrees of closure: as the pressure of the tongue is relaxed the friction-noise decreases and the element of musical resonance becomes more and more audible. Such spirants as the American English [ɹ], the laterals, and an open [j] are on the border line; if anything, the resonance-element is, in the [ɹ] and [l] at least, dominant. The traditional division of sounds into 'consonants' and 'vowels', while often convenient, is therefore untenable for purposes of exact terminology. Instead, the sounds of speech represent an unbroken series of relations between noise and resonance: the latter element is at a minimum in the unvoiced stops; then come, in order, the voiced stops, the unvoiced and the voiced spirants, the nasals, the laterals, the *r*-sounds, and, finally, the most open musical sounds, in the production of which the mouth is merely shaped into a resonance-chamber.

In this shaping the chief factor is the tongue-position. It is customary to distinguish nine typical tongue-positions, three along the horizontal plane, *front*, *mixed*, and *back*, and three along the vertical, *high*, *mid*, and *low*. The former three indicate the region in which the tongue approaches most closely to the roof of the mouth, the latter three, the degree of approximation. Other factors modifying the quality of the resonance are the tensity or relaxation of the oral muscles, especially those of the tongue, and the position, normal, drawn back, or rounded, of the lips. It is customary to distinguish two typical states of each of these factors: *wide* (that is, loose) and *narrow* (that is, tense) vowels, and *rounded* (lips protruded and rounded) and *unrounded* vowels.

a) *Front vowels*. A high front vowel, narrow and unrounded, is produced, if one pronounces the spirant [j] more and more openly, so that the friction-sound disappears. This vowel [i] occurs in a very characteristic form in French, where the corners of the mouth are drawn back to emphasize the shape of the resonance-chamber: this is the regular French *i*, as in *fini* 'done'. In German the lips are not so far drawn back; the sound so produced is the German long *i*-vowel, spelled *ie* or *ih*. In English it is the initial sound of such words as *year*, *yes*.

The corresponding articulation with muscles relaxed produces a very different acoustic effect, for the resonance-chamber in a high vowel is so narrow that even the slight increase in width produced by the relaxation of the tongue-muscles is a relatively large change. This wide high unrounded front vowel [ı] is the German short *i*, as in *bin* 'am' and, in slightly lower position, the English short *i*, as in *bin*.

If, while pronouncing [i], one strongly rounds the lips, the result is the high front narrow rounded vowel [y], as in the French *lune* 'moon'. Decidedly lower, but still of the same type is the German long *ü*, as in *kühn* 'bold'.

The rounded wide vowel of this position [ẏ], — i. e. a rounded [ı], — appears, in a lowered variety, in the German short *ü*, as in *Hütte* 'hut'.

If the tongue is lowered to mid-position from these vowels, the narrow unrounded vowel is [e]. This vowel occurs in German, as in *geht* 'goes', and in French, as in *été* 'summer'.

The corresponding wide vowel [è] does not differ from [e] so characteristically as does [ı] from [i], for, what with the greater width of the resonance-channel, the width added by the loosening of the tongue-muscles is here not so apparent. The [è] occurs in standard German and (slightly lower) in American[1]) English as the regular short *e*-vowel, as in the English *men, get*.

The rounded form of [e] has usually less lip-rounding than that of [i], but a form with as great lip-rounding is conceivable, since this factor is in no wise bound to that of tongue-position, but can vary freely. The typical mid front narrow rounded vowel [ø] is the French vowel in such words as *peu* 'little', *jeune* 'young'. A lowered variety is the German long *ö*-vowel, as in *schön* 'beautiful'.

The wide form of this vowel occurs, again in a lowered variety, as the short German *ö*-sound, e. g. in *Götter* 'gods'.

---

1) By 'American English' I mean my own Chicago pronunciation, common generally to the North Central States.

The low front position, which is reached from that of the preceding vowels by lowering the tongue, scarcely admits of any distinction between narrow and wide vowels. The unrounded vowel produced in it, [ε], is the British English vowel in *men, get;* in both British and American English it is the long vowel before *r* in such words as *air, care;* it occurs in French in such words as *lait* [lε] 'milk' and *père* 'father'. A wide and lowered variety [æ] is the American English vowel of such words as *man, can.*

The narrow rounded vowel [œ] occurs in French, as in *peur* 'fear' and *seul* 'alone'.

b) *Back vowels.* It will be simplest to speak next of the back vowels. In these the rear of the tongue is near velar articulation and the front concavely lowered, so that the mouth is in the shape of a long, wide, hollow resonance-chamber. This shape is accentuated, in most cases, by protrusion and rounding of the lips. The unrounded back vowels are very hard to analyze, owing to the inaccessibility to touch and sight and to the relatively undeveloped muscular consciousness of the back of the mouth.

The high back narrow rounded vowel [u] is typically represented by the French sound in *tour* 'tower', *pousse* 'grows'. The German long *u* has a little less characteristic lip-rounding; it occurs, for instance, in *du* 'thou'.

The wide rounded vowel [ù] is the short sound in English words such as *book, foot* and is the German short *u*, as in *Mutter* 'mother'.

The unrounded vowel in this position is rare; it occurs as a variant of another vowel in Russian and is said also to be spoken in Armenian and in Turkish; its symbol is [ɯ].

The mid back narrow rounded vowel [o] is most typically represented by the French *o* as in *rose* 'a rose'. The German long *o*, as in *Rose*, has less distinct rounding; in

Norwegian and Swedish, on the other hand, there is an [oʊ] with the extreme lip-rounding which French, for instance, gives to [u].

The wide form [ò] is the German short *o*, as in *Gott* 'god'.

The same wide vowel, unrounded, [ʌ̀], is in American pronunciation the vowel of such words as *cut, but*.

The low back rounded vowel [ɔ] occurs in English before *r* in such words as *hoarse, more*. Within the sphere of this symbol, though perhaps lower than the preceding sound, is the British English vowel in *got, collar*, and the like. A narrower forward variety is spoken in such French words as *mort* 'death' and one still more forward, — almost a mixed vowel, — in such as *comme* 'how'. A lowered variety of [ɔ] sometimes expressed by the special symbol [ɒ] is the English vowel in such words as *all, law*. It exists in Swedish and Norwegian with the greater lip-rounding normally given to [o].

The unrounded vowel corresponding to [ɔ] is the [ʌᵀ] in the British pronunciation of *cut, but*. Much commoner is the unrounded vowel coresponding to [ɒ], namely [ɑ]. We may take the variety which occurs long in English *father, car* as the normal type. Then the German long vowel in *Kahn* 'skiff', *Staat* 'state' and its wider short form in *kann* 'is able', *Stadt* 'city' are a little lower and the French vowel in *pas* 'a step' and *pâte* 'dough' is a little lower and a little farther back. Higher than this normal type is the [ɑ⊥] in the American pronunciation of such words as *got, collar*. A divergent variety of this vowel is [a], pronounced much farther forward than [ɑ]; it is the vowel of such French words as *patte* 'paw', *part* 'part', and, slightly fronted and raised, of the British pronunciation of *man, can*, and the like.

c) *Mixed vowels*. The mixed vowels are less common

than the front or the back. The high mixed vowel, narrow and unrounded, [ï], alternates with [ɯ] in the Russian vowel of such words as [sïn] 'son'; it is pronounced somewhat back of the ideal mixed position.

Its rounded correspondent is the [ü] of Norwegian, written *u*, as in *hus* 'house'.

The mid mixed unrounded vowel [ë], in both narrow and wide pronunciation, is found in German unaccented syllables where *e* is written, as in *alle* 'all'.

The low mixed vowel, unrounded, [ɛ̈] is used in the British pronunciation of such words as *heard* [hɛ̈ɹd], *nurse* [nɛ̈ɹs].

I shall not attempt to discuss the vowels of the unaccented syllables of English and some other languages, as they present many and complicated problems and have been but imperfectly analyzed. It is customary to express the commonest unaccented vowel of a language, — such as in the second syllable of the English *started* (really [ë˞]) or the German [ë], as in *alle*, or the French '*e*-mute' (really [œ˞˞]), as in *je* 'I', — by the symbol [ə], which thus has different values for different languages and is a practical rather than a descriptive symbol.

There remain the nazalized vowels, of which French can give us good examples. In these the velum is well lowered, so that much of the breath escapes through the nose, producing the peculiar nasal resonance. Thus in French there is a nazalized [ɔ], [ɔ̃], as in *bon* [bɔ̃] 'good', an [ã], as in *banc* [bã] 'bench', an [ɛ̃], as in *bain* [bɛ̃] 'bath', and an [œ̃], as in *brun* [brœ̃] 'brown'.

8. Infinite variety of possible sounds. It will be seen that even the comparatively few of the most typical sounds here described form a large list. By way of summary we may unite the most important of them in the following table.

INFINITE VARIETY OF POSSIBLE SOUNDS 39

	Laryngeal.	Uvular.	Velar.	Palatal.	Dental and alveolar.	Labial and labio-dental.
Stops, unvoiced.....	ʔ	q	k	c	t	p
Stops, voiced......		ɢ	g	ɟ	d	b
Nasals, voiced.....		ɴ	ŋ	ɲ	n	m
Spirants, unvoiced...	h, ʜ	χ	x	ç	ʃ s θ	f
Spirants, voiced. ...	ɦ, ʕ	ʁ	ɣ	j	ʒ z ð	v
Laterals, voiced.....			ɫ	ʎ	l	
Trills, voiced......		ʀ			r	
Musical sounds, high..			u ɯ ü ï y i			
Musical sounds, mid...			o ʌ ë ø e			
Musical sounds, low...			ɔ ë œ ɛ			
Musical sounds, lowest.			ɒ ɑ a æ			

We have seen that these sounds, which may be selected as typical, are only single instances from among an infinite variety. Even the stops, which might seem fairly inflexible, occur in a number of varieties. We have already spoken of the many variations as to point of articulation and of the difference of voiced [b, d, g] and unvoiced [p, t, k]. In English, standard German, and French this difference is accompanied by another, that of energy of articulation: the unvoiced stops of these languages are pronounced with greater muscular tension at the point of closure than the voiced stops. Our [p, t, k], therefore, are *fortes*, our [b, d, g] *lenes*. These two differences do not always go hand in hand: in many German dialects, for instance, there are unvoiced lenes. Another kind of variation in stops will appear in § 9. The various possible pronunciations of spirants, trills, vowels, and so forth, and their variations as to place of articulation are more obvious and have in part been mentioned.

9. Glides and mixtures of articulation. In the actual current of speech another factor of variation appears: the transition or *glide* from one sound to another, or from inactivity of the vocal organs to the production of some sound (or vice versa). I shall mention only the two most important instances. In passing from an unvoiced stop to a vowel, we have to perform two movements: to change the mouth-position and to begin voicing. If these two movements are performed simultaneously, the result is a *pure* stop, as spoken in the Romance languages (e. g. French) or in the Slavic (e. g. Russian). If the stop is opened before voicing is begun, so that a puff of unvoiced breath first escapes, we hear an *aspirated* stop [pʻ, tʻ, kʻ], as in English and German, or, even more pronouncedly, in Danish. Finally, the glottis may be closed during the stop and opened at the same time with the latter, — this is the pronunciation in some Armenian dialects, — or shortly after it, — this type occurs in Georgian, — producing *choke* stops. The other instance I shall mention is the on-glide of initial vowels. Here the oral vowel-position is first taken: if voicing now begins immediately, we hear a pure vowel initial, as in American English or French; if the vocal chords are gradually brought from the breathing-position into that for voicing, they must pass through that of an [h] (p. 26), producing the aspirated initial of our words such as *heel, have, hoop*, etc. If, finally, the vocal chords are first closed and then suddenly opened into the voicing position, we hear a choke initial, the glottal stop followed by the vowel: this is the way German words written with initial vowel are pronounced, such as *arm* [ʼɑrm] 'poor' (p. 24).

While there are a number of other instances, notably in connection with stop-articulation, of various glide-possibilities, the glide is in the majority of cases determined by the positions of the two successive sounds. In passing from [ɑ] to [u], for instance, there is only one movement to be performed and only one path for that movement; similarly, in passing from [n] to [d] all one needs to do is to raise the velum, and this can be done in only one way.

Beside glides from articulation to articulation there is often possibility of *mixture of articulations*. An [m], for instance, before an [i], may be pronounced either indifferently or with the tongue-position and lip-widening of the [i]. The latter is the habit of the Slavic languages. This mixing in of part of the position of a front vowel, called *palatalization*, is very common. In English it occurs only in the case of [k] and [g], which are pronounced farther forward before [i], as in *kin, give* (p. 32). In the Slavic languages almost every consonant can be palatalized; in writing an accent mark may be used to indicate this (cf. p. 31), for instance, in Russian [p′i ʃu·] 'I am writing', — [p′] spoken with the tongue-position of [i] and the corners of the mouth drawn back for the articulation of this vowel. In *labialization* sounds are pronounced with the lip-rounding of a rounded vowel. An instance is the American pronunciation of *wh*, as in *which, whale*: the vocal chords are pronouncing an [h] while the tongue and lips are in the [u]-position, [h̨)] or [hẘ].

10. Syllables. While much more could be said about the different articulations and their glides and mixtures, it must suffice for our purpose to understand how varied the possibilities are. Great as is this variety, everyone who has heard a foreign language spoken will realize that, aside from the strange sounds, the general manner of pronunciation or 'accent' of a language is even more characteristic. Here, of course, the possibilities are again unlimited. Pitch, stress, kind of voice (e. g. full voice and murmur), and duration (speed) are all variable factors.

Even aside from the factors just mentioned, a sequence of articulations never appeals to the ear as a series of coordinate sounds. Some sounds are, in themselves and aside from any distinction of stress or pitch we may give them, more sonorous than others. Voiced sounds are more audible than unvoiced, for the obvious reason that to the oral noise they add the tone produced in the larynx. It is equally obvious that the more open a sound, the greater its volume. In a sequence of articulatiŏns, accordingly, we hear a constant up and down of sonority. The less sonorous articulations are heard, to speak metaphorically, as valleys between crests of greater sonority. The sound-sequence between the least sonorous instants of two such successive valleys we call a *syllable*. The most sonorous sounds are the low vowels. Even in a word like *away* [æuei] or [əuei], which is composed entirely of vowels, we hear two syllables, for the [u], less sonorous than the preceding and following lower vowels, is heard as a valley; similarly the [i] is less sonorous than the preceding mid vowel [è]: we write [æ ŭeĭ] or [ə ŭeĭ]. The lower sonority of the [i] appears in a combination like *away again* [ə ŭeĭ ə gen]. The most sonorous sound of a syllable is called the *syllabic*, the others are the *non-syllabics*. Vowels used as non-syllabics, like the [u] and [i] above are often called *semi-vowels*. The semi-vowel [ŭ] is often, especially if the lips are tenser than in the syllabic occurrence of [u] in the same language, written [w], and, as [ĭ], if the friction is at all above a minimum, approaches a [j], this character is often used to express a non-syllabic [i]. The combination of non-syllabic with syllabic vowels is called a *diphthong*. If the syllabic vowel precedes, as in the English *he* [hiĭ], *do* [duŭ], *day* [deĭ], *toe* [toŭ], *boy* [bɒĕ], *die* [daĕ], *how* [haŏ], we speak of a *falling* diphthong; if the semi-vowel precedes, as in *yes* [ĭes], *year* [ĭiɹ], *your* [ĭuɹ], *wag* [ŭæg], *wall* [ŭɒl], of a *rising* diphthong. A *triphthong* occurs, for instance, in *use* [ĭuŭz], [ĭuŭs], *wait* [ŭeĭt], etc. One can also write [hij, duw, dej, tow, jes, jiɹ, juɹ, wæg, wɒl, juwz, juws, wejt].

Next to the vowels in sonority are the trills, laterals, and nasals; all of them may figure as syllabics. Thus the American pronunciation of words like *sir, skirt, heard, nurse* is [sɹ̩, skɹ̩t, hɹ̩d, nɹ̩s], and words like *bottle, butter, button, bottom* are pronounced [batl̩, bʌtɹ̩, bʌtn̩, batm̩]. In *work* [wɹ̩k], the [u] or [w] is non-syllabic, the [ɹ] syllabic.

The boundary between two natural syllables is thus always the least sonorous sound between the syllabics: in *bottle, butter*, etc. it is the [t].

11. Stress. a) *Syllable-stress.* The inherent sonority of the speech-sounds is partly offset by the possibility of speaking one sound more loudly than another, — that is, of distributing the stress (p. 25). Thus the sequence [ui] can be spoken with the [u] louder, so that the [i] becomes non-syllabic: [uj], or with the [i] louder and the u non-syllabic: [wi], — for the most sonorous sound is always the syllabic. Even an [aŏ] may thus be turned into an [ăe] and an [ĕa] into an [eā] by speaking the [e] more loudly than the [a]. On the other hand, stress cannot wholly offset natural lack of sonority: in an [as], no matter how loud we try to make the [s], the [a] will aways be the syllabic, for any voiced [a] is appreciably louder than the loudest [s].

Some languages regulate the stress within the syllable in conformity with the natural sonority, pronouncing the syllabic of each natural syllable with greater stress than the non-syllabics. This, for instance, is the case in the Romance and the Slavic languages. In all languages there is some approximation to this distribution. English and German depart from it as far as any. In these languages it often happens that a succession of two or even more natural syllables is spoken with but one effort of stress. While in French, for instance, one would say [ʒə ma pɛl sɔ lɛːj], 'I am called the sun', with higher stress on each syllabic than on the preceding and following non-syllabics, an English word like *utter* [ʌtɹ̩] begins with highest stress, which is maintained through the syllabic [ʌ], and then sinks steadily to the end of the word, without regard to the presence of the second syllabic. In a word like *pity* [piti] the stress rises through the [p], reaches its height at the beginning of the first [i], maintains it through this syllabic, and then uninterruptedly sinks. The same is true of German words like *bitte* [bitə] 'please' or *hasse* [hasə] 'hate'. There are in all these words two natural syllables, but they consist of only one *stress-syllable*. Since stress-weakening by means of separation of the vocal chords (p. 25) easily passes over into the slightly wider-open murmur-position (p. 25), the unstressed parts of such words are often spoken with murmur instead of voice.

The distribution of stress may thus conflict as to syllable-boundaries with the inherent relations of natural sonority. The boundary between natural syllables is, of course, within the least sonorous articulation that intervenes between the syllabics. Thus in *utter, bottle, butter, button, bottom, pity* it is in the [t], in the German *hasse* [hasə] in the [s], in the German *bitte* [bitə] in the [t]:

in short, the least sonorous sound belongs as much to one syllable as to the other, — it is the valley between the two crests of sonority. In these words there is, however, as we have just seen, but one stress-syllable and therefore no valley or boundary of stress. The boundary between two stress-rises may, on the other hand, coincide with the natural syllable-boundary. That is, the stress of one stress-syllable may come to its minimum and that of the next stress-syllable begin to rise within the least sonorous sound. This is the case in such Italian words as *anno* [ɑn no] 'year' and *atto* [ɑt to] 'act'. The effect on the ear is that of a definite separation between the beginning and the end of the articulation concerned. Hence we write the symbol twice, once for each stress-syllable, and call such sounds *double* or *geminate* sounds.

In by far the most instances, however, the minimum of stress does not fall within an articulation: English, German, and French, for instance, have no double sounds. In the Romance and the Slavic languages the stress-boundary falls, when there is but one non-syllabic, always before the latter: the minimum of stress is reached at the end of the preceding syllabic, and the new stress begins to rise with the non-syllabic. Hence the division in the preceding French sentence, or in such Russian words as [vɔ· dï] 'waters', [bɑ· bɑ] 'woman', [pə tə rɑ pʼi·s] 'hurry up'. When there is more than one non-syllabic these languages recognize certain groups of articulations which may begin a stress-syllable: such groups are treated like a single sound; thus in French [a ple] 'to call' or in Russian [prɑ ʃtʃʼɑ·j tʼɛ] 'farewell'. Sequences of sounds which may not begin a stress-syllable must be divided: thus in the above French sentence [ls] cannot begin a stress-syllable, hence the division [pɛl sɔ]. In English and German, on the other hand, the conditions are not so simple. 1. In passing from a less highly stressed syllable to one more highly stressed, we usually pronounce a single non-syllabic with the following stress-syllable, as in *away* [ə wej], *again* [ə gen], *a name* [ə nejm]; but we do not always do so, certain meanings demanding a different division, as in *an aim* [ən ejm], in contrast with *a name*. 2. In passing from a stressed syllabic followed by a single non-syllabic to a less stressed syllabic, we ignore the natural syllable-boundary, as in *utter, pity, bottle*, etc. above, — speaking but one stress-syllable. 3. If two or more non-syllabics intervene, we put the stress-boundary between them, as in *until* [ən til], *hating* [hej tiŋ], *wholesome* [howl səm]. — German differs from English only in that in case 2 it does make a stress-boundary (taking the non-syllabic with the following stress-syllable), provided the preceding syllabic is long; thus, in contrast with *bitte* [bitə], *hasse* [hasə], spoken as but one stress-syllable each, it says *biete* [bi: tə] 'offer', *Hase* [ha: zə] 'hare' with two each. After the longer English vowels the same distribution is often made; one may say [fɑ: ðɹ̩, æ pl̩] as well as [fɑ:ðɹ̩, æpl̩].

Within each stress-syllable also, different relations of stress are possible. Two forms are common: the syllable either begins with highest stress, which then decreases, or it begins with less than the highest stress, rises to the highest, and then falls off. In each case the highest stress may for a short time be maintained. In English we use the former type for syllables beginning with the syllabic, such as *all, are, utter, apple*, the latter for those beginning with a non-syllabic, in which we reach the highest stress only at the beginning of the syllabic, as in *mid, lid, pity, bottle*, etc. (It is best to try these and the following examples of stress-relations in a whisper, as pitch-variations — see next § — may otherwise be confusing.)

In all the preceding instances the stress is maintained at its height throughout the syllabic and sinks only after the following non-syllabic is reached. This is why the [d] in *lid*, for example, is so much more stressed than that in *lead* (verb) [lijd], the [n] in *bin* so much more than that in *bean* [bijn]: the former [d] and [n], respectively, begin with highest stress and descend, but those in *lead* and *bean* begin only after the stress has already decreased during the preceding non-syllabic, [j]. This maintenance of highest stress throughout the syllabic is called *close* syllable-stress.

The decrescendo of the stress may, on the other hand, take place within the syllabic. In the Romance and the Slavic languages this is almost always necessarily the case, for most of the stress-syllables of these languages end with the syllabic. This is called *open* syllable-stress. In English it is less common, occurring chiefly in our longer vowels, which often stand at the end of a stress-syllable and therefore must needs include the descrescendo, as in *mama* [məmɑ:] and frequently (cf. above) in *father* fɑ:ðɹ̩], *apple* [æpl̩]. German has open syllable-stress in syllables with long syllabic, as in *Wien* [vi:n] 'Vienna', *Kahn* [kɑ:n] 'skiff', and in the first syllable of *biete* [bi:tə] 'offer', *Hase* [hɑ:zə] 'hare', and close in syllables with short syllabic, as in *bin* [bin] 'am', *kann* [kɑn] 'is able', *bitte* [bitə] 'please', *hasse* [hɑsə] 'hate'.

The stress may, further, rise, reach its highest point, and fall within the syllabic; this is called *compound* stress. It is found regularly in certain syllables in Ancient Greek and in Lithuanian. In English it is heard in a surprised, displeased *What!?* and in a peeved, irritable *No!* (most clearly if the whispering test is used).

These differences in syllable-stress constitute one of the chief difficulties in acquiring a foreign pronounciation and are perhaps the most important factor in the peculiar 'accent' of a language.

b) *Group-stress.* Of the several stress-syllables in an utterance some receive louder stress than others. In this distribution of varying degrees of stress among the syllables, *group-stress*, the different languages also diverge. In French the last syllable of an utterance or of such parts of an utterance as are fairly independent in meaning, alone receives higher stress, the other syllables being fairly equal. Thus the French sentence above quoted, receives, in contrast with the English equivalent, *I am 'called the 'sun*, but one highest stress: [ʒə ma pɛl so'lɛ:j], or at most also a weaker secondary stress on [pɛl], the last syllable of the part of the utterance which corresponds in meaning to 'I am called': [ʒə ma 'pɛl so ''lɛ:j]. In Japanese there is even less difference between the syllables. English and German, on the other hand, divide every utterance into small groups of syllables within each of which there is one highest stress, — *stress-groups*. But even these two languages differ from each other; English, for instance, normally gives highest stress to one syllable each of an adjective and a following noun, as in *a 'young 'man* or *'rotten po'tato*, so that such a combination contains two stress-groups, while German normally gives higher stress to the noun: *ein 'junger ''Herr, 'faule Kar''toffel*, one stress-group each. Russian also, in spite of its entirely different syllable-stress, has much the same group-stress as English or German, but differs, for instance, in often giving higher stress to a preposition than to a following noun, as though we should say *'at the foot, 'under the head*: ['zɑ· nə gu, 'po·d gə łə vu]. English, German, or Russian, with their frequent high stresses, can distinguish different meanings by their distribution of group-stress; thus in English *'torment* noun, but *tor-*

'ment, verb; in German *übersetzen* ["ˀyːberˈzɛt sn̩] 'to set across' but ["ˀyːbɹ̩ "zɛt sn̩] 'to translate'; in Russian [ˈmuˑka] 'torment' (noun) but [muˈkaˑ] 'flour'. Other languages with frequent high stress give it a uniform place with regard to the word, — which, as we shall see, is a division based entirely on meaning. Thus Čechish and Icelandic have highest stress on the first syllable of every word; short words of relational meaning, such as pronouns, prepositions, conjunctions, may, however, lack this stress. In Polish the next-to-last syllable of words is similarly, in almost all instances, accented. German departs widely and English very widely from a fundamental principle of stressing the first syllable of every word. There remains, however, the principle that in these languages every word is a stress-group, containing one syllable with highest stress and, in longer words, one or more with intermediate stress (the degrees of stress are indicated by the varying number of accent marks before the syllable), e. g. *procrastination* ["pɹʌˈkɹæs ti ‴nej ʃn̩], with four degrees of stress, highest on [nej], least on [ti] and [ʃn̩] and intermediate degrees on [pɹʌ] and [kɹæs]. Short relational words, such as *a, the, he, her, in*, and the like, have, however, as a rule, low stress and stand to the preceding or following higher stress in the same relation as do less stressed syllables of the same word. Further, the highest stress of some words is in certain connections weaker than that of others, so that the stress-groups which represent words fall under a higher unity of the phrase; examples are the German combinations of adjective with noun (see above) or such expressions as *a ˈgreat ˈbig ″man*, which, however, in nearly all cases, are really examples of *sentence-stress*, to which we shall now turn.

c) *Sentence-stress.* Among stress-groups the highest

stress of some is in turn higher than that of others. This highest stress or sentence-stress is in all languages given to the emotionally most vivid part of the sentence, — a result of the fundamental character of speech as an expressive movement varying in intensity according to the intensity of emotion (p. 1). We may illustrate this by speaking an English sentence with emotional stress on different words, — as though in answer, for instance, to various contradicting statements. E. g.: *"I 'saw the 'young 'man, — I "saw the 'young 'man, — I 'saw the "young 'man, — I 'saw the 'young "man,* and even *I 'saw "the 'young 'man.*

We find, thus, a threefold distribution of stress. First, there is the up-and-down of stress within the syllable, fixed for each language. Secondly, every language habitually gives certain syllables higher stress than others: we have our accented and unaccented syllables and our unaccented short words. Finally, the emotionally dominant elements of the sentence receive higher stress than all others. Usually these elements are words, in which case the emotional stress is given in most languages to the syllable which otherwise also bears higher stress than the others. Thus when we say *It 'wasn't dis"honesty, it was "sheer procrasti"'nation,* the emotional stress of *procrastination* is placed on the same syllable which habitually has highest stress in this word. If, however, the emotionally most charged part of the sentence is not a word, but only part of a word, the emotional stress may conflict with the group-stress. Thus, while we say *for'give,* as in *for'give and for'get,* we say *"for'give* in *"give and "for'give.* In French, where not a syllable of every word, but only the last syllable of sentences and phrases receives habitual group-stress, the emotional sentence-stress is given to the first syllable that begins with a consonant of the dominant word. Thus it is almost always a part of a sentence or even of a word which usually is unstressed, that now receives highest stress, 'It's the same person' is [sə la mɛ:m pɐr'son] but 'It's the very same person' is [sə la ″mɛ:m pɐr ′son]; 'It's impossible' is [sə tš po ′sibl] but 'It's *impos*sible' is [sə tš: ″po ′sibl].

The rhythmic effects of stress-distribution are heightened in English and Russian by the habit of speaking in the less stressed syllables shorter and less extreme vowels than in the stressed. Other languages, like German, go still farther and restrict the least stressed syllables to a single vowel, — in German [ë].

12. Pitch. Pitch, like stress, can be infinitely varied. The modulation of pitch may correspond to the syllable-division, each syllable being spoken with a unified pitch-scheme. This is the case in Chinese; thus in Peking [ˈxŭaˀ] with even high pitch means 'flower', [ˌxŭa\] with low falling pitch, 'speech' or 'picture', [ˌĭy/] with low rising pitch means 'rain' and [ˈĭy/] with high rising pitch means 'fish'. While the Peking speech has only these four pitch-schemes, some dialects have as many as nine. In Norwegian and Swedish stress-groups (words) of one syllable are spoken with rising pitch and stress-groups of two or more syllables (corresponding in most, but not in all cases, to words) are spoken with either rising or falling and then rising pitch, according to fixed habits; thus in Norwegian [bün/] 'ground', [′bü nən/] 'the ground', [″bü\ ′nən/] 'bound'. In Lithuanian, Ancient Greek, and the oldest Sanskrit we find compound (rising-falling) pitch belonging habitually to certain syllables.

In other languages, such as English, the different syllables have no fixed pitch-relations, but pitch is used in the whole sentence to express emotional relations. We use falling pitch for statements, as in *He cáme back* or the answer-word *Yes*, rising pitch for questions that contain no question-word, such as *Did you say that?* or for question-words used alone, as *What?*; the compound pitches are similarly used, thus rising-falling in questions that contain a question-word, such as *What was he doing?*, or in an irritated *No*, and the falling-rising in an angrily surprised *What?* Compound pitch is usually, if confined to one syllable, accompanied, as in these examples, by compound stress (cf. p. 47).

13. Duration. *Duration* or *quantity*, — that is, the length of the different sounds, syllables, and stress-groups, — is another important factor.

Thus in English some of the vowels are longer than others, [æ] and [ɒ], especially, longer than [ı̆] and [ŭ]. All our vowels, moreover, are longer before voiced sounds, as in *bid*, than before unvoiced sounds, as in *bit*. In one case only have we, in American pronunciation, approximately the same vowel in two distinct quantities, namely [ɑː] long, as in *father*, and the same sound (with a slight difference, p. 37) short [ɑ], as in *got, collar, god;* in accordance with the preceding rule the [ɑ] before the voiced sounds in the last two examples is, however, longer than in *got*. In standard German the tense vowels are long, the loose vowels short; in the case of [ɑ] there is, however, scarcely any difference except that of quantity, e. g. *Stadt* [ʃtɑt] 'city', *Staat* [ʃtɑːt] 'state'

In English our non-syllabics are longer, the shorter the preceding syllabic; thus the [n] in *bin* is longer than that in *men*, which is in turn longer than that in *man*. In other languages the duration of non-syllabics is not automatic (i. e. does not depend on the surrounding sounds) but is fixed for each word. Such long non-syllabics differ from doubled sounds (p. 45) in that no stress-boundary occurs during their articulation. Accordingly a difference exists between the Norwegian *otte* ["ɔ\ 'tːə/] 'eight' with long [t] beginning the second syllable and the Italian *otto* ['ɔt to] 'eight' with double [t], the stress-boundary coming after the closure and before the opening of the [t]-stop.

The duration of the various parts of a sentence is less fixed. Certain tendencies, however, such as that to speak a parenthetic clause very rapidly (as in *This man, — who for that matter, had very little to do with the affair, — ...*), can here be distinguished. No doubt there are also differences between the different languages, but they have never been ascertained, owing to the difficulty of abstracting from factors of mood, personal habit, and the like, which here have comparatively free play.

14. Limitation of the articulations in each dialect. A language which significantly used any considerable part of the articulations and variations of stress, pitch, and quantity that are possible, could be understood only by the closest application of the attention, and, if it used too many, could not be understood at all, for the intelligibility of language depends, of course, on repetition and recognition.

As a matter of fact every language limits itself to certain sounds and to certain ways of combining them. Some, like English and German, employ constant stress-relations for certain syllables, leaving pitch-modulation for the sentence as a whole; others, like French, use both pitch and stress only in the sentence; still others, like Chinese, assign a definite pitch-relation to each syllable and use stress only to modulate the sentence; Norwegian and Swedish use pitch and stress both for the syllable and for the sentence. The same is true of the individual articulations. Thus English and standard German use unvoiced aspirated fortis [p‛, t‛, k‛] and voiced plain lenis stops [b, d, g]; the Romance and the Slavic languages use only plain stops, unvoiced fortes [p, t, k] and voiced lenes [b, d, g]; the Peking pronunciation of Chinese uses only unvoiced stops, aspirate fortes [pʻ, tʻ, kʻ] and plain fortes or lenes [b̥, d̥, g̊]; other languages, such as the Polynesian, have but one series of stops; Sanskrit had four, unvoiced fortes and voiced lenes, each in aspirate and plain form. Such distinctions are recognized by speakers of the language, and forms not so recognized are interpreted as standard forms by the hearer. Thus, though unaspirated [p, t, k] and unvoiced lenes [b̥, d̥, g̊] are occasionally spoken in English, they are not recognized as different from the more usual forms; such a distinction as that between [pʻ] and [p] is not even noticed. Whether we speak a [t, d, n, l, ɹ] a little farther forward or a little farther back is a matter of indifference in English; it is left to personal habit, mood, or the influence of the surrounding sounds; but in Sanskrit and in many modern languages of India the difference between dental and cerebral articulation is as important as that between any other sounds; thus in Canarese *kondu* means 'killed' but *koṇḍu*, 'taken'. Whether we pronounce a *k* farther forward or back depends mainly on the following vowel and is never significant, but in Greenlandish or in Arabic [k] and [q] must be strictly kept apart.

In other words, each language, or, better, each dialect distinguishes only a limited number of places of articulation, and in each place only a limited number of manners of articulation, and any variations from these are never significant.

15. Automatic variations. The variations that occur, while not significant, may be very regular. Our English vowels, for instance, are longer in final position and before voiced sounds than before unvoiced, longer, to repeat our example, in *bid* than in *bit*, in *bee*, *bead* than in *beat*, and English spoken without this variation would strike our ear as very foreign-sounding, even though most of us would be unable to determine exactly what the peculiarity was. Yet in spite of this universal occurrence, — really because of it, — this difference of vowel-quantity is never significant. It depends solely on the following sound and can never be determined by the meaning of the word: it is an *automatic sound-variation*. Before and after unvoiced sounds we pronounce our [m, n, l, ɹ] partly or wholly unvoiced, e. g. in *try, belt, hemp, sent, snow*, but we are not even conscious of this variation: it also is purely automatic. So is the German and English variation between [k, g] farther forward or back according to the following vowel, as in *kin, give, — cap, gap, — coop, goose*, but in Arabic, as above mentioned, such pairs as [kaːla] 'he spoke' and [qaːla] 'he measured' could never be confused.

Every language has, further, limitations as to what combinations of sounds can occur and as to where, in the syllable, a given sound or combination may be spoken. Thus no English syllable can begin with the combinations [kn, gn, ts, ʃpɹ, tsv, ʃv], which are common in German, — even though, distributed between two syllables or at the end of a syllable, all of these do occur in English, as in *acknowledge, bigness, its, cash price, it's very cold, cash value*. The sound [ŋ] cannot occur at the beginning of a German or an English syllable but it does so in many languages. In Peking Chinese a syllable can end only in a vowel, [n], or [ŋ]. In the Polynesian languages no syllable ends in any other than a vowel sound.

Each language, therefore, has a limited sound-system, which, if only significant distinctions are counted and non-significant variations, whether automatic or merely casual, are ignored, is never very great.

CHAPTER III.

THE MENTAL BASIS OF LANGUAGE.

1. The place of language in our mental life. Language plays a very important part in most of our mental processes, few of which, indeed, are entirely free from linguistic elements. While it is possible, for instance, with some effort, to picture in purely visual terms the actions we have in mind for the morrow, we hardly ever do so, but rather plan our day not only by visualizing but also by wording what we intend to do. If, further, we try to think of our reasons for these intended actions, or of their effects, or of anything else not in immediate physical connection with them, we must resort to language, framing our thought in words and sentences. In short, a very little introspection shows that nearly all of our mental life contains speech-elements. We cannot conceive of the human mind without speech. The development of language, accordingly, must have advanced in inseparable connection with that of the mental powers generally. To demonstrate in detail the role of language in our mental processes would be to outline the facts of psychology. We are here concerned, of course, only with those mental processes which most immediately underlie the use of language.

2. Total experiences. The animals have in common with us a process which may be called the formation of *total experiences*. Like us, they experience the outside world not as a chaotic jumble of sensations, but as a system of complex recurrent units, as a world of objects. The perceptual and emotional elements which we group together, for instance, as a rabbit, appear to a dog also coherent and distinct from other perceptions and emotions, such as those of the surrounding trees, the sky, other smells and noises, the internal bodily sensations, and so on. Like ours, the dog's apperception, — or, as we subjectively say, his attention, — may focus the rabbit as the central object, for the time being, of consciousness. The coherence and unity of such a total experience are due to habits of association formed in earlier related experiences: in our instance the surrounding trees and the sky, the bystanders, and those of our internal sensations and emotions that are not connected with the present experience, have all entered into various combinations in earlier experiences and have thereby become familiar enough not to be irrelevantly confused with the present one.

Animals respond to a total experience by an expression varying at best for a few widely distinct emotional qualities; thus the dog barks at the rabbit as he does at a great many other things. Man differs from the animals first of all in that he has a distinctive sound-reaction for each one of a great many types of experience, — e. g. for the type of experience which we call a 'rabbit'. Whenever an experience of a given type occurs, the sound-reaction connected with that type is associatively recalled and reproduced. When we saw the rabbit, for instance, we did not 'inarticulately' cry out, but exclaimed 'a rabbit.'

This also, to be sure, is not an exact way of dealing with experiences. We react to countless experiences of a single type (such as 'rabbit') with one and the same utterance, while in fact no two experiences are wholly alike. When we associate the present experience with certain past experiences and utter with it the sound-sequence which we heard and uttered with them, we do so not because the present experience is exactly like the past ones, — it is not, — but because certain elementary features are common to it and each of them. These elementary features are known as *dominant elements*. Thus a rabbit of different size or color, or one running in the opposite direction might call forth the same utterance. We use the word 'book' for objects of many sizes, shapes, and colors, provided they present certain features. Even a clearly defined scientific term, such as 'triangle' applies to an infinite variety of experiences with but a simple common element. In short, our reaction to experiences, though much more differentiated than that of animals, is not just to the individuality of each experience, but groups great numbers of experiences together under types within each of which all the experiences are designated by one and the same reaction.

The association of experience-types with fixed and distinctive sound-utterances represents an important step in mental progress. It makes possible attentive and connected thought. When we recall the experience, we repeat, actually or in imagination, the sounds with which it is connected. They are a convenient means of holding the experience in the attention; by recalling the sounds (or their visual symbols) over and over again, — at first as young children do, aloud, but, after practice, in imagination alone, — we can keep the experience before us much longer than is possible in speechless picturing.

An advantage of the grouping together of hosts of individual experiences under one type is this, that all experiences belonging to the type can be dealt with en masse and need not be recalled one by one, if we use the linguistic expression, which deals with all of them alike. This is conceptual or general thinking.

3. The analysis of total experiences.

The existence of a fixed sound-reaction, which enables us to hold an experience vividly in our attention, also makes possible the *analysis* of experiences. Every experience is composed of a number of elements whose individuality is due to their having occurred in other contexts in past experiences. Thus we have seen the color of the rabbit, other four-footed animals, other running animals, and the like. Each element recalls those past experiences in which it figured. But it does this obscurely, until language has given the experience a fixed and easily handled symbol with which we can keep it from slipping, as it were, through our fingers. Once language exists, however, the analysis of the experience into these elements is bound to develop. At least it takes place in all known languages and is in all of them, as time goes on, being perfected by a gradual but unceasing process of development, to which we must ascribe also its origin.

This process is the assimilation of expression-relations to experience-relations. We may illustrate it by a schematic example. Suppose that in some language the utterance connected with the experience of a white rabbit is *patilu* and that connected with a white fox is *meko*, — in other words, that these experiences, of different emotional value, are attended by two totally unlike expressions. Nevertheless, owing to such elements as they have in common, whenever a white rabbit is seen, not only the past white-rabbit experiences, with their *patilu*, but also, among others, the white-fox experiences, with their *meko*, will be awakened. Sooner or later one of these types will assimilate the other's expression; such assimilative processes are constantly occurring, as we shall see, in every language, — as when, in English, Chaucer's word *fader* became the *father* of present English, under the influence of *mother, brother*. For instance, instead of *patilu*, someone will, under the influence of *meko*, say *metilu*. At first this will happen occasionally, but it will be the more likely to happen again when one has once spoken or heard the new form. The associational circumstances are all in favor of it. Finally the new habit will completely supersede the old. When this has happened, there are two utterances: *me-tilu* 'white-rabbit' and *me-ko* 'white-fox'. Corresponding to the perceptual element 'white' is the phonetic element *me-*. When one now utters *me-tilu* a certain amount of analysis is involved: *me-* expresses the color, *-tilu* (or *-ko*) the kind of animal. These phonetic elements may ultimately attain independent use: in answer to such a question as 'What kind of a rabbit (fox) did you see?' one may say *me* 'White', and one may designate 'rabbit' in general by *tilu*, 'fox' in general by *ko*.

When this development has taken place, such an utterance as *me tilu* or *white rabbit* involves an analysis of the total experience into these two elements. When we say *white rabbit* we more or less vividly separate the two elements of the total experience. Sometimes we may not attend closely to the analysis, but at others we shall insist on it, as when we say 'No, a *white* rabbit' or 'No, a white *rabbit*'. Such an utterance analyzing an experience into elements we call a *sentence*.

The relation of the elements of a sentence to each other has a distinctive psychological tone. It is called the *logical* or *discursive* relation. It consists of a transition of the attention from the total experience, which throughout remains in consciousness, to the successive elements, which are one after another focused by it.

The attention of an individual, — that is, apperception, — is a unified process: we can attend to but one thing at a time. Consequently the analysis of a total experience always proceeds by single binary divisions into a part for the time being focused and a remainder. In the primary division of an experience into two parts, the one focused is called the *subject* and the one left for later attention the *predicate*; the relation between them is called *predication*. If, after this first division, either subject or predicate or both receive further analysis, the elements in each case first singled out are again called subjects and the elements in relation to them, *attributes*. The subject is always the present thing, the known thing, or the concrete thing, the predicate or attribute, its quality, action, or relation or the thing to which it is like. Thus in the sentence *Lean horses run fast* the subject is *lean horses* and the horses' action, *run fast*, is the predicate. Within the subject there is the further analysis into a subject *horses* and its attribute *lean*, expressing the horses' quality. In the predicate *fast* is an attribute of the subject *run*.

Constant repetition, to be sure, mechanizing these processes, saves us the trouble of repeating the entire discursive analysis in every sentence we utter. Such groups, especially, as are very common are no longer felt as attributions (predication is always vividly discursive), the concrete relation alone remaining uppermost. Thus, in a sentence such as *A white rabbit ran across the field*, the first three words are plainly felt to be the subject, and the rest the predicate, and within the subject *white*, within the predicate *across the field* are in vivid attributive relation, respectively, to *a rabbit* and *ran;* but the groups *across the field* and *a rabbit* are not by the normal speaker felt as discursive relations. He would say simply that *a* expresses the 'indefiniteness' and that *the* expresses the 'definiteness' of the thing, while *across* is expressive of local relation. It is only when we give the parts of the utterance much more than the usual degree of attention, that we may feel these relations as discursive, — as, for instance, when we say 'It was *a* house, but I don't think it was *the* house', where *a* and *the* are plainly attributes. In short, a frequently recurring arrangement of elements may become habitual and not require a vivid discursive analysis for its utterance.

As this circumstance shows, discursive analysis is not an absolute thing: associational identification shades into it. In most languages we find, accordingly, elements that are but partially independent. In our schematic representation above, the stage in which *me-tilu* 'white-rabbit' and *me-ko* 'white-fox' are used, but neither *me-* nor *-tilu* nor *-ko* are as yet used independently illustrates this. In such an English sentence as *He suddenly ran across the field* there are several such partly analyzed elements. The element *suddenly*, for instance, divides itself into *sudden* and *-ly*, but since the latter cannot be used alone, the analysis is not discursive but merely associative. The same is true of *across*, where *cross* does, in related senses, occur alone, but not so *a-*. The *r*-vowel-*n* of *ran* occurs also in *run*, and the vowels [æ] and [ʌ] of these two forms are felt to express the relative time of the action, but neither is an abstract *r*-vowel-*n*, as a term for the action itself regardless of time, in English conceivable, nor is an [æ] or an [ʌ] ever spoken separately to express the time alone. In *father*, *mother*, *brother*, the *-ther* is common to all and thus expresses a common element of all three; or, if we add *sister*, we may say that dental-plus-*r* does so, but neither *-ther* nor a dental-plus-*r* can be used alone in some such sense as 'near relative': there is but the suggestion of an analysis. Such imperfectly separable elements are called *formational elements*, as opposed to the independently recurrent units of analysis, *words*. Words only and scarcely ever formational elements, can be dealt with as conceptual units of general thinking.

4. The naming of objects. If we look into concrete experience, we find that all of it centers round objects. An independent (or, as we say, abstract) quality, action, or relation never occurs. The sound-reactions, therefore, which form language can originally have been called forth, in so far as they refer to perceptual experience, only by objects. Words for qualities, actions, and relations we must suppose to have been evolved in the later course of speech-history.

The linguistic expression of an object-experience, then, is the simplest type, psychologically, of such expression. It is a sound-complex heard and uttered in connection with a number of successive concrete experiences, each of which exhibits certain dominant elements. The words *rabbit* or *book* are associated for each speaker with a long series of experiences having certain dominant features in common, much as these experiences may have diverged in their other features.

Even here we see a certain degree of abstraction. In speech or thought the sound-expression may be used not only for a given object exhibiting the dominant features, but also as a representative of all objects exhibiting them. In a general statement about 'the rabbit', 'books', or 'a triangle' these words save us the task of picturing successively all the rabbits, books, or triangles we can recall or imagine: we need only dwell on the word and the associated dominant features, such as a vague visual image of a rabbit, a book, or three intersecting lines. Thus, to repeat, the easily handled general concept, — the basis of logical thought, — is a product of language.

There are numerous languages, especially on the American continent, which have not gone beyond the naming of objects. In these languages the qualities and actions of objects, which in concrete experience never occur apart from objects, are in expression also always connected with them. Thus one cannot, at this stage, speak of 'white' or of 'runs', but only of such objects as 'white-rabbit' or 'running-rabbit', or, at best, of 'white-thing' or of 'running-thing' — in terms of our diagram, of *me-tilu* or *me-ko*, never of *me*. Every word is an object-expression; qualities or actions are never as such expressed by separate words. One cannot say 'kills' or 'killing', for instance, but only 'his-killing-of-it' or the like. This state of things forbids any distinction in speech between predication and attribution, for, as predication usually has as its subject an object and as its predicate an action or quality, its explicit expression depends on the existence of action-words and quality-words as separate words. Hence in these 'nominal' or 'attributing' languages such utterances as 'white-rabbit' correspond equally to our predication 'It is a white rabbit' and to our attributive 'white rabbit', and such a locution as our 'The rabbit is white' is inconceivable: one could only say 'This-rabbit (is a) white-rabbit' or 'This-rabbit (is a) white-thing'. Owing to the constant possibility of use as what we feel to be complete predications, the words of such languages are often called 'sentence-words'.

In addition to the object-expressions such languages have only *pronominal* words. These are expressions of purely deictic value, referring to the speaker in words for 'I', the one spoken to in words for 'you', the object near the speaker in words for 'this', the object farther away in words for 'that', and so on. Their origin is probably to be sought in sounds uttered in connection with deictic movements. At any rate, in most languages they resemble exclamations: as in English, they are usually short words, and occasionally they differ phonetically from the rest of the word-stock, as when in Russian the word for 'that', [ˈsˑtet], is the only native word beginning with the sound [s]. These pronominal words thus resemble the purely emotional responses to experience which we shall meet as 'interjections'.

5. The development of abstract words. Language at the nominal or attributive stage has not attained a habit of abstraction which English, for instance, has, — namely the habit of separating, as independent expressions, the qualities and actions of objects. That our concepts of quality and action are purely linguistic is evident upon a little introspection. Experience contains qualities and actions only in connection with objects. If we try to think, apart from the word, of 'white', we can do so only by picturing an object (such as a flat surface) or a succession of fleeting objects whose white color we hold dominantly in our attention, neglecting their other features. Similarly, the concept of 'run', 'running', if we exclude word-images, can be pictured only as a man or an animal or a succession of such running. This is due to the fact that in actual experience there is no such thing as a quality or an action apart from an object. What language does is to furnish a fictitious object, namely the word-symbol, by which we represent the unimaginable abstract concept of quality or action.

The historical origin of words independently expressing quality or action is various. In English such words as *white* used to mean 'white-thing', the 'thing' being defined as to gender, number, and case, and such words as 'runs' used to involve also an actor, meaning 'he-runs'. As to the psychologic character of the expressions as we have them today, the historic origin is, however, immaterial.

In the words expressive of quality the dominant element is a single common feature, permanent in each of a number of objects whose other elements are various. This permanence of the dominant element allows it, in its association with the word, to remain vivid: such a word as *white* is joined to a lively image of a single object or of successive shifting objects of white color. In the action-words the dominant element is a feature also common to a number of objects, but in all of them impermanent. As soon as we attempt to picture the object vividly, the action is lost: the object stands immovable, however suggestive of action we may allow its pose to be. Consequently the perceptual dominant element, aside from the word, of an action-word is never vivid: as a rule, in fact, we do not attend, in thought, to any element except the word itself, which has thus become dominant in the whole complex. That is why the experiment of thinking of an action-concept without using words is much more difficult than in the case of a quality-concept.

The psychologic character of the more abstract words, such as in English, the prepositions (e. g. *under, over, in, by, across*), the conjunctions (e. g. *if, though, because*), and the abstract nouns, (e. g. *cause, result, essence, being, relation*), while in itself interesting, need not further concern us here, if we remember that the principle is the same as in the case of action-words. The dominant element when these words are used is always the word itself; in any given occurrence they resolve themselves into concrete collocations or successions of objects, which objects we do not stop to picture more than vaguely when the word is being used.

6. Psychologic composition of the word. The word is thus psychologically a complicative association of those perceptual and emotional elements which we call its meaning or experience-content with the auditory and motor elements which constitute the linguistic symbol. Where reading and writing are practised the visual and motor elements of the printed and written word join the auditory and motor of the spoken. Disturbances of these associational habits are the much-discussed phenomena of the aphasias.

Among the elements constituting this complex the dominant may, according to individual disposition, be visual, auditory, or motor; whether the linguistic elements alone or the experience-elements also shall be dominant, depends, as we have seen, on the character of the word: in object-words, and, in a different sense, in quality-words, elements of perceptual experience may dominate, while in action-words and more abstract expressions the linguistic symbol is dominant, the experience-elements being but vaguely imaged. This is why in absent-mindedness or aphasic conditions the most concrete object-words (such as proper names) are first and most frequently forgotten, the quality-words next and the abstract words last of all. In learning languages, on the other hand, we succeed better in remembering object-words and quality-words, which we can associate directly with perceptual images, than action-words and abstract words (prepositions, conjunctions, particles, etc.) which we tend to associate only with words of our own language which either do not correspond exactly, or, in any case, remain dominant to the exclusion of the foreign words.

7. Grammatical categories. In the analysis of the total experience into independent elements and in the partial analysis of the latter into formational elements, certain types may become habitual and finally universal in a language. For instance, in analyzing a total experience we who speak English always speak of an actor performing an action. Many total experiences really are of this type, e. g. *The rabbit ran;* in English, however, this type has been generalized to furnish the mould for expressing all total experiences, — that is, for all sentences, — including those which really involve no actor or action, such as *The rabbit is white.* Here we use a fictitious action-word, *is,* of whose action the rabbit is supposedly the agent. In Latin, for instance, this would not have to be done: one could say *Cunīculus albus,* literally 'Rabbit white', where no such fiction is maintained, — and the same would be true in Russian. In short, actor and action are grammatical *categories* in the English language. Categories like this one, which universalize certain relations between words, are *syntactic* categories.

In the imperfect analysis of words into formational elements also there may be categories. These are called *morphologic* categories. An English verb-form, for instance, always contains an imperfect analysis into a formational element expressive of the action itself and one expressive of its relative time: one can say *he runs* or *he ran,* but there is no indifferent form, as, for instance, in Chinese, where [ˌpʻɑ ɒ̆/] means, from our point of view, 'runs', 'ran', or 'shall run', indifferently, but, if the element of time is vivid in the total experience, one can say also, in two words, [ˌpʻɑ ɒ̆/ lɑ] 'ran' or [ˌjɑɒ̆\ ˌpʻɑ ɒ̆/] 'will run'. That is, just as we always express future time in a separate word (*will run*), so Chinese also analyzes out the past-element as a separate word. Latin, on the other hand, has also a future category: *currit* 'he runs', *cucurrit* 'he ran', *curret* 'he will run'. We say, then, that the formational expression of present or of past time with actions is a morphologic category in English, that of present, past, or future time, in Latin.

The grammatical categories, then, though always based

on relations common in experience, universalize these, so that they must be formally expressed even where they are not actually present or where there is no occasion for focusing them, even though they are present. We must express actor and action in a sentence and tense in a verb even where they are not very vivid in the total experience, — where, respectively, a Latin or a Chinese speaker could ignore them, just as we ignore numerous unessential elements of every experience, — and also where they are not present at all, as in *Mount Blanc is high*, where the experience presents neither action and actor nor any particular tense.

The normal speaker, however, blindly accepts the categories of his language. If he reflects upon them at all, he usually ends by supposing them to be universal forms of thought. In linguistics, of course, we must be careful to distinguish between categories of a language, be it our own or another, and the features of experience, as apart from any particular language.

8. Psychologic character of the linguistic forms. The categories of a language originate in the extension of some oft-repeated type of expression. In this they are like all linguistic forms. To the speaker they seem fixed and universal forms of expression and even of thought; actually they are habits of association in vogue in a community. Owing to the similarity of dominant elements, an experience awakens a series of past experiences and is designated by the same word. Owing to the uniformity of the process of analyzing a total experience, all such analyses, — that is, all sentences, — may receive the form of certain numerous past ones: thus arise our syntactic categories. All words presenting certain common features, — belonging, for instance to a certain class, — may take on formational features that corresponded to experience in only a limited part of their occurrences, — such features as time-expression: morphologic categories.

The best evidence of the purely associational nature of linguistic forms lies in their change in history. The word *dog* once meant 'mastiff'; it came, however, to awaken predominantly the idea of dogs in general, with the species, not the breed, as dominant feature, until it became the universal expression for all these experiences. At one time English sentences could be formed without an actor and an action, but the process of forming a sentence came, in the course of time, always to awaken the process of forming actor-and-action sentences, until this type became universal. Similarly, when a new action-word comes into the language, such as the German *waltz* or the Japanese *hara-kiri*, it recalls the verbs of our language with their time-forms and unconsciously and immediately submits to the morphologic tense-categories, receiving the past-forms *waltzed, hara-kiried*.

Thus language is not, as the sight of a grammar and dictionary might lead us to suppose, a system of unalterably fixed and indivisible elements. It is rather a complex set of associations of experiences in groups, each of which is accompanied by a habitual sound-utterance, — and all these associations are, like all others, certain of displacement in the course of time.

9. Psychologic motives of utterance. True to its original form of an outcry under the most violent experiences, language is most easily realized under emotional stress. Some violence of experience must normally be present to call forth loud expression. If this emotional violence is the dominant cause of the utterance, we speak of *exclamation*. Under the social conditions of linguistic development utterance with predominantly communicative motive, *declarative* utterance, is a natural sequel. Likewise the *question*, an utterance expressive of uncertainty or incompleteness of an experience, is a weakening, as to dominance of the emotional motive, and a transference to communicative use, of the exclamation.

10. Interpretation of the linguistic phenomena. I have troubled the reader with a psychologic description which, though perhaps difficult, would have been all the more so, had there been appended to each step the examples from various languages that would illustrate the specific linguistic phases of the phenomena in question. The most important of these shall in the next chapter be so illustrated. After what follows the reader may find the psychologic description more intelligible, if he will go back to it; so much is certain, however, that the phenomena themselves, without consideration of their mental significance are unintelligible or rather, what is worse, liable to a post factum logical interpretation which substitutes for the actual state of things our reflections upon them.

The points of view from which linguistic phenomena can be regarded are of course various. For those unfamiliar with them the greatest importance lies in the realization that the categoric and other distinctions of one's own language are not universal forms of expression or of experience. It is important also to remember that the meaning of any linguistic expression is due to the associative habits of those who use it. A deictic or a representative gesture is intelligible at once, because it owes its meaning to universal psycho-physiologic characteristics of man. Even a suggestive or symbolic gesture hardly ever fails of immediate understanding, for the constant analogy of the simpler gestures predominates over associative transference. Vocal language, quite otherwise, though it has its origin in the direct reactions of our organism to experience, is the result of a very different development. The reactions which gave rise to it were reactions of movement, but the effect which became of self-satisfying and of communicative value, was the acoustic effect of these movements. Consequently even the simplest utterances furnished no analogy, comparable to that of the simplest gestures, by which every kind of associative transference and innovation might have been counteracted. The result is that no language has the character of a set of sounds in some way logically derivable from the experiences which they express.

CHAPTER IV.
THE FORMS OF LANGUAGE.

1. The inarticulate outcry. We have seen that our linguistic utterances are part of the expressive movements which attend every experience. In many lower animals also some of the expressive movements produce sound. The bodily expression of experiences of pain, for instance, may include not only a sudden withdrawal, but also a contraction of the thorax forcing out breath through the glottis, which, likewise contracted, produces the sound that we describe as a cry of pain. We have seen that human language is a developed and varied form of such vocal reflexes.

Even where language in the highest form exists, however, these most primitive reflexes occur by its side; the inarticulate cry of pain or anger is uttered by human beings under an extremely violent experience. As a direct result of this experience, this cry has nothing to do with any earlier experiences of the individual. It is independent, accordingly, as to its form, of the utterer's personal or social history: its sounds need not be speech-sounds used in his community, and it is no more intelligible in his speech-community than in any other; even an animal may utter its like.

2. Primary interjections. It is only under the most violent experiences that such purely reflex vocal utterances are used by man. If the experience is somewhat less radical, the vocal utterance is less completely dependent upon it alone, for, owing to the universal laws of habit, the utterance now tends to take that form which the individual happens to have most used or heard under similar conditions. This factor will, of course, vary according to the earlier history of the individual. Another individual who has had, in this respect, the same history and has, accordingly, formed the same habit of association, will, on hearing the utterance, at once associate the same experience: that is, he will understand. An individual, on the other hand, who has not had the same history, and has never heard the utterance in question, will make no such association, and will not know what kind of an experience the utterer is undergoing. Hearing the exclamations of a Zulu or a Fiji-islander, we may be in doubt as to whether it is joy, sorrow, anger, or surprise that he is expressing.

Even in these less radical vocal expressions there is some element of direct reflex. This appears, on the one hand, in the rather extended intelligibility of these *interjections*, as we call them, and, on the other, in their occasionally departing somewhat from the regular sound-system of the language. An example of both features is the labial trill, which is used all over northern Europe as an expression of intense cold and of abhorrence, although as a regular speech-sound it does not occur in the languages concerned; in writing it is usually reproduced as *brrr!* Similarly, various sound-complexes with the unusual feature of a syllabic [s] or [ʃ], written *Sh..!* or *Pst!* are used as an urgent demand for silence. Our peculiar whistling expulsion of breath, written *Whew!* to express extreme heat as well as surprise, is another instance of divergence from the usual sound-system. On the other hand, interjections may remain within the usual sound-system and may also vary in the different communities; thus the interjection of pain is in English *ouch!* and in German *au!* This, indeed, is by far the commoner case.

In the utterance of an interjection there is thus beside the mere vocal reflex another element: the experience is lived through as similar to certain earlier experiences, and is accompanied by the same vocal utterances as were these earlier experiences. We may say that these experiences together constitute a class recognized by the speech-community, in that they are always accompanied by the utterance of these particular sounds. A certain degree of pain might, for instance, be called in English an *ouch!*-experience.

3. Secondary interjections. Experiences less intense, — that is, having less predominantly emotional value, — than those so far discussed, are accompanied by utterances of more specific descriptive value. While a person who inadvertently got his hand into the fire might give an inarticulate shriek, and one who got his finger blistered might utter the interjection *ouch!*, one who merely saw a fire where he did not expect it, — saw, for instance, that a barn was burning, — would utter the more deliberate and specific, though still exclamatory cry of *Fire, fire!*

The more specific character of this utterance consists in its perceptual value. In the inarticulate cry and such interjections as *ouch!* only an emotional element of the experience is expressed; in the utterance *Fire!* the sounds uttered are associated by speakers of the language with the specific perceptual content of fire. Exclamatory utterances of this kind are called *secondary interjections*. There is no limit to the amount of material detail which they may contain. Other examples are cries of *Help!*, *Murder!*, *Man overboard!*, and the like; also exclamations describing noises or movements, such as *Bang!*, *Crash!*, *Snap!*, *Fizz!*, *Puff!*, *Whoop!*, *Rip!* Here belong also utterances which name the principal object concerned in the experience, such as *The child, the child!*, *Gold!*, *Forgery!*, *Mother!*, *A shooting star!*, *A white rabbit!* The calling of descriptive names is, of course, also exclamatory: *You thief!*, *Villain!*, *Generous man!* Of especial importance are commands: *March!*, *Get up!*, *Bring me a glass of water, please!*, or the use of people's or animals' names to call their attention: *O stranger!*, *John!*, *Child!*, *Doggie!*

The reflex element may here be present in various degrees and find expression in modulations of pitch, stress, duration, and the like. The modulations so permissible are different in different languages: the articulations which form the basis of the utterance, however, are in each case determined by their association with the kind of experience concerned. A foreigner does not understand them, because he possesses an entirely different set of associative habits in this regard. It will be noticed, also, that some of these secondary interjections involve a considerable degree of discursive analysis (though not, usually, a predication); in so far as they do so, they are exclamatory sentences.

The same articulations may be used at other times with a minimum emotional content. A chemist, after long investigation of what a certain component of a preparation was, could turn to his client or his pupils and, holding up a test-tube, quietly say *Gold*. A lawyer, after some consideration of the technical validity of a paper, could say, with very little emotion, *Forgery*. The significance of all these utterances, in other words, is due not to the emotional value with which they may be used, but only to their association, in speaker's and hearer's mind, with certain material contents of experience. This association has to be formed by every member of the speech-community before he can speak or understand what is spoken. It is only in the inarticulate outcry, and, to a lesser extent, in the primary interjection, that the universal reflexes of the human body undergoing an experience determine the form of utterance; in the words of material content this association is, so to speak, an external one and differs greatly in the different speech-communities.

4. The arbitrary value of non-interjectional utterances. We saw in Chapter I how most new members of a speech-community, namely children, are taught to make these associations. The problem of the origin of language, we further saw, resolves itself into the question as to how these associations originally came into being. The answer we found (p. 14, f.) was that the movement which produces the sound was originally an expressive movement, but, as the sound produced by the movement was in communication the striking element, further development proceeded from the sound and not from the movement. As no essential connection between sounds and experience was felt by the speaker, transferences and changes had free play, so that even between movement and experience there soon remained no recognizable connection. For instance, the experience of a bitter taste produces a very characteristic expressive movement of the facial and oral muscles which, if the experience is violent enough, may be accompanied by sound-production. The sounds resulting from this expressive movement may have been, in some time and place, the current expression for 'bitter'. As time went on, however, there happened that which, as we shall see, is universal in language: the manner of articulating the sounds gradually changed until they were very different from those formerly spoken. Even by this time the movements which made up the articulation of the sound-sequence were no longer those of the 'bitter' face-expression. But another, even more radical and equally universal kind of change must also be considered: people do not go on using the same expressions for ever. There is a constant tendency, as we have seen and shall in greater detail later see, to assimilate expressions to one another when the experiences are at all alike. Thus our expression for 'bitter' might be somewhat changed so as to resemble the expression for 'sharp', or 'bad' or even 'sweet', for 'almond-like' or 'uneatable' or 'nasty'. Of these processes we shall see many examples when we come to speak of the changes of language. For the present it is clear that the immediate physiologic connection between expression and experience, which at some particular time must have existed in a great many expressions, can in the case of no expression be of indefinite duration. The English word *bitter*, for instance, cannot be interpreted as an expressive movement, for we know that thousands of years ago, if it then existed at all, it had some such form as *bhidrom* and further that, whenever it began to be used, it was not an expression arising directly from the experience of a bitter taste, but rather a descriptive term which meant literally 'biting', for it was originally an adjective derived from the verb *to bite*. The expressive habits of the community, in other words, are in a constant process of change, and though, for language to begin, it was necessary that certain sound-sequences should be called forth by certain stimuli, it was neither necessary, once given this beginning, nor even possible that this direct connection should continue to exist.

It may be asked, then, if there are in use to-day any expressions which are still at the stage where there is a direct connection between experience and movement. If we look into our own feeling with regard to certain of our words, there might appear in English to be a great many such. For instance, our words *flame, flare, flicker, flimmer, flash* seem to us highly expressive of certain features of the experience of fire. Other words that might seem directly expressive are *puff, fizz, bang, zip, diddle, snap, smash, whack, squeak,* and so on. We are very much surprised to learn that to a foreigner these words are as unintelligible as any others, — until, of course, he learns English.

Let us look a little more closely at these expressions. In the words *flame, flare, flash, flimmer, flicker* we find, corresponding to the common half-emotional, half-perceptual element of meaning, the common initial sound-group *fl-*. In *flare, flash, flimmer,* and *flicker* the rest of the meaning also seems to be directly and immediately expressed; and here again, if we look for words with similar meaning, we shall find the same sound-groups recurring. Thus *flare* relates itself to *glare* and *blare*. The *-icker* of *flicker,* which expresses to our feeling the small repeated movements of the flame, performs a similar function in *snicker*. The *-immer* of *flimmer,* expressive to us of a quiet, small, continued action, is similarly expressive in *simmer, shimmer, glimmer*. In *flash* the sounds *-ash* express to us a very different, more rapid and violent kind of movement also conveyed in *clash, crash, dash, lash, mash, slash, smash, splash*. Or, to leave our *fl-* words, the articulation of *b-* in *bang, biff, bump, buffer, box, beat* corresponds to a common element of meaning which, we feel, is *directly* expressed by all these words. In the common parlance of school-room and dictionary they are 'onomatopoeias'.

This peculiar feeling on the part of those who know the language is in all probability, however, due to nothing other than the existence of parallel words expressing the same shade of meaning with the same sounds. When we utter any such word the other words of similar meaning are awakened, and their similarity of form adds corroborative strength to the impulse of articulation. That is, if we had only *flash* and not the other words in *fl-* and in *-ash*, it would not seem to us any more aptly and immediately expressive of its meaning than such terms as *chair, throw, combustion*. In short, there is no ulterior connection between these words and their meanings, or even between such formational sound-groups as *fl-* or *-ash* or *b-* and the elements of meaning conveyed by them. Even if it should be found with any certainty that the movements producing these sounds are, in a psycho-physiologic sense, the natural expressive movements attending the experiences which they in present English express, this would not alter the case. We might at first wonder at the correspondence and then realize that a selective process by which associations and assimilations occur had favored in each case the most suitable articulations. All this, however, would not change the fact that these words, like others, are limited to their language and outside of it are understood no more than others, and that these words have arisen and changed in the course of time by exactly the same processes that affect all words. The peculiar feeling of directness of meaning which they give us is due, then, entirely to the associative conditions of our vocabulary and not to these words' being any such thing as primitive reactions to experience: their history is the same as that of other words. Aside from primary interjections, the forms of language owe their function entirely to their association with experiences in the speakers' minds. The peculiar value in the speakers' feeling of such expressions as the above, is called *sound-symbolism*, — a term which is useful, if we remember that the 'symbolism' is such only within the expressive habits of the given community.

There are still other cases in which there seems to be an actual connection between the sounds uttered and the experience, this time in the sense that the experience contains a noise which is imitated in the expression. This is especially the case in bird-names, such as *cuckoo*. Such investigation as there has been shows that among the Germans, for instance, there have been in use great numbers of bird-names explicable only in this way, — that is, as *onomatopoeias*. This, however, is not a general principle, but only a special instance of the way in which language is expressive. It happens that some birds, — and there are probably few other such fields in human experience, — are naturally recognizable by their calls, and it is not surprising that, if the call became the dominant element in these experiences, the expressive habit of designating the birds by a more or less rough imitation of it should have come into currency. In English this is far less the case, our bird-names being mostly descriptive of the birds' appearance or habits (*red-breast, blue-bird, mocking-bird*), and, where an onomatopoetic name seems to exist, its form is usually determined by association with usual words of the language, as in the case of *Bob-White* and *whip-poor-Will*. The range of onomatopoeia is thus at best very limited, and where it occurs it can take rank only as one of the many forms of associational habit that occur in language.

As we look first at inarticulate outcries, then at interjections, and finally at the words of ordinary speech, we thus find a continuous gradation. The outcry is entirely the product of the present circumstances, of the primary interjection this is not fully true, and the utterance with material content depends for its form entirely on the habits of the speaker, which he shares with his speech-community. These habits are in a sense arbitrary, differing for the different communities and changing gradually in the course of time. A new member of a community must learn its speech-habits as he would any other set of communal habits.

5. The classifying nature of linguistic expression. The arbitrary nature of speech-expressions is directly due to the fruitful principle which makes communication by means of any such expressions possible. If each speaker reacted under each experience in such a way that no trace of his earlier history affected the reaction, communication would be impossible. No two speakers would ever react alike and no one speaker would ever react twice alike. Fortunately we are so constituted that our past does unceasingly modify our present: a present experience is inevitably assimilated by past ones of a similar nature and is attended by the same or similar expressive actions as were these. Thus the circumstance that an English-speaking person and a German will express similar experiences, respectively, by *horse* and *Pferd*, — an arbitrary divergence, — is due to the very fact that each expression is moulded by the past history of the speaker. The one has heard and spoken *horse* when such an experience occurred, the other *Pferd*.

The identity of the several experiences that are in each case designated by the same expression (e. g. *horse* or *fire*) is not actually inherent in them. This is obvious, if we recall the psychologic truth that no two experiences, whether belonging to one person or to different persons, are ever exactly alike. When we express each of a great number of experiences by the sound-sequence *fire*, we are associating them on the basis of an only partial similarity.

In our survey of the sounds of speech we saw that language would be unintelligible, if all of the infinity of possible sounds were employed, that the difficulty of understanding would grow as this infinity were approached, and that actually each community uses only a limited number of the possible sounds; that this limitation alone makes possible well-fixed habits of articulation and hearing. We are now again face to face with this principle. If each experience, owing to its indisputable individuality, were to be accompanied by a special utterance, no sound-sequence would ever be uttered more than once, and communication by means of speech would be impossible. It is the habitual inclusion under one form of expression, — that is, under one specific sound-sequence, — of vast numbers of experiences presenting certain dominant features, which enables us to understand one another.

We are so accustomed to think and express ourselves in the terms of our language that we are not ordinarily conscious of the subjective character of this inclusion or classification. Only the poet, who looks directly at the experience and seeks for an exact expression of it, must constantly realize this fact. Science also, on the basis of objective analysis, can make an extended classification of experiences and then arbitrarily determine that a given expression shall be used whenever certain features are present: this, of course, is the process of scientific definition. In ordinary life no such analysis is made: certain general, often very complex features are associated with the expression and all experiences in which these features are dominant are classed together and expressed alike.

Yet, even in ordinary life, there are circumstances when the uncertain character of our classifications is thrust upon our notice, — and that is in the face of some novel experience. A man who for the first time confronts a phenomenon which, let us say, looks like fire but gives out no heat, or one that presents a different exterior, being, say, a liquid, but produces the same charring effect, combined with smoke, as a fire, — this man will ask 'Is this fire or not?' — or, if he is more philosophical, 'Am I to call this *fire* or not?' The answer to the question must come, if it be given at all, from the consensus of the speech-community, which may or may not in turn call upon a scientific definition to settle the usage by determining a logically recognizable dominant feature.[1] The subjective character of our speech-classifications is brought home most of all, however, by the study of language itself; for here we constantly find that different speech-communities make very different classifications. There may be languages, for instance, where no such classification as 'fire' is made, but where there is an entirely different expression for each of such classes as 'camp-fire', 'cooking-fire', 'forest-fire', and so on: in such a language experiences which we should regard as falling into a single class would fall into several distinct classes. In other words, a number of experiences that are classed together in one speech-community may not be classed together at all, or may form but a small part of a larger class, or may be in some other way distributed in another speech-community. All depends on the expressive habits, — that is, on the linguistic tradition, — of the speech-

---

[1] The vagueness with which these dominant features may be defined is the motive in the anecdote of the traditional Irishman who for the first time in his life saw a parrot. It had escaped from its owner and perched in a tree, which the Irishman at once climbed. As he was about to lay his hand on the parrot, it exclaimed 'Hands off! Hands off!' The Irishman was dumbfounded, raised his hat, bowed, and said, 'Excuse me, sir; I thought ye were a bird.' — That is, speech was for him a dominant feature of human beings, dominant even to the exclusion of factors of visual appearance. General usage could have corrected him by changing his associational habits, — the science of zoology, by giving him criteria of logical validity.

community. It is especially important to remember that, except for the case of terms of purely scientific character, this classification is due to associative tendencies and is not affected by any logical considerations which individual speakers may undertake. People of a nation whose language had no expression for 'fire' but only for 'camp-fire', 'forest-fire', 'cooking-fire', and so on, might know very well that all these have certain features in common, and might even study physics and chemistry and arrive at the scientific concept of combustion, — but their language would remain the same. It would provide, always in accordance with its existing habits, some analytic expression, such as 'camp-fires, kitchen-fires, forest-fires, and the like', which would be used for the scientific concept of 'fire'. This may be illustrated by a few actual instances.

In Malay the experiences which may be logically defined by us as 'offspring of the same parents' are classed together, and for such an experience is used the word *sudara*. In English we form no such class; we form two classes, according to the sex, and speak of a *brother* or a *sister*. Now, it would be manifestly absurd to say that a Malay does not know his brother from his sister; it would be no less absurd, however, to say that English-speaking people are unable to form the general idea conveyed by the Malay word. Both languages can express the experiences for which no single designation exists by a compound expression which analyzes them, — the Malay by saying *sudara lakilaki* and *sudara perampuwan*, where the added modifying words resemble our terms 'male' and 'female'; and the English by saying *brother or sister* or *child of the same parents*.

There are still other possibilities. In Chinese the experiences of which we are speaking fall into four classes: [⌐ciuŋ⌐, ˌti\, ⌐tsə⌐, ˌmei\]. The first two denote males, the second two, females; and in each of these pairs the former denotes an older, the latter a younger member of the family. While we make no such classes, we can analytically designate these relatives by saying *older brother, younger brother, older sister, younger sister*. The Chinese, on the other hand, can express the idea of 'brother' by saying [⌐çĭuŋ⌐ ̩ti\], of 'sister' by saying [⌐tszə⌐ ̩meĭ\], and of the Malay *sudara* by [⌐çĭuŋ⌐ ̩ti\ ⌐tszə⌐ ̩meĭ\], — all of which expressions are comparable to our expression of the Malay term by *brother or sister*. It would be as absurd to say that the Chinese classification shows the Chinese to lack power of generalization or else to have a particularly strong feeling for relationship as it would be to say that we have less power of generalization than a Malay or more feeling for the difference of sex; or else that we have little feeling for the distinction between older and younger brothers and sisters, — when, to take the last point, English law has from time immemorial made much of it.

If any final demonstration were needed of how independent linguistic classification is of logical insight, it would be furnished by the German form of these words. This language, when speaking of one person, makes the same classification as English: *Bruder, Schwester*, but when speaking of more than one, makes also that of the Malay, using the term *Geschwister*, for experiences which in English would have to be analyzed into *brothers and sisters, brothers or sisters, brother and sister, brother and sisters, brothers and sister*, as the case might be. It is evident that whatever hasty conclusions were drawn from the contrast between the Malay and English expressions would have to be applied in turn to one and the same German, from moment to moment, according to the number of people he happened to be talking about.

CLASSIFYING NATURE OF LINGUISTIC EXPRESSION

The English translations given for the German *Geschwister*, however, show that, where a classification is not made and an experience is instead expressed by some analytic phrase, the analysis is constantly open to the speaker. If the expression is very frequently used, it may, to some extent nevertheless become mechanized, and need not involve the entire conscious analysis every time it is used.

A few more instances of divergent classification may be of value. The general word in English for locomotion is *go*, in German *gehen*. To begin with, however, while we can say *I go*, a German cannot say *ich gehen*, but must in this connection use a slightly different form, *gehe: ich gehe*. Aside from this, the German word is more inclusive, in that it is used also of the specific form of locomotion separately classed in English as *walk*. On the other hand, our word *ride* is more inclusive than the German terms *reiten*, used of riding on the back of an animal, and *fahren*, of riding in a vehicle or vessel. A black horse is in German *Rappe*, a white horse *Schimmel*; compare our *bay, roan, sorrel* when used as nouns. The relation expressed by our *on* in *on the table* is in German *auf*, but that in *on the wall* is in German *an: auf dem Tisch, an der Wand*. It will also be seen from this example how our word *the* corresponds to an element variously expressed in German. In French there are no simple expressions corresponding to our *stand* or *sit*; the idea must in each case be analyzed into *être debout (assis)* 'be upright (sitting)', *rester debout (assis)* 'remain upright (sitting)', *se tenir debout (assis)* 'hold oneself upright (sitting)'.

Even pronominal expressions (p. 64), in which the simple deictic value might lead us to expect entire uniformity, differ greatly. Three 'persons', that of the speaker, the one spoken to, and the person or thing spoken of, are everywhere distinguished. Some languages, however, use material object-words instead of the first and second persons; so the Malay for 'I' *sahaya* 'companion', *hamba*, *beta*, or *patek* 'slave', rather than the purely pronominal *aku*, and for 'you' rather the name of the person addressed or *tuwan* 'master' or *datoh* 'grandfather', than *ankau* 'you' In Japanese such object-expressions are exclusively used, no purely pronominal terms for 'you' and 'I' being known. Similarly, Polish uses *pan* 'gentleman', 'sir', *pani* 'lady', 'mistress', 'madam' to all but intimates and servants, rather than *ty* 'you'. Other languages identify different persons: thus the Italian uses *ella* or *lei*, literally 'she', 'it', for 'you', the German similarly *Sie* 'they' for 'you'; these pronouns originally referred to such nouns as 'your grace', singular and plural, and are thus results of the preceding type of usage. All these forms had their origin in polite phrases. The same was once true of the English *you*: it was the plural, politely used instead of the singular *thou*, — a use which finds its parallel today in the French *vous* instead of singular *tu* and the Russian [vī] instead of singular [tĭ]. In Italian, German, and French the substitute-forms are almost universal, the old words for 'you' (singular), — German *du*, French *tu*, Italian *tu*, — being used only to intimates, children, and in prayer. In the plural some languages differ from ours in distinguishing two kinds of 'we', one including, the other excluding the person or persons addressed: thus, in Malay, inclusive *kita*, exclusive *kami*.

Related to this is the expression of varieties of deixis, such as the 'here' and 'this', the 'there' and 'that'. In this, too, languages differ somewhat. In the Scotch dialects of English three types of deixis occur: not only a 'here' and a 'there', but also a 'yonder', and not only a 'this' and a 'that', but also a 'yon'. Likewise in Latin one used *hic* for an object near one, *ille* for one farther off, and *iste* for one near the person addressed; in German, too, one says *hier* 'here', *da* 'there', and *dort* 'yonder'.

Beside the deictic expressions most languages distinguish anaphoric reference: mention of things known or spoken of, as, for instance, in English: *he, she, it, they*; other languages make no distinction between anaphoric and deictic reference. Within the anaphoric relations a single instance may be cited of a distinction absent in some languages (including English) but observed in others; namely, the distinction between anaphoric reference to an object immediately concerned and that to another object. So in Latin: *Amat sorōrem suam* 'He loves his sister', that is, his own sister, but *Amat sorōrem eius* 'He loves his sister', that is, someone else's (who has been spoken of) sister. Similarly in Norwegian 'he took his hat' is *Han tok sin hat*, if the hat belongs to the one who took it, but *Han tok hans hat*, if it belongs to someone else. The same distinction is made in the Slavic languages.

A striking example of differences in classification is furnished by the numerals. In most languages the numbers are divided, as in English, into series of ten, the multiples of ten receiving analytic expression: the decimal system. This had its origin in counting on the fingers, — an origin plainly apparent, also, in the quinary or fives system of the Arowak, a Carib language, in which the expression for 'five' is the same as that for 'one hand', *aba-tekabe*, for 'ten' as for 'two hands', *biaman-tekabe*; that for 'fifteen' means 'one-foot-toes' (sc. 'added'), *aba-maria-kutihibena*, while 'twenty' is 'one man', *aba luku*. Our peculiar words *eleven* and *twelve* (instead of *oneteen, twoteen*) may be traces of a duodecimal system with which speakers of English may have come in contact in prehistoric times. In French one counts from sixty twenty units to eighty: 'sixty-nine, seventy, seventy-one' are *soixante-neuf, soixante-dix* ('sixty-ten'), *soixante-onze* ('sixty-eleven'), and so on; 'eighty' is *quatre-vingt* ('four-twenties'). This is a trace of a vigesimal system, probably used by the prehistoric inhabitants of France. At any rate, in the Basque (which probably represents the speech of prehistoric times in this part of Europe), the vigesimal system prevails, though the decimal has encroached upon it. Thus 'twenty' is *hogei*, 'twenty-one' *hogei-ta-bat*, 'twenty-two' *hogei eta bi*, 'thirty' *hogei eta hamar* ('twenty and ten'), and so on, while 'forty' is *be-ogei*, 'sixty' *hirur-ogei* ('three twenties') and 'eighty' *laur hogei* ('four twenties'). Wild peoples who have little occasion for systematic use of numbers, often have less extensive systems. Thus the Kham [t*kham] Bushmen in South Africa have a trial system, with words for 'one', 'two', and 'three'; higher numbers are expressed by combinations: 'four people' are 'two people, two people', 'five people' are 'two people, two people, one person', — or else one simply uses the word for 'many'.

In short, just as each language uses only a limited set out of the infinity of sounds possible to the human vocal organ, so each language divides the infinitely various experiences of life into a limited number of classes within each of which all experiences are named by the same expression. The classes so recognized by the different languages are, as we have just seen, very different. It need hardly be said that the description of the various experience-classes and of the sound-complexes used to express them, constitutes the *lexicon* or *dictionary* of a language.

6. Expression of the three types of utterances. There are, as we have seen, three types of psychic conditions under which speech occurs (p. 70). The simplest and most fundamental one is that in which an experience by its violence forces a sound-producing expressive movement. The most typical instance of this is the insuppressable cry of pain or rage. Almost as characteristic are the circumstances under which the primary interjections are uttered, and finally, the endless variety of expressions which may be used as secondary interjections. All these utterances, in which the dominant motive is the emotional stress contained in the experience, are exclamatory utterances. We have seen that language must have had its beginning in these, since it is a developed form of expressive movement (p. 9).

We have also seen that there is no fixed boundary between an exclamatory utterance and one in which the emotional prompting is at a minimum and the communication of a material content is the determining motive, as in the chemist's *Gold* or the lawyer's *Forgery* (p. 76). Most of our speech today is of the latter kind, declarative utterance. Some emotional tone is, to be sure, present in every experience, and the minimum of emotional tone must be greatly exceeded before the experience will receive loud expression, but the declarative utterance is always chiefly prompted not by the emotional content itself but by some material content connected with sufficient value to bring about utterance.

Finally we have interrogative utterance, unified by the peculiar emotional tone of doubt or hesitation at the acceptance of an experience into a particular sphere. In this form also the emotional tone may be so great that the utterance merges with the exclamatory type, as in *What!?* — *Gold!?* — *Forgery!?*

The constellation under which an experience receives expression always modifies the form, though it may do so in the most diverse ways. In English, for instance, interrogative and declarative utterances are distinguished not only by pitch-modulation, as in *Your father has gone out* (even, then falling pich) and *Your father has gone out?* (rising pitch), — see p. 51, f. — but also often by word-order, as when the interrogative of the preceding is *Has your father gone out?*, as well as by particular question-words: *Where is your father?* (rising, then falling pitch). In Latin the three question-words *ne, nōnne,* and *num* have no content except that of expressing the interrogative situation, and the same is true of the Slavic *li*, — e. g. Russian [zdaˊroˑva lˊi vaʃaˊmaˑt] 'Is your mother well?', literally 'Well (*li*) your mother?' — and of the Chinese [ˌmo/].

On the other hand, very much the same pitch-modulation that with us is expressive of interrogation is in Norwegian usual in declarative utterances. Similarly, exclamatory sentences have in English a peculiar pitch-modulation of greater range than that of other utterances, but Italians use a very similar modulation for declarative and interrogative speech, which makes them in our ears seem to be excited when really they are not. The accompaniment of the utterance by a primary interjection may also be used to express exclamatory value, as in *O stranger!, Oh, come on!* The names of persons or animals used as secondary interjections, to call them, have in many languages a particular form when so used, called a *vocative*; e. g. Latin *Fīlī!* 'Son!' (otherwise, for instance, *Fīlius abest* 'The son is away') or ancient Greek *Páter* 'Father!' (as opposed, for instance, to *Patḕr apēn* 'The father was away'). An action expressed exclamatorily as desired or commanded has in many languages a particular form for this use, an *imperative*, as in Latin *Audī!* 'Hear!' or *Da!* 'Give!' (as opposed, for instance, to *Audīs* 'Thou hearest' or *Dare vult* 'He wants to give').

7. The parts of utterances. We have so far in this

THE PARTS OF UTTERANCES

chapter been speaking of utterances as units and ignoring the fact that most of them consist of definite parts (p. 60, ff.).

Many of the utterances of which we have spoken are, in fact, indivisible, — for instance, *Ouch!* or *Fire!* or *Gold!* or in Malay the word *sudara* or each of the four Chinese words [⌈çĭuŋ⌉, ˌti\, ⌈tsze⌉, ˌmeĭ\]. They present the simple instance of a sound-complex used in its entirety for the expression of an experience lived through as falling into a class with certain earlier ones.

Many other of the utterances I have quoted are, however, more complex, containing formational elements (p. 62). The English word *flash*, for instance, is felt to belong, on the one hand, to a group with *flame, flare, flicker, flimmer*, on the other, with *clash, crash, dash, slash*, etc. This word is, to be sure, used repeatedly to express a certain type of experience; but to this value is added another factor: it relates the experience, on the one hand, to such as would be expressed by *flame, flare*, and so on, and, on the other, to such as would be designated by *crash, dash, slash*, and the like. It does this subtly, without analytic consciousness on the speaker's part, and yet certainly, as is shown by the peculiar feeling of pregnant significance (p. 79, f.). Or, to take one of several other instances of formationally composed words that have occurred, the German *gehen* 'go' or 'walk' relates the experience, on the one side, to that of *gehe* in *ich gehe* 'I walk' and other similar forms, and, on the other side, to *reiten, fahren*, and many others with final *-en* and the meaning of general verb-forms.

That is to say, beside expressing the classification of the experience with those past experiences with which it is unconditionally thrown into one class, these utterances at the same time imply that the experience is similar to a number of others, — this implication being made by a partial similarity of form. We thus obtain, beside the total assimilation of experiences into a single class or word, a grouping of such single classes into larger and looser classes, the 'morphologic word-classes'. The associational character of the grouping appears in the fact that we cannot, for instance, say *-ash* for a violent movement or *fl-* for an experience of fire, and so on: these are formational elements, not words (p. 62). Though the value — especially the emotional value — of these words is due very greatly to the associations which their formational elements express, the normal speech-feeling, no matter how often it associates these words with one another, never stops to analyze them. Such utterances as *flash* or *father* (p. 62), therefore, though composed of parts, are nevertheless conceptually units.

The unity of such expressions as these may outweigh the divisibility in various degrees. In the case of *flare, flash, flimmer, flicker, flame* the sound-complex *fl-* is a formational element, the expression of a similarity of the the experiences, which can never occur alone. In fact, it can not be added at liberty to any other utterance, but occurs fixedly and exclusively in certain words. What is more significant still, the same sounds occur in other words, such as *flow, float, fly, flutter*, with a different value entirely, or, at any rate, if there is association with our first set of words, in a much extended and vaguer value.

If, now, we look at an English expression, such as the plural *fires*, the parts at once appear to possess a much greater degree of independence than in the instances so far mentioned. Even the normal speaker feels at once that the first, larger part, *fire-*, of the expression is identical with the singular, *fire*, and that the last part, *-s* [z], is identical with the same sound in other expressions, such as *fathers, boys, sisters* and with the similar sounds [s] and [əz] in *cats, ropes* and *watches, peaches*.[1]) In fact, even the normal speaker would not need to think long before he could define the common element by saying that the *-s* expresses plurality. Nevertheless, as the *-s* cannot be used in this sense in certain words, such as *man, deer, goose, foot*, — and, further, as it could not be used independently in the sense, let us say, of 'several' or 'many', it is but a formational part of the expression *fires*, even if a more independent part than, say, the *fl-* in *flash*.

In the possessive *father's* the first and larger element, *father*, has as much independence as *fire* in the last instance, but the second element, *-s* [z], has more. For, beside occurring also, with the same value, in such expressions as *boy's, king's, man's*, it may even occur with some measure of independence, as in *the King of England's son* and *the man I saw yesterday's father*. Nevertheless its independence is not complete. One who said '*s*', meaning some such thing as 'possession' or 'belonging', would not be understood, nor is the speaker of English, no matter how conscious he may be of the value of the possessive *s* as a part of the larger expressions, ever tempted to essay this independent use.

Another type of the same phenomenon is illustrated by Turkish plurals, such as *kullar* 'slaves', *evler* 'houses'. The Turkish speaker could not use *-lar* or *-ler* alone in some such sense as 'several', any more than the English speaker could so use his *-s*. Moreover the vowel of this element is *a*, if the preceding part of the word has a

---

[1] Owing to the similarity of the writing and to the automatism of the sound-variation, the normal speaker is not conscious of the difference between the endings [s], [z], and [əz].

back vowel, *e*, if it has a front vowel, — obviously an indication of the unity of the whole expression in the speaker's analysis of experience. On the other hand, side by side with this dependence, there are features which show the sound-sequence *-lar* or *-ler* to have a more independent value than the English plural-suffix; most important among them the fact that, if the plurality is otherwise expressed, the suffix is left off, as in *dört adam* 'four men', not *dört adamlar*.

Of a different character, again, is an English expression such as *thirteen*. The transparency of the meaning, due to the association with such forms as, on the one hand, *fourteen, fifteen, sixteen,* etc., *ten, tenth,* and, on the other, *three, third, thirty,* makes it certain that every speaker feels the *thir-* to mean the units above ten and the *-teen* to mean the ten. Nevertheless, no one would say independently, *thir* instead of *three* or *teen* instead of *ten*. Yet cases like *sixteen, seventeen, nineteen,* where the first part, *six, seven, nine* does occur independently, make the second part so distinct in the feeling of speakers that we have come to speak of 'a girl in her *teens*'. The formational element *-teen* is more nearly independent, therefore, than any we have yet analyzed out of a unified expression.

If we look finally, at an English word like *bulldog*, there can be no question, from the outset, but that the elements *bull* and *dog* are used independently. Still, there is a reservation: for *bulldog* does not mean 'a bull and a dog', but only a certain kind of a dog that may be supposed in some way to resemble a bull. The word *bull* independently used has never this meaning; it means a 'bull' and not 'like a bull', — it is a noun and not an adjective. In the expression *bulldog*, therefore, the element *bull* is not fully independent, for, though closely associated with the independent use of the same sound-sequence, its value is not exactly the same; the expression *bulldog*, consequently, retains a considerable degree of unity; as we shall see, it is technically a *compound* word.

The independence of the parts is even greater in a Chinese expression such as [ˈɕĭuŋ˥ ˌti\] for 'brother'. The elements [ˈɕĭuŋ˥] and [ˌti\] occur independently in the respective senses of 'older brother' and 'younger brother'; the unity of the whole expression consists only in its habitual use, with this order of the parts, in the sense of 'brother' or 'brothers' — a very 'loose' compound.

8. The word: phonetic character. An expression in which the independence of the parts is fully realized can no longer be said to have unity in the sense of the preceding cases. The English expression *older brother*, for instance, contains two parts, *older* and *brother*, each of which is used to designate a class of experiences and can recur in this capacity in the most varied connections, as in *I am older, older men* and *my brother, Where is brother? younger brother.* Such elements of speech, independently recurring as expressions of experiences viewed as similar, are, of course, words (p. 62). It will be evident from the foregoing illustrations of less independent elements approaching the independent use of words, that the word is by no means a mathematically definable concept; in fact it is sometimes very hard to decide what is and what is not a word. It may be a puzzle, even in one's own language, to decide whether an element can or cannot be independently used. Does the usage in *bull terrier, bull pup*, and a few similar instances justify us in setting up an adjective *bull* and calling *bulldog* two words? Probably not, for all these expressions may be looked upon as compounds of uniform type, — but the point is disputable: a dog-fancier who spoke of 'three terriers, two fox and one bull' would be using *bull* in this sense as an independent adjective, no different from *small, large, white,* or *black.*[1])

It is also clear that the unity or plurality of words used to express a given experience must vary greatly in different languages. We have seen how what a Malay expresses by *sudara* is expressed in Chinese by a very loose compound of four parts, and in English by three independent words: *brother or sister.* What we express by the word *brother*, a fairly close-knit unit, the Chinese express by a compound of two parts, and the Malays by the two words *sudara lakilaki.* Finally, the Chinese unit [ˌti\] would be in English two words, *younger brother*, and in Malay, — where we might expect three or four words, — again but one: *adek.* To take another example, — our expression *I am eating meat*, corresponds to the German one of three words: *Ich esse Fleisch*, to the Latin of two: *Carnem edo*, and in Aztec to a single fairly close-knit compound word: *Ninakakwa.*

It is especially to be observed that the unity of such expressions as we found above to be unified, was in no way due to any phonetic peculiarity in these words. If we found *thirteen*, for instance, to be a single word, this was not due to anything in the immediate phonetic form of the expression, but only to the fact that *thir-* does not occur independently. Likewise, where an expression consists of several words, phonetic observation does not reveal any pause between them. Indeed such pronunciations as

---

1) The written form of the expressions gives, of course, no answer, for the graphic (p. 20, f.) separation of the words is only a half-conscious and unscientific attempt at answering the question we are here dealing with; genuine compound words may be found in good English printing as separate words, as hyphenated combinations, or run together as one word, e. g. *bull moose, bull-pup, bulldog.*

that shown by Latin versification of something like [kɑrnẽːdo] for *Carnem edo*, or in English of [ætʃu] for *at you*, show this most plainly; and it is safe to challenge anyone who does not understand a language, be it English or any other, to divide the current of speech into words. The word, in short, is a semantic, not a phonetic unit. It is only through a process of analyzing the meaning that people can come to distinguish the word-boundaries, as we imperfectly do in our writing.

Secondarily, however, every language does make some phonetic recognition of the word: but this differs greatly in different languages.

A language which shows little phonetic recognition of word-boundaries is modern French. In a French sentence there is no feature which shows where one word ends and the next begins. The stress-accent, for instance, is not distributed according to the words, but rests on the last syllable of the sentence, or, in longer sentences, on the last syllable of connected word-groups (p. 48). On account of this lack of phonetic word-boundaries French has been called, par excellence, 'the language of the pun. A good illustration is the couplet quoted by Passy in his *Petite phonétique*[2], page 22. The two verses are pronounced exactly alike. They each read:

[ga la mā də la 'rɛːn a la tur ma pa 'niːm];

the word-division, however, is seen in the conventional orthography:

Gal, amant de la Reine, alla, tour magnanime,
Galamment de l'Arène à la Tour Magne, à Nîmes.

'Gal, lover of the Queen, went, brave feat, gallantly from the Arena to the Large Tower, at Nîmes.' For the same reason uneducated Frenchmen have great difficulty in separating their words in writing; Passy quotes an instance in which [ʒə sÿi 'sa:ʒ a vɛk man mŭa 'zɛl] 'I am being good with Miss (the governess)' was written by a child: *je suisage avecmane moisel*, the conventional orthography (and real word-division) being: *Je suis sage avec Mademoiselle*. The one-sound utterance *au* [o] 'to the' is two words, for it is semantically composed of the fully analyzable elements *à* [a] 'to' and *le* [lə] 'the', the substitution of *au* whenever they come together being a purely phonetic automatism.

All this is in some contrast to languages like English, in which nearly every word has a high stress-accent on one of its syllables (p. 49). Certain small words which lack this stress, — commonly, for instance, such words as *the, a, is, in, and* (p. 49), — we call *enclitics*, if they are semantically joined to the preceding word (*hasn't, let 'im*), and *proclitics*, if to the word that follows (*a rabbit, in speaking*); they alone can offer difficulty as to the number of words in a sentence. This clearness is increased by the fact that we use an almost entirely different set of vowels in unstressed syllables from that of the stressed. It is only the presence of stressless words that makes halfway possible the pun which answers the question, 'What's the difference between a rheumatic man and a healthy man who lives with his parents?' by saying, 'One is well at some times and has a rheumatism others, and the other is well at all times and has a room at his mother's'. It will be noticed, however, that the boundary between words is sufficiently marked by certain stress-relations to rob such similarities of their full effect: in the latter phrase our stress begins to increase with the *m* of *mother's*, in the other the *m* is weak and stress begins on the initial vowel of *others*. There is the same difference, for instance, between *a name* and *an aim* (p. 46).

In Norwegian and Swedish all words not enclitically

THE WORD: PHONETIC CHARACTER 101

or proclitically used have one of two pitch-melodies, rising or falling-rising (p. 51). Čechish has a stress-accent regularly on the first syllable of all but enclitically used words, and Icelandic has a similar habit; Polish stresses almost always the next-to-last syllable of its words (p. 49). In Chinese the phonetic recognition of the word is especially striking. Every word here consists of only one syllable ending in vowel, [n], or [ŋ], and uttered on one of a limited number of pitch-melodies (p. 51); the only exceptions are enclitics.

If we look beyond the single utterance, we find another set of phenomena involving phonetic recognition of word-boundaries. These phenomena may be described as sound-variation in word-initial and word-final, and are spoken of by the name which the grammarians of ancient India gave them, *sandhi*. The beginning or the end of a word often varies phonetically according to the phonetic character of the preceding or the following word. In English, for instance, the word *you* [juŭ] or [ju] when coming after a final [t] is pronounced [ʃu], and after a final [d], [ʒu], e. g. *won't you, did you*. We thus find one word occurring with three different initials, — a variation which does not occur within any word, and therefore marks phonetically the word-boundary. The most familiar example of sandhi is the so-called 'liaison' of French. The word *vous* 'you', for instance, is [vu] except before a word closely connected in meaning that begins with a vowel, where it is [vuz]; thus *vous avez* 'you have' is [vu za 've] but *vous faites* 'you make' is [vu 'fɛt]. Such a variation without change of meaning, as that between [vu] and [vuz] occurs only at the end of words and is therefore a sign of active recognition of the word-boundary even in French. Another of the many instances is the word *a* 'has' [a], which before a semantically closely joined vowel-initial becomes [at], written *a-t*, e. g. *elle a sonné* 'she rang' [ɛ la sɔ 'ne], but *a-t-elle?* 'has she?' [a 'tɛl]. The most extreme instance of the use of sandhi, at least in writing, is Sanskrit, the language from which the name of the phenomenon is taken; here the end of every word has a number of forms that appear according to the nature of the following initial, which also is sometimes affected. Thus: *devaḥ patati* 'the god falls', *devas tatra* 'the god there', *devaś carati* 'the god wanders', *deva eti* 'the god goes', *devo gacchati* 'the god walks', and, with change also of the following initial, before *atra* 'here', *devo 'tra* 'the god here'. Sandhi, however, does not imply so vivid a recognition of the word as do those features which appear in each single utterance; for sandhi makes itself felt only when several utterances containing the same word are taken in view, and under these conditions the very reappearance of the word already constitutes such a recognition.

There is always a tendency, when a word has several sandhi-forms, that these may come to vary not in automatic sound-variation, according to the character of the preceding or the following sound, (as is the case in Sanskrit), but that the difference of form may come to imply some semantic difference. A transition to the latter type is the French liaison, which limits the longer forms, such as [vuz] and [at] to occurrence before words closely connected in sense. An instance still farther along toward semantic differentiation occurs in Irish. This language has a sound-variation in word-initial which, however, does not depend upon the phonetic character of the preceding word-final, but arbitrarily on the preceding word; that is, Irish words may be divided into a number of otherwise arbitrary classes, according to the effect they have on a closely following word-initial. Examples are: *tá ba* 'there are cows' but *a va* 'his cows'; *uv* 'an egg', *an tuv* 'the egg', *na nuv* 'of the eggs', *a huv* 'her egg'. This variation has semantic value in that it does not depend automatically on the adjoining sounds but implies a division of words into classes, — in this instance, however, not of the words in which the variation occurs, but of the words that may closely precede them. A great many other semantic classifications as we shall see, are expressed by sound-variations and affixed sounds in almost all languages: in so far as these sound-variations and affixations affect either the end or the beginning of words, they involve, of course, a recognition of the word as a unit.

9. The word: semantic character. The word, then, is not a phonetic unit, but is to be defined as a semantically independent and recurrent element which can be dealt with as a conceptual whole. We have seen that, in spite of this, a language may recognize within its words a relation to other words of partially similar meaning. This relation expresses itself, as we have seen, by partial phonetic similarity, as in *flame, flare, flimmer, flash* or in *flash, crash, dash*, etc., or in *fathers, boys, fires*. It may, however, receive no phonetic expression, but inhere entirely in a parallelism of use, especially as to categoric distinctions, as in the plurals *fathers, men, geese, children,* or the verbs, present tense, third person singular, *eats, is, has, may, can*. Here there is no phonetic similarity between the forms, but their function with regard to the English categories of actor and action, number, and tense (p. 68) is in each group uniform. The formational elements, as we have seen, may stand in various degrees of dependence, from the comparative unity of *flash, clash,* and the like, where the normal speaker is unconscious of the relating values, to such comparative independence as that of the English possessive -*s* (p. 95), or of the members of a compound like *bulldog*, which, in slightly divergent use, occur as independent words. Semantically, the elements can be of the most various significance, from the almost purely emotional tinge of *fl-*, *cl-*, *-ash*, *-immer* to the explicit relational value of a plural or possessive sign, or the material explicitness of the elements of compounds such as *bulldog*.

Different languages vary, of course, widely in the meanings of the formational elements into which imperfect analysis divides a word. The greatest complexes of semantic elements in single words are found in the attributing languages, where every word is an object-expression (p. 64). For here the expression of experiences of action and quality cannot dissociate these elements from objects; one cannot say 'white' but only 'white-rabbit' (as a single word) or, at best 'white-thing', and cannot express 'runs' or 'running' except in 'rabbit's-running' or 'running-rabbit' (again, as a single word) or, at best, in 'he-runs', 'running-thing', 'his-running'. Consequently, any expression of quality or action must be in a word containing these elements together with that of an object. We find such words, therefore, as the Greenlandish [tusaʀp-a-ʀa] 'hearing-his-mine', that is, 'I hear him': the action is viewed as an object possessed by the actor and by the object affected, or, to put it more justly, the actor is expressed as an object possessing the action. Similarly, where quality is to be expressed, it appears as an element of the word which also expresses the object that has the quality; thus 'liar' (or 'he is a liar', cf. p. 64) is [sal̥uto:q], 'big liar' [sal̥uto:qaoq]. Only an object-experience can be independently expressed, as in [qim:eq] 'dog' (or 'it is a dog'). All this corresponds, as we have seen, to the concrete facts of outer experience, where we never meet qualities or actions apart from objects. The same objective character of the word is responsible for the inclusion of objects standing in some relation to another object, for these, too, are qualifying elements. Here belong such words as [iḷːu-a] 'house-his', 'his house' and [qitoʀna-ʀa] 'child-mine', 'my child': the 'he' or 'I' as possessor is, of course, not present in the actual experience as an object; all that is there present is the house or the child associatively standing out as 'his' or 'my' possession: the inclusion in the same word is, therefore, concretely justified. This is true also of such words as [kia-gu-nːeq] 'heat-suffering-result', 'perspiration', — for here the heat and the suffering are not objects figuring in the experience, but are associatively presented features of the 'result'. Our abstract relational words, finally, are, of course, by no means found in such a language, where the relation is expressed as an associative feature of the object. Thus our 'in' appears in [nuna-me] 'land-in', 'in the land', our 'across' in [nuna-kːut] 'land-across', 'across the land', and our conjunction 'when' in such a form as [tuawioʀ-toʀ-sːʼuo-ḷːu-ne aneʀlaʀpoq] 'hurry-using-very-when-his he-returns', i. e. 'hurrying very much, he goes home'.

In many languages which, like our own, are not confined to this objective expression, we find, nevertheless, frequent inclusion of several partly analyzed elements under one word. It is possible that extended investigation will determine that these features are always, as they surely sometimes are, traces of an older objective habit of expression.

The inclusion of qualities of an object in one word with the object, as in the Greenlandish [saḷːutoː-qaoq] 'liar-big', 'big liar', appears in 'diminutive', 'augmentative', 'pejorative' and similar formations, as in the Italian *sorellina* 'little sister' beside *sorella* 'sister', *librone* 'big book' beside *libro* 'book', *tempaccio* 'nasty weather' beside *tempo* 'weather', or the German *Männchen* or *Männlein* 'little man' beside *Mann* 'man', compare our *manikin*. Such forms are common in many languages, especially the Romance, Slavic, and Baltic (Lithuanian). The value, especially as to emotional tone, of these formations is different enough from that of the analytic expression by means of adjective and noun to prevent interference. Much rarer are compounds whose elements correspond to adjective and noun, like the Sanskrit *mahā-dhanam* 'big-booty'. Such compounds are almost equal to the analytic expression, *mahad dhanam* 'big booty'. The only difference, in fact, lies in the very slight tone of unity expressed by the fixed order of the members and by the non-inflection of the one element, as in the plural *mahā-dhanāni* 'big-booties', opposed to the two-word *mahānti dhanāni* 'big booties'. The presence of genuine adjectives, which tend to be awakened in the production of the sentence, is the cause for the rarity of these forms. These genuine adjectives are themselves probably sprung from nominal expressions. In the oldest scientifically attainable stage of English, Primitive Indo-European, the value of such an adjective as 'white', for instance, seems to have been 'white-person' or 'white-thing' as often as the present purely qualitative meaning. Thus in Latin, which is another historic descendant of Primitive Indo-European, adjectives are frequently used as substantives. So *bonus, bona, bonum* mean not only 'good', but also, respectively, 'good man', 'good woman', 'good thing' or 'blessing'; *juvenis* means both 'young' and 'young man, youth'; *sapiens* both 'wise' and 'wise man', and so on; this appears also in some of the Latin adjectives borrowed in English, as *German, Italian* both noun (person of this nationality) and adjective, — but not so the native English forms, such as *English, Danish*, which are adjectives only.

The verb, like the adjective, is in English an independent word, inclusive of the action-meaning only; *sing* or *sings* or *sang* does not express the actor, even though the first two of these forms can occur only with certain actors. In Italian *canta* can be used as well as *egli canta* to include the actor: 'he sings'; in Latin and many other languages this is the regular usage, there being no other way of saying 'he sings' than the one-word expression *cantat;* the verb, in other words, does not occur independently of an object-element, namely that of the actor. When we say in Latin *Puella cantat* 'The girl sings', the latter word expresses the idea not only of 'sings', but also of an actor, 'she-sings', more exactly defined by *puella*. This resembles the expressions of an objective language, like the Greenlandish [takuwaː] 'seeing-of-him-his', 'he sees him', which reappears in its entirety even where the actor is specifically expressed: [qimːip takuwaː] 'to-the-dog seeing-of-him-his', 'the dog sees him'.

Inclusion of objects in some relation to other objects is also common. It appears most of all in compound words. Thus *bulldog* includes in one word with the object 'dog' the other object to which the dog stands in an associative relation, here that of resemblance; similar instances are *sofa-cushion*, *pay-day*, *schoolboy*, and the like. In many languages we find pronominal elements expressing these relational object-ideas; so, especially, in the Semitic languages, e. g. Egyptian Arabic *dulāb-i* 'my cupboard', *dulāb-oh* 'his cupboard', *dulāb-ha* 'her cupboard', *dulāb-hum* 'their cupboard', and so on, like the Greenlandish [qitoʀna-ʀa] 'my child'.

The abstract relational elements, finally, which pertain to an object, are very extensively found formationally combined with it. The extreme of this is seen in the Uralic languages, as in Finnish, for instance, which has twelve 'cases' expressing local relations, such as the 'inessive', e. g. *silmä-ssä* 'in the eye', the 'adessive' *silmä-llä* 'by the eye', the 'ablative' *silmä-ltä* 'from the eye', the 'comitative' *silmä-ne* along with the eye', and so on. The case-forms of the more familiar languages are in part of this type; in Latin, for instance, there are a number of locutions in which the case-form expresses the object together with a relational element. So especially the 'ablative of means': *manū* 'by hand', *lacte vīvunt* 'by means of milk they live'. Less common in Latin are forms like *Rōmae* 'at Rome', *Rōmam* 'to Rome', *Galliā* 'from Gaul'. The genitive or possessive case is another example: *John's*, as in *John's hat*, expresses the possessive relation in partial analysis in one word with the object-element, *John*. But, as we have seen (p. 95), the analysis is almost equal to that into a separate word, for we can use such turns of speech as *the man I saw yesterday's father*. Even here the use of the independent word *of* expressing the relation is more frequent: we say not *the table's legs* but *the legs of the table*. The relational element of number, also, is in most languages included in the object-expression, as in *boy: boys, man: men*. A language in which this is not the case is Chinese. Here a word like [⌜ʒʌn/] 'man, men, people' expresses only the object, not its number; only if the number is a vivid element in the experience, is it expressed, and then by an independent word.

10. Word-classes. Partial analysis, such as just described, is due to association of experiences with others like them. Consequently, we may say that the words containing a given formational element fall into a class. Thus those English nouns which express, by means of an element -*s*, plural number in addition to the object-content, form a class, e. g. *boys, fathers, rabbits, stones, trees, fires, eggs*, etc. Or, again, all the words containing a given material formational element, as *boy, boy's, boys, boyish, boyishly*. Where a relational element expresses a categoric distinction, it is the basis of a class, even though it has no uniform expression. Thus the English plurals just quoted are only a smaller class within a larger one containing also such forms as *knives, houses, men, geese, feet, children, oxen*, etc., which have not the same plural-formation and, in some cases, not even the final *-s*, but fulfil the same function with regard to the grammatical categories of the language.

We find, however, other word-classes which are not expressed by formational similarity at all, but seem to go back, none the less, to emotional associations of the speakers. The well-known three 'genders' of nouns in German, Latin, and Greek, or the two of French and Dano-Norwegian are an example. To only a minimal extent do these agree with any perceptual reality, such, for instance, as animal sex. Thus in German two nouns for 'woman' will be found in different genders: *die Frau* 'feminine' gender, *das Weib* 'neuter' gender; similarly, of men: *der Mann* 'the man', 'masculine' gender and *die Schildwache* 'the sentry', 'feminine' gender, *das Männchen* 'the little man', 'neuter'; sexless objects appear equally in all three genders; *der Tisch* 'the table', is 'masculine', *die Tür* 'the door', is 'feminine', and *das Fenster* 'the window' is 'neuter'. Similar are the 'animate' and 'inanimate' genders of many American languages, or the dozen and more gender-classes of certain African languages.

Naturally, we cannot expect the associational habits of speech-communities, which underlie these morphologic classifications, to coincide with the results of conscious scientific study of the universe. The noun-genders are an example of this. Another instance is furnished by the English action-words. In these we make no distinction between the performance of an action, as in *I eat*, *I walk*, *I write*, and the undergoing of a sensational process, as in *I hear*, *I see*. Our expression seems everywhere to correspond to the former type of occurrence. In other languages, such as Greenlandish, the second type is generalized; one says, in accordance with reality, [takuwaː] 'appearing-of-it-to-him' i. e. 'he sees it', but also [tukaʀpaː] 'stamping-of-it-to-him', i. e. 'he stamps on it, tramples it', where the English type of expression is more appropriate. In Georgian both types exist: one very justly says [v-t'ser] 'I-write' and, differently, [m-e-smi-s] 'me-to-sounding-is', i. e. 'sound comes to me', 'I hear'. Yet, as we must in such cases expect, the distinction is by no means carried through with scientific correctness; seeing, for instance, is viewed as if it were an activity, not a sensation: [v-naxav] 'I-see'.

The phase of linguistics which studies these classes, — that is, the structure of words, — is *morphology*.

11. The sentence. When the analysis of experience arrives at independently recurring and therefore separately imaginable elements, words, the interrelations of these in the sentence appear in varied and interesting linguistic phenomena. Psychologically the basis of these interrelations is the passing of the unitary apperception from one to the other of the elements of an experience (p. 60, f.). The leading binary division so made is into two parts, subject and predicate, each of which may be further analyzed into successive binary groups of attribute and subject, the attribute being felt as a property of its subject. The subject of the sentence is analyzed out of the total experience as the substratum, more or less permanent, and, owing to earlier experiences, the relatively familiar element, which in the predicate receives definition (*The rabbit is an animal*) or description (*The rabbit is white*), or is apperceived as the substratum of an action (*The rabbit runs across the field, The rabbit is being chased*).

The explicit predication of quality or action is impossible for languages in which every word expresses an object (p. 64). In these languages the sentence consists of one or more object-words. Each of these, since it can occur alone as a sentence, is capable of expressing what we look upon as a predication; any series of them, consequently, contains no expression as to where the predication lies. These words, then, are sentence-words. The Greenlandish [qim:eq] thus can mean 'dog' or 'It is a dog', [saḷuto:qaoq] 'big liar', 'He is a big liar', or 'He lies very much', and so on.

In contrast with this stands such a language as English, in which the existence of independent action-words and quality-words removes all obstacles to the expression of predication. Among such languages, also, there are, however, a great many differences. Latin, for instance, presents some features that remind one of the nominal languages. Its verb always includes expression not only of the action, but also of the acting object. Accordingly, predication can in Latin also be expressed in one word, — a sentence-word, — even though only a limited portion of the words, the verbs, can be so used: *cantat* 'he, she, it sings', *edo* 'I eat', and so on. Where a quality-word, — an adjective, — forms the predicate, there is often no difference between predication and attribution. Thus *māgna culpa* means either '(a) great fault' (attributing adjective) or '(The) fault (is) great' (predicating adjective). Russian makes this distinction by using different forms of the adjective; thus, in [mu′ʒï·k ′b′e·d′in] the adjective is the predicate: '(The) peasant (is) poor', and in [′b′ɛ·dnï mu′ʒï·k] it is an attribute: '(the) poor peasant'. English has gone farther. It expresses predication only and always by means of the verb; where no action is involved, the abstract verb *is*, expressive only of the relation of predication (in the form of an action), is used (p. 67, ff.); we cannot say *fault great* or *peasant poor* but only *The fault is great, The peasant is poor*. Moreover, the English verb does not, like the Latin, include the expression of an acting object: we cannot say *sings* or *eat*, but only *He sings, I eat*, — so that no sentence-word exists.

By thus confining the function of predication to our action-words and that of subject to our object-words, we have produced the syntactic categories of action and actor (p. 68). If, now, it happens that the subject of a total experience is not an object, but an action, this action cannot be expressed by a verb, but must be put in the form of a noun. This is the function of our abstract nouns, such as *skating* in *Skating strengthens the ankles*. Similarly, if the subject of the statement is really a quality, no genuine quality-word (adjective) can be used, but only an abstract noun of quality, such as *length* in *The length of the wall was two miles*. When the predicate does not really involve an action, we have seen that the abstract verb *is* fulfils the predicative function. Attribution is always expressed by adjectives with nouns, by adverbs with verbs. Hence the use of nominal and verbal adjectives and adverbs when an object or an action is attributive: *a boyish man, he spoke boyishly, skating boys, he spoke drawlingly*. For attributive occurrence of objects we have, however, also our possessive form: *John's hat*.

The categoric distinction between these 'parts of speech', — verbs, nouns, and so on, — is by no means a necessary attendant of independent words for quality and action. Chinese, for instance, also has such words, [e. g. [₁xaŏ/] 'good' or [₁mař/] 'buy', — but the functions of subject, predicate, attribute are not confined to any

THE SENTENCE 113

such classes. Thus the quality-word [ˌxaðˈ] appears as attribute in [ˌxaðˈ/ˈʒʌn/] 'good man' and as predicate in [ˈtʼaˈ ˌxaðˈ/] 'He (is) good'. The action-words [ˌmašˈ/] 'buy' and [ˌmašˈ\] 'sell' appear as attributes (where we in English should have to use verbal adjectives 'buying', 'selling') in [ˌmašˈ/ ˌmašˈ\ ˈʒʌn/] 'a trader, merchant', and so on. In the modern speech there are also the independent words [ˈtiˈ] and [ˌʃəˈ] which independently express the relations, respectively, of attribution and predication; thus one can say also [ˌxaðˈ/ ti ˈʒʌn/] 'good (attribution) man', and [ˈtʼaˈ ti ˌmaðˈ\] 'he (attribution) hat', 'his hat', and [ˌmašˈ/ ˌmašˈ\ ti ˈʒʌn/] 'trader', as well as [ˈtʼaˈ ʃə ˌxaðˈ/] 'He (predication) good', almost exactly our 'He is good'.

The process of analyzing an experience may be temporarily interrupted by the associative addition of elements viewed as entering into the same discursive relation as some one of the original elements. As well as we say *He is a good student*, we can include other attributes of *student* suggesting themselves as parallel to *good: He is a good, intelligent, industrious student*. Such groups are called *serial* groups. It is possible that they represent a specialized, automatized form of the discursive relation. They are especially common in English and the languages most closely related to it; we say *John and Mary ran* rather than *John ran, Mary ran*, but this condensed habit of expression is not everywhere so common.

While the sentence has its foundation in the discursive analysis, other forces also play a part in determining its form. Most important of these are perhaps the *emotional relations* of the elements. The relations of emotional stress find expression especially in the modulation of loudness (p. 50). In addition to this, however, they affect the sentence in various ways in different languages. A method in English, for instance, is to place the emotionally dominant element[1]) in some way out of its usual position, preferably first or last. Thus *He came last* is turned into *Last came he*. This inversion can be effected also by making the dominant element predicate of an introductory sentence: *It was he who came last, It was last that he came, It was me they beat*. The introductory words are here entirely abstract and are spoken with very low stress, so that phonetically the dominant element practically comes first. This construction is the regular one, as we shall see, in some languages.

The *material* or *concrete relations* between the elements of a sentence may also play a part in its structure.) These relations are, of course, endless in variety, and their linguistic expression is scarcely less manifold; we are interested, however, only in those cases where such a concrete relation receives some other expression than that of the underlying discursive construction. \Such specialized expression of concrete, non-discursive relations is of course, always a sequence of words that once stood only in discursive relation but then became mechanized in the particular use. Are the two words *in Rome* in discursive relation? Which is attribute, which subject? We cannot answer: for our feeling the relation is simply this, that *in* expresses a local inclusion with regard to *Rome*. Our feeling is due to the fact that this type of expression has become mechanized: we reel it off without entering upon the discursive analysis, which, when such locutions were first used, was vividly present.

---

[1] The term 'psychological (as opposed to the 'logical' or 'grammatical') subject', used in this meaning by many writers, is to be avoided as confusing. There is nothing more 'psychological' about an emotionally dominant element than about the subject of a discursive analysis, and 'subject' is a discursive, not an emotional concept.

Thus, as we have seen, the concrete relation of an actor performing an action has in English furnished the universal form for the sentence. When, for instance, the subject is not an actor but the goal (object affected) of an action, we make it actor-subject of the abstract verb *is* and use in the predicate a verbal adjective denoting the quality of something that has undergone an action. Thus we say *He is hurt, The rabbit was killed, The house was being built*. For such locutions Latin has special verb-forms, the 'passive', which express an action as being undergone, allowing the object affected to be expressed as actor: *Domus struēbātur* 'The house was being built'. Where there is no actor at all, we use in English a purely formal word: *It is raining, It was four years ago*.

Another concrete relation which we feel as entirely unique is that of the goal or object affected of an action. Originally this seems to have been an ordinary attribute of the predicate verb. In Latin, as in Old English, there are two case-forms of nouns used in this way: the 'accusative' for the object fully affected and the 'dative' for the object less fully affected. Thus in *Pater filiō librum dat* 'the father gives the son a book', *librum* is in the 'accusative' *filiō* in the 'dative' case. In present English these distinctions of word-form are almost entirely lost. Nevertheless the expression of these relations has remained a thing by itself. The object fully affected follows the verb; that less fully affected either stands between the two or is viewed as in prepositional (local) relation: this latter usage amounts to an analysis of the relation of object less fully affected into an independent word. Thus we say either *The father gives the son a book* or *The father gives a book to the son*. In Chinese also the object fully affected has a construction all its own: while all other attributes precede their subject, the object affected follows its action-word. Thus [ˌwo/ ˌpʻa\ ⌈tʼa⌉] 'I fear him', [⌈tʼa⌉ ˌpʻa\ ˌwo/] 'He fears me'. The object less fully affected has a different expression, which, however looks like a specialized form of the preceding: a few action-words take it as their goal, forming a phrase which then as attribute precedes the main action-word of the sentence. For instance [⌈tʼa⌉ ˌkeɏ/ ˌwo/ ˌsuŋ\ ⌈cçiĕ/ ˌli/] 'He sends me festival-presents' (more literally: 'He, giving me, sends festival-presents'). Here [⌈tʼa⌉], the subject, is followed by the predicate, in which [ˌkeɏ/ ˌwo/] is an attribute composed of the action-word [ˌkeɏ/] 'give' followed by its object affected, [ˌwo/] 'I'. This two-word attribute, according to the general principle, precedes its subject [ˌsuŋ\], an action-word meaning 'send', which is followed by its object affected [⌈cçiĕ/ ˌli/], in which the former word 'festival' is an attribute of the latter 'presents'.

Coming, finally, to our English preposition-groups, with which we began as an example of crystallized concrete relations, we may seek their origin in older constructions of attribution. Local relations are always, concretely, relations with regard to objects; we find them, accordingly, in many languages expressed by case-forms of object-words, as in the Latin *Fugit Corinthō* 'He-flees from-Corinth', ('ablative' case), *Rōmam venit* ('He-comes to-Rome' ('accusative' case), the Sanskrit *parvate tiṣṭhati* 'On-the-mountain he-stands' ('locative' case) *prayacchati savyena* 'He-hands-out with-(his)-left-(hand)' ('instrumental' case); compare also the Finnish case-forms on p. 108. This purely attributive usage is still seen in a later stage, when there come into use set phrases of certain adverbial attributive words with these case-forms of nouns. Thus, to take an example from Ancient Greek, we find such sentences as *Kephalēs ápo phāros héleske* 'From-(his)-head off the-cloak he-drew', 'He drew the cloak from his head'. Here the verb *héleske* 'He-drew' has, beside the object fully affected *phāros*, the attributes *apo* 'off', an adverbial word, and the case-form, of ablative value, *kephalēs* 'from-the-head'. Later such combinations of adverbial word and case-form became habitual and were crystallized into a standard expression of the concrete local relations with regard to objects: *apò kephalēs* 'from the head'. The same occurred in English, and even today, when our case-forms are practically lost, such phrases are our regular expression for local relations: *from Corinth, to Rome, from his head, into the fields*. Thus we obtain the collocation of preposition plus noun which would be entirely inexplicable on the basis of the purely discursive relations from which history shows it has grown. In Chinese similar phrases have a very different origin. One can there say [ˈtʼaˀ ˌtaðˌ ˈtʼIen/ ˌli/ ˌcɕ́y\] 'He goes into the fields', but it would perhaps be more literal to translate 'He, entering (the) fields' interior, goes'. For the central element of the predicate is here [ˌcɕ́y\], preceded by its attribute of three words, which consists of the action-word [ˌtaðˌ] 'enter' followed by its object fully affected [ˈtʼIen/ ˌli/] 'fields' interior'.

λ Of similar nature are our words *the* and *a*. The relation of *the* to *rabbit* in *the rabbit* or of *a* in *a rabbit* is scarcely the regular discursive one of attribution. Originally the word *the* was probably a deictic word similar to our *that*: it was used attributively with a noun; in time, however, it came to be used anaphorically (of objects not actually present, but of those which had been mentioned or were otherwise specifically known), until today the use of *the* is a peculiar and categoric expression of definiteness of an object. Likewise, *a, an* was originally the numeral 'one', attributively used. It came in time to be used whenever only one object was meant and the definite *the* could not be used. Today, in consequence, we have three syntactic categories affecting nouns: every object must be spoken of either as definite (at least with *the*), or as indefinite (at least with *a*), or as collective, without the article, as in *Man wants but little* . . . or *Men are easily moved by such things*. This is in contrast with most languages. In Latin, for instance, *homo* means 'the man', 'a man', or 'man', and such attributes as *ille* 'that' or *ūnus* 'one' or *quīdam* 'some' are used only where such elements are actually and vividly present in the experience; they stand, then, in regular attributive relation to their noun.

As a last example I shall cite our 'infinitive' verb-forms. These express the action as complement of another preceding verb, e. g. *I shall go, He can speak, You must write a letter, I want to forget it, They tried to deceive us*, — the relation between the two verbs being in many instances expressed by the word *to*. This form of expression would baffle all attempts at reducing it to terms of attribution or predication. But it was not always so. In the older forms of English the infinitive is a verbal noun, comparable to those we now use in *-ing* (as *skating*), occurring most frequently in two case-forms, an accusative, e. g. Old English *bindan* 'to bind' and a dative case, Old English *bindanne, bindenne*. The accusative form was used as the object fully affected of a verb; thus *I shall go*, for instance, meant originally 'I owe going' and was parallel to such expressions as 'I owe money'. The dative form, after the preposition *to*, was used like any other noun with a preposition (see above), such a sentence as *He went to eat* meaning 'He went to eating', parallel to 'He went to London'. The scheme of these expressions has long ago, however, become so automatized that they are used where the original discursive relation could not be interpreted into them, — for any feeling for this historically underlying relation has long ago disappeared. The preposition *to*, by the same token, has here become an abstract relational element, expressing the relation between the two verb-forms; its independent value can be seen in such expressions as *He doesn't want to*.

These peculiar developments, beyond predication and attribution, of the sentence-relations of a language, are, of course, an important part of its *syntax*. The description of typical cases could be greatly expanded. The principle, however, is everywhere the same: the discursive relations of predication and attribution, which are inherent in the formation of the sentence, lie at the basis of all set locutions in which the material content becomes dominant. While a Chinese speaker, on reflection, will realize that 'fields' in the above sentence (p. 117) is the object affected by the action-word 'enter', — for the word [ˌtaδ\] can thus occur in a sentence without any other action-word, as the central element of the predicate: [ˈtˈaˈ ˌtaδ\ ˈtˈĭen/ ˌli/] 'He enters the fields', — he would perhaps have difficulty in appreciating the relation of 'enter' to 'go' as the regular attributive relation of his language, just as an English speaker would undoubtedly be at a loss, were we to require him to explain in terms of attribution and predication, the relations of the words in *He goes into the fields*. In short, the change of language produces such relation-words as our prepositions, with the simple and direct forms of expression which they make possible, out of the concrete, cumbersome habits of an older time. This change is at the same time a development of the mind: the conceptual values of our words of quality, action, and relation would be impossible without these words (p. 65), just as the latter can exist only as the result of a definite mental-linguistic development.

CHAPTER V.
MORPHOLOGY.

1. The significance of morphologic phenomena. The morphologic classes of a language represent communal associative habits: they express the associative connections which the national mental life of a people has made between the types of experience which the language expresses in words. Thus we in English find some connection between *flare* and *flash*, between *father* and *mother*, between *boys* and *stones*. Every formational element common to a number of words involves a grouping together of these words on the basis of what to the community has appealed as a common element in the experiences expressed by these words. The classifications of language are, in fact, the clearest expressions of the associations made by the community as a whole. They are, accordingly, of great ethnologic significance. This significance is increased by the fact that they are far less subject to reflection than other communal activities (such as religion) and are never, in any but the most highly cultured communities, modified by such reflection.

2. Morphologic classification by syntactic use (Parts of speech). The first kind of morphologic word-class of which we shall speak, — and it is in many languages the most fundamental, — is really a syntactic phenomenon. It is the division into parts of speech. This

MORPHOLOGIC CLASSIFICATION BY SYNTACTIC USE 121

division is due to the existence of syntactic categories, — in English mainly to that of actor and action. The English parts of speech received some mention in the last chapter, where our classification of noun, verb, and adjective was spoken of. The classification may in its entirety be described as follows:

a) The verbs express an action *(I eat, they danced)* or another element viewed as such *(he is)*. Their distinctive characteristics are several. They always form the nucleus of the predicate; predication cannot be expressed in any other way in the English language. The actor, real or formally viewed as such, must always be explicitly mentioned with the verb. Nearly every verb expresses by its form the time, present or past, of the action. In the present-time forms most verbs vary according to the number and person of the actor, in that a third-person singular actor requires a special form: *I, we, you, they eat*, but *he, she, it eats*.

The only exception to all this is the non-committal or infinitive verb-form, e. g. *eat* in *I shall eat this apple*. This form expresses the action apart from any actor. It can be used only in exclamatory utterance, where it serves as a command *(Eat!)*, and as a supplement to another verb (p. 118). The infinitive differs from the present-tense form in only one verb: *be* (present tense: *we are*); it is lacking in several others *(can, may, shall, will)*.

Verbs are modified by adverbs (see below).

b) The nouns express an object-experience, be it really such *(stone, house, man)* or viewed as such *(skating, length, greenness)*. They are distinguished by a number of characteristics from verbs (e. g. they cannot express predication) and from the other parts of speech. They express the actor or the objects affected by an action *(The man gave his son a book)*, as well as that to which something is equated or under which it is subsumed by the predication *(He is a merchant, The whale is a mammal)*. They can stand in attribution to other nouns only when in their possessive form *(the man's hat)*. Nearly every noun shows by its form whether one or more than one of the objects is intended. The nouns are modified by the attributive nouns already mentioned, by adjectives, and by attributively used pronouns, among which *the* and *a, an* are especially frequent, owing to certain syntactic habits of the language (p. 117, f.), and they are used in set phrases with prepositions (p. 117). The constrast with verbs is thus complete.

This contrast is, however, less in the verbal nouns (ending in *-ing*) which express what is usually looked upon as an action (e. g. *skating* in *Skating strengthens the ankles*), for these verbal nouns can, like a verb, be followed by mention of the objects affected: *Giving them alms is no remedy, I am tired of hearing him grumble*.

c) The adjectives express a quality *(green, large, long)* or what is viewed as such *(growing, burning, boyish)*. They can be used to express neither predication nor action, actor, or objects affected, but stand only in attribution with nouns or, in the predicate, as qualities predicated of the subject *(The man is good)*. Beside the usual form they have two variations which express a superior and a superlative degree of a quality *(better, best)*. Adjectives are modified attributively by adverbs.

A peculiar variety of adjectives are the verbal adjectives or participles, which express as a quality what is usually viewed as an action, e. g. *a running boy, broken toys*. These verbal adjectives are used in set phrases with the verbs *is, has,* to express durative and perfectic manner of action (see below, p. 145), as in *I am reading a book, He was dreaming, I have written him a letter, Have you written?, He had arrived.* Like the verbal nouns, the verbal adjectives can be followed by expression of the objects affected, as in several of the above examples.

A few of our adjectives may be said to form a sub-class in that they can be used in the predicate only: *He is asleep, awake; The ship ran aground.*

d) The pronominal words are unified by their relational value, personal, deictic, anaphoric, numeral, etc.; in their syntactic use they can be divided into a number of sub-classes. They are used to express actor or objects affected *(He gave me it)* or, in the predicate, that relational element to which something is equated *(Is it I, It is mine),* — differing in these uses from nouns in that they never are attributively modified by adjectives, though some of them are so modified by other pronouns. They are used, further, as attributive modifiers of nouns and of other pronouns *(the man, this man, three men, the other),* but differ in this use, as well as in the predicate, from adjectives in that they always precede the latter when both are present *(three good men, the old house).* Some pronouns occur in the nominal uses only *(who, I, mine),* these and a few others *(what)* are never modified by another preceding pronoun; two, *the* and *a,* never occur in the nominal, but only in the modifying uses. While less homogeneous as to syntactic use, then, than the other parts of speech, the pronouns, taken together, yet constitute as distinct a class as any, owing to their peculiar meaning and to their resistance to material modifying elements.

e) The adverbs attributively express the circumstances of qualities and actions, such as place *(here, there, where),* time *(then, yesterday, afterwards),* degree *(more, very),* manner *(rapidly, slowly, kindly),* and the like. They alone have the function of modifying adjectives and, in a direct sense, verbs. As in the case of adjectives, their form may express a superior or superlative degree of the experience *(kindlier, kindliest)* but no other relations.

f) Prepositions express a relation, usually spatial, with regard to an object. Accordingly, they are used only with nouns or with nominally used pronouns, preceding them and their modifiers in a unique construction, the set phrase of preposition plus noun (p. 117).

g) The conjunctions express relations between coordinate parts of speech and between predications. Subordinating conjunctions express a relation of time, condition, cause, and the like *(when, if, because, though)* with regard to a predication. Thus they relate a predication, as a whole, subordinately to another predication *(When he saw the house, he ... .)*. Coordinating conjunctions express serial relations of all kinds *(and, or, but, both ... and, either ... or)*. Externally, this function involves their appearing between coordinate words, phrases, and predications.

h) Interjections (of the primary type) are, of course, opposed to all the other classes of words, in content, use, and form.

The most striking circumstance about this classification is that the normal speaker is utterly unconscious of it. It requires a considerable degree of mental training and even of linguistic habit of thought before one can by introspection analyze these classes. And yet they are used correctly every day by millions of speakers who would be utterly incapable of making such an introspective analysis, and perhaps even of understanding it, if it were made for them. With all the complexity of the classification, confusion between the different parts of speech never occurs. This is a most important fact, especially in view of the unconscious nature of the habits, and one which could be illustrated by many features of English usage. It is attested, for instance, by the failure of homonyms to introduce even the slightest confusion. Such homonyms as *wood* (noun) and *would* (verb), for instance, could be confused only in the dream-world of Alice in Wonderland. The noun *wood* occurs with preceding adjectives, prepositions, and pronominal modifiers, in the function of actor, object affected, or predicate noun; the verb *would* expresses only and always a predication, must be accompanied by mention of an actor, is modified by adverbs only, and is followed by an infinitive supplement. Even where the homonymy is significant, corresponding to some resemblance of semantic content, as in the case of *stone*, noun in *a stone*, verb in *they stone him*, and adjective in *a stone gate*, the same distinctions hold true, and a single syntactically joined word will show which of the homonyms is present: all that is necessary to show that the noun is meant is the modifier *a*, the verb is at once identified by a preceding actor, and the adjective by a following subject. In short such homonymy never obscures the boundaries between these classes, as it well might, were they less clearly drawn; thus one is never tempted to confuse *house* [haŏs] noun and *house* [haŏz] verb, or *gun, bullet, arrow,* nouns and *shoot* verb, in spite of the corresponding homonymy in *stone*. Likewise there is no confusion between adverb and preposition in spite of such homonymy as that of *in*, preposition *(in the house)* and *in*, adverb *(He walked in)*; no confusion between preposition and conjunction in spite of the homonymy of *after*, preposition *(after the meal)* and *after*, conjunction *(after they had gone)*. For instance, the conjunction corresponding to *in* would never be expressed as *in*, no matter how ignorant the speaker, but would be *while, during*, or the like; and the adverb corresponding to *after* would (in spite of homonymy of adverb and preposition in such cases as *in*) never be *after*, but always *afterwards* or *then*. In short, the classification into parts of speech, though not appearing in the phonetic form of the single word, is as distinct as any other classification in the language. Self-explanatory and self-understood as it seems to us when once we are made conscious of its existence, it is by no means universal in linguistic expression. In fact, the parts of speech used in English occur in only a limited number of languages. In Chinese, for instance, as we have seen (p. 112, f.), a word, no matter whether it expresses object, quality, or action, is externally treated alike, and may express subject, predicate, or attribute; thus we saw on p. 113 the word [ˌxaŏ⸴] 'good' (quality) as attribute and as predicate, and the words [ˌmaš/ ˌmaš\] 'buy' and 'sell' (action) as attributes; as predicate they appear in such sentences as [ˌmaš/ ⸢ji/ ˌpʌn/ ⸢ʃuꜞ] 'buy one volume book', i. e. 'buy a book'. Similarly the action-word [⸢ʃŭoꜞ] 'speak' appears as predicate in [⸢ťaꜞ ⸢ʃŭoꜞ ˌpeɥ/ ⸢cçiŋꜞ ˌxŭa\] 'He speaks North-capital (Peking) language', but as subject in [⸢ťaꜞ ˌpeɥ/ ⸢cçiŋꜞ ˌxŭa\ ⸢ʃŭoꜞ ʃə ˌxaŏ/] 'His North-capital language speaking is good', i. e. 'He speaks the Peking language well', where we must translate the uniform [⸢ʃuoꜞ] by a verb in the one case, where it is predicate, and by an abstract noun of action in the second, where it is subject.

Chinese may, indeed, serve us as an example of a language with parts of speech entirely different from ours. It has no such parts of speech as noun, verb, adjective, and adverb. 'Good' is a quality, 'man' an object, 'speaks' an action in China as everywhere else, but the fact that these experiences belong to these different spheres is not expressed in the Chinese sentence. In Chinese we can distinguish primarily two parts of speech. One, by far the more numerous, is used according to certain rules of word-order, chiefly the following: subject precedes predicate, attribute its subject. Example: [ˈtʻaˀ ˌxað/ ˈʒʌn/] 'he good man', to be taken as subject and predicate, the latter consisting of an attribute and its subject, i. e. 'He is a good man'. Other examples have occurred earlier in this book (p. 113).

Within this first class of words a subdivision can be made between intransitive and transitive words. The object affected by a transitive word follows it (in opposition to the usual rule of attribute-subject), e. g. [ˈtʻaˀ ˈʃuoˀ ˌpeǐ/ ˈcçiŋˀ ˌxŭa\] 'He speaks North-capital language'. The word [ˌxŭa\], for instance, is intransitive, and could never, like [ˈʃuoˀ], be followed by the expression of an object affected. Other examples will be found on pages 116, 119, 126. The words of the transitive class thus resemble some of our verbs (or, again, our prepositions, see page 117); but the resemblance is distant, for the Chinese transitive words by no means, as we have seen, either occur only as predicates or monopolize this function; further they alone can, by definition, be followed by expression of objects affected, whereas in English this is exactly the feature in which verbal nouns and adjectives (p. 122, f.) compete with verbs; and our verbs, on the other hand, can by no means all of them take an object affected.

The other part of speech consists of words not subject to these rules of word-order, but used, sometimes invariably, sometimes at will, between words of the former type to express explicitly the relation between them. Thus [ˌʃǝ\] expresses predication, [ˈtiˀ] attribution, and the sentence above could read [ˈtʻaˀ ʃǝ ˌxað/ ti ˈʒʌn/], the meaning being unchanged but more fully stated (cf. p. 113).

3. Classification by congruence. A peculiarity of the classifications by use in the sentence, — parts of speech, — which we have just seen in Chinese and English, is that the phonetic form of the word itself does not express the classification. Thus *stone* noun, verb, and adjective are alike in form; similarly *in* preposition and *in* adverb, *after* preposition and *after* conjunction, or in Chinese [ˈtiˀ] expressing attribution and [ˈtiˀ] 'low'. It would be impossible to find in such words as *street*, *house* [haŏs], *gun*, *arrow* any formal feature to show that they are nouns, as opposed to such adjectives as *sweet*, *narrow* or to such verbs as *beat*, *souse*, *run*.

The next type of morphologic word-class that demands discussion, has the same feature of not involving formal identification of the classes. It also is really a syntactic rather than a morphologic phenomenon.

We had occasion in the last chapter to notice that word-boundaries are sometimes phonetically recognized by the fact that word-initial or word-final may vary according to the sounds that precede or follow (p. 101, ff.). In some cases, as in the Sanskrit example there quoted, the variation is an automatic sound-variation and therefore of no morphologic significance. In another example this was different; in the Irish *tá ba* 'there are cows' and *a va* 'his cows' (p. 102, f.), the variation of *ba: va* does not depend upon the preceding sound. One says also *na ba* 'the cows'; further, *bog* 'soft' but *ró vog* 'very soft', *bán* 'white' but *bó ván* 'white cow', *brish* 'break' but *do vrish* 'did break', and so on. The speaker must have a class-feeling for words such as *tá*, *na*, after which *b-* is spoken, as opposed to words such as *a*, *ró*, *bó*, *do*, after which *v-* is spoken. The words in these two classes possess no distinguishing characteristics, by themselves, as to form or meaning: they constitute a class, in each case, by virtue of the effect they have on other, — in our instance, the following, — words in the utterance. These are word-classes by *congruence*. That there are several such classes in Irish appears from *bó* 'cow': *an vó* 'the cow: *ar mó*' 'our cow' and from *uv* 'egg': *an tuv* 'the egg': *na nuv* 'of the eggs': *a huv* 'her egg'. Each of these classes has one distinctive feature, and that is simply the fact that the words in it are felt to have this phonetic effect on following words, as it were necessarily and as part of the expression of the meaning. To the Irish speech-consciousness nothing else seems possible: here, as always, the morphologic classification of a word is, in the feeling of the speakers, part of its semantic value. For this very reason most speakers of a language are unconscious of their morphologic classifications, taking the classification-element for granted as an inevitable part of the meaning.

Another example of classification apparent not in the classified word itself, but in its effect on other words, — classification by congruence, — is that of the German noun-genders. There is nothing in such German nouns as *Leib* 'body', *Anker* 'anchor', *Auster* 'oyster', *Frau* 'woman', *Weib* 'woman', *Fenster* 'window', either in form or in material meaning, to indicate a classification. All attributive words, however, such as adjectives and pronouns, and all later anaphoric reference to these or other nouns at once show them to fall into three separate classes. Thus the definite article 'the' has in the nominative case singular three forms, one being used with each class of nouns: *der Leib, der Anker,* — *die Auster, die Frau,* — *das Weib, das Fenster;* and similarly in anaphoric reference, the pronoun referring to nouns of the first or 'masculine' gender is *er*, to the second or 'feminine', *sie*, to the third, 'neuter', *es*. This German classification differs, then, from the Irish in that not the next word, but all the attributively modifying words and all words expressing anaphoric reference, even though spoken much later, are affected.

Speakers of English can contrast this German gender-classification with their own language. In English such words as *the* or *good* are the same for all nouns, and, though we have in the singular three anaphoric pronouns, *he, she, it*, these differ not in being assigned to different classes of nouns, but only in actual meaning, just as any three other words may differ. While we refer to human beings beyond infancy according to sex as *he* or *she*, we are in other cases free to recognize sex or not: *the horse.... he* or *the horse... it*. When we use the sex-forms to refer to a sexless object, we are, by a genuine metaphor, attributing personal and sexual character to it, as when we refer to a ship or a steam-engine or the moon as *she*. In short, *he* and *she* differ as any other words may differ, e. g. *man, woman, child*, and do not, like the three German forms of the pronoun, involve the constant presence of a classification of nouns. Chinese, which has but one anaphoric word [ˈt'aˈ], does not in this differ much from English. The difference is merely parallel to that between the Chinese [ˈçĭuŋˈ] 'older brother', [ˌtiˌ] 'younger brother' and our *brother*, where the Chinese has two different words to our one: in the anaphoric pronoun we have three words to the Chinese one. Both languages are in this respect widely different from the German with its *er, sie, es*, which demand a complete and always present classification of the nouns in that language.

Another type of classification by congruence is seen in Chinese. Anything counted is expressed in this language by the numeral-word and the designation of the thing counted, and the latter is preceded by a modifying word of fairly material content expressing the unit of the object-idea; e. g. [ˈji/ko ˈʒʌn/] 'one piece man', i. e. 'one man'. Now, there is a considerable number of such numerative words, and the choice of the numerative word depends upon the thing counted. Thus one says:

[ˈsan˥ ko ˈʒʌn/] 'three piece man', i. e. 'three men',
[ˈsan˥ ko ˈcç'ɩen/] 'three piece mace', i. e. 'three mace (coin)', but:
[ˈsan˥ ˌpʌn/ˈʃu˥] 'three root book', 'three books',
[ˈsan˥ ˌweɩ/ˈjy/] 'three tail fish', 'three fishes',
[ˈsan˥ ˌweɩ\ ˈçɩen˥ ˈʃʌŋ˥] 'three rank earlier born', 'three teachers',
[ˈsan˥ ˈt'ɩað/ˌçɩen\] 'three branch thread', 'three threads',
[ˈsan˥ ˈt'ɩað/ˌpeɩ\] 'three coverlets', —
very much as we speak of *three head of cattle*. Owing to the material content of these numeratives there is a certain amount of freedom in their use: in the North, for instance, [ˌko\] encroaches on the others, but this freedom has definite limits; each of the forty or more numeratives has its range of objects with which it is used. It is apparent that the Chinese speech-feeling divides everything that may be counted into a number of classes which receive distinction in the numerative word. Here again we see a classification by congruence, though of a very different kind from those which we examined in Irish and German.

4. Phonetic-semantic classes. The two kinds of classification so far considered have this in common, that the words classified in no way show the classification in their immediate form. In the classification by syntactic use it is in the sentence that the classification appears, the different classes here performing entirely different functions; and in the classifications by congruence it is in the form of following words or of attributively or anaphorically connected words or in the choice of certain other words, never in the classified word itself, that the classification is expressed.

Now, it is conceivable that such classifications may receive expression in the classified word itself. For instance, there are in Italian two gender-classes of nouns, the classification receiving expression, as in German, by variation in the form of attributive and anaphoric words. In addition to this, however, very many of the masculine nouns end in *-o* and very many of the feminine in *-a*. Although there is one feminine in *-o* (*la mano* 'the hand') and there are a few foreign masculines, usually, however characterized by peculiar accent, in *-a* (e. g. *il sofà* 'the sofa'), the feeling that nouns in *-o* are masculine, those in *-a* feminine is part of the Italian speech-feeling. In German and English the prepositions, pronouns, and conjunctions tend to be shorter than other words, and similar tendencies occur in other languages, notably in the Semitic and the Malayan. All this shows that a word-classification may express itself in more than one way, although, as a rule, the expression is in only one direction complete and regular, and in the others imperfect and irregular, as in the Italian *-o* and *-a* endings.

There are, however, word-classes which receive expression in the form of the classified words alone. These are the commonest of all classes: most of our instances in the third and fourth chapters illustrated them. Thus we there set up a formula by which *metilu* might be used for 'white rabbit' and *meko* for 'white fox'. In these two hypothetical expressions the phonetic element *me-* corresponds to the common semantic element of 'white'. To turn, now, to our actual instances, we may recall a number of them.

English *father, mother, brother, sister:* common phonetic element, dental plus *-er*; these words form a semantic class in that they are all nouns designating a near relative.

English *flame, flare, flash, flimmer, flicker:* the common phonetic element is the initial *fl-*; the words fall into a semantic class in that all of them express phenomena of fire with especial reference to its peculiar moving light. This class is of interest in the present connection, because it illustrates the emotional rather than perceptual value and the ill-defined rather than clear-cut extent of many of these classes. For there can be no doubt that, in the feeling of many speakers, *flicker* again associates itself with such words as *flutter, fly,* and even, further, with *flit, flip, flop, flap,* and so on. All these words share the initial *fl-* and are more or less vaguely related in meaning; indeed, the feeling for the semantic connection may vary in the same speaker under different circumstances. In short, the extent or the existence of a phonetic-semantic word-class may be very doubtful, and could be determined with accuracy only for a given person at a given time, and here only if a full insight into his associative disposition at the moment were attainable.

The different members of such word-classes, may, moreover, cohere in differing degrees. Thus *flare* and *flash* readily and vividly associate each other; so do *flicker* and *flimmer;* so, perhaps, though in lesser degree, do *flicker* and *flutter;* then, again, *flip, flop,* and *flap* form a smaller class within the larger, their coherence being expressed by the common final *-p;* or, further, *flicker, flimmer, flit, flip* possess a common semantic value in the smallness and fineness of the movement designated, to which corresponds, in form, the common vowel *-i-*. We are dealing here with complex and delicate habits of association of emotional rather than perceptual significance.

This appears, further, in the fact that these classes cross each other. We have seen (p. 79), in our instance, that *flicker* also connects itself with *snicker;* likewise, *flimmer* with *glimmer, shimmer, simmer,* where the first two words are closely associated, the last one perhaps more loosely. The word *flash* belongs also to the large but coherent class of *clash, crash, dash, gash, gnash, hash, lash, mash, plash, slash, splash*. To this there join *quash, squash*, even among us, who pronounce the vowel in these words as [ɒ] instead of [æ]. Further, the word *sash*, no doubt belongs with *lash*, even though it is far from the other words of the class, and *plash, splash* weakly join to *wash*. Then again, crossing this class is the association of *mash* with *mush*.

English *bang, biff, bump, buffer, box, beat* form a more or less homogeneous class, but *bed* or *buy* or *boat*, which also have initial *b-*, surely do not belong to it. The best illustration of the peculiar character of these classes is, however, *box* ('to strike blows with the fist'), which decidedly belongs to this class, while the homonymous *box* ('receptacle') surely does not. If the reader, in first reading the list, took *box* in the latter sense, he no doubt felt a disturbing value when he came to it; yet, keeping the former sense in mind, he will be able to re-read the list without this feeling. This is comparable, of course, to the drawings which may be interpreted as a concave or a convex object, according to one's momentary predisposition. So *beat* above is homonymous with *beet*.

Phonetic-semantic classes are also the following, some of which were quoted in the fourth chapter:

English *thirteen, fourteen, fifteen*, etc., to which come, more loosely, *ten* and *tenth*.

English *thirteen, thirty, third, three*, crossing the latter class.

English *fires, fathers, boys, sisters, cats, ropes, watches, peaches*, etc., all expressing a plurality of objects with the common phonetic element [z] and, by an automatic sound-variation peculiar to this ending, [s] and [əz].

English *father's, boy's, king's, man's, priest's, boss's*, etc.; the common phonetic element is homonymous with that

PHONETIC-SEMANTIC CLASSES 135

in the last class, but the attributive use puts these words into different connections; notice, moreover, such oppositions as *men*, but *man's*.

English *dance, dances, danced, dancing, dancer*, with a common material element expressed by the common sounds [dæns].

English *eat, eats, ate, eaten, eating, eater, eatable:* common phonetic element, front diphthong plus *t*, with material content of the action 'eat'.

English *danced, walked, rocked, loved, cried, landed, bounded*, etc.; common phonetic element [t] and, by an automatic variation, [d] and [ed], the content being the past time of the action relative to that of speaking.

Russian ['b′ɛ· dnĭ] 'poor' in attributive use, ['b′e· d′in] 'poor' in predicative use (p. 111). Here the common material content finds expression in the common phonetic element ['b′ɛ·dn .., ′b′e·d′.. n], the sound-variations being common in the language.

Greenlandish [tusaʀpaʀa] 'I hear him', [tusaʀpat] 'thou hearest him', [tusaʀpa:] 'he hears him', etc., where the common phonetic element [tusaʀpa] corresponds to the common meaning, 'sounding of him' (cf. p. 104).

Semantically similar are the Nahwatl (Aztec) forms *niktlamaka* 'I give him something', *niktemaka* 'I give it to someone', *nikmaka* 'I give it to him', and so on.

The crossing of the classes is very apparent in a language like Latin, in which, for instance, words like *edo* 'I eat', *edis* 'thou eatest', *edit* 'he eats', *edimus* 'we eat', etc. have the common phonetic element *ed-* and the common semantic element of the material content 'eat', while such groups as *edo* 'I eat', *rego* 'I rule', *lego* 'I read', and so on, have a common *-o* expressing the actor as the speaker, *edis* 'thou eatest', *regis* 'thou rulest', *legis* 'thou readest', a common *-is* expressing the actor as the one addressed, and so on.

5. Classes on a partially phonetic basis. Still other morphologic classes depend partly, but not entirely on phonetic similarities.

English nouns, for instance, fall into two categoric classes: every noun expresses an object either as one or as more than one. Now, this classification of nouns into singular nouns and plural nouns is, to begin with, classification by congruence, for our present-tense verbs and many of our pronouns vary in form according to whether a singular or a plural noun is the actor, or, respectively, that modified or referred to, e. g. *The boy skates, The boys skate, The man smokes, The men smoke, this boy, these boys, my hat...it, my hats...they.* In addition to this, however, almost every singular noun has by its side, closely associated with it and falling with it into a semantic-phonetic class, a plural noun of the same material content: *boy, boys* (belonging to the larger semantic-phonetic class *boy, boys, boy's, boyish, boyhood,* etc.); *man, men* (*manhood, manly, mannish,* etc.); *hat, hats; knife, knives;* and vice versa. Our singular nouns form a class, consequently, in that nearly all of them are related, in uniform semantic relation, to plural nouns which resemble them in form; and our plural nouns form a class because each of them has by its side a similarly related singular. Now, within these classes there are a number of sub-classes according to the formal relation to the corresponding word of the other class. Thus the plural nouns, *boys, fathers, hats, rocks, peaches, watches* and the great majority of other plural nouns form a large class in that they add [z], [s], or [əz], — these three endings varying automatically, — to the form of the corresponding singulars. A smaller class is formed by those which also add a sibilant, but at the same time substitute [v] for the final [f] of the singular: *calves, knives, loaves* (as opposed to *cliff, bluff*, etc. in the preceding class; all these plural nouns together however belong to a single phonetic-semantic class, see page 134). *Houses*, beside adding the ending [əz], substitutes [z] for the final [s] of the corresponding singular *house*, and thus forms a class by itself. *Men, women, geese, mice, children, oxen, sheep*, etc. form a class in that they lack the usual sibilant ending; and within this class the first four words belong with a few others to a sub-class, the members of which differ from their singulars in vowel only; within this, again, *mice* and *lice* form a smaller class in having exactly the same vowel, corresponding to the same singular vowel in *mouse, louse*. *Children* and *oxen*, further, probably form a class in that they add an -*n* suffix, within which class each word again stands by itself. *Sheep, fish*, and *deer* constitute a sub-class by virtue of homonymy with their singulars.

Owing, finally, to the close association between corresponding singulars and plurals, the singulars corresponding to the plurals within each of these classes, larger or smaller, also form a class. Thus most singular nouns belong to the large class of *boy, father, hat, rock, peach, watch*, because they correspond to plurals with the regular sibilant addition; *knife, calf, loaf*, etc. form a class because they correspond to plurals with [v] for the final [f]; *house* forms a class; so do *man, woman, mouse, louse, goose*, etc., within which *mouse* and *louse* are a smaller class, and so on.

We see thus in the English nouns two kinds of word-classification not entirely marked by phonetic common elements, namely:

Classes due to the association of each word with another word in uniform semantic relation to it; for instance: all singular nouns; all plural nouns;

Classes due to the association of each word with another

word in uniform semantic and phonetic relation to it; for instance: the plural nouns *calves, knives, lives, wives, loaves*, etc., or the singular nouns *mouse* and *louse*, or the singulars or plurals, respectively, corresponding to these classes.

We may illustrate such classes by our verbs also. Classes by semantic parallelism are: a) all infinitives: *be, have, eat, sing, love, dance;* b) all forms used of the present tense, when the speaker himself is the actor: *am, have, eat, sing, love, dance,* homonymous in all cases except *am* with a) and d); c) all present-tense verbs used with a third person singular actor: *is, has, eats, sings, loves, dances,* — in a few instances homonymous with b) and d), e. g. *can, shall, will;* d) all present-tense verbs used with actor in the second person ('you') or in the plural: *are, have, eat, sing, love, dance,* — homonymous in all instances except *are* with a) and b).

As in the instance of all singulars and all plurals of nouns, these classes are at the same time classes by congruence, for b) is used only with the actor *I,* c) only with a singular-noun or singular-pronoun actor, and so on. However, all these together constitute a large class, again by semantic parallelism, as opposed to those that now follow, and this classification is not supported by any features of congruence. For, while all the preceding refer to an action viewed as present in relative time, those which follow express the action as past in relative time or unreal in modal character (cf. below):

e) all verbs expressing the action as past, used with a singular actor of first or third person: (*I, he, John*) *was, had, ate, sang, loved, danced,* — rarely homonymous with a), b), d), e. g. *let, put, cost;* f) all past tense verbs used with an actor in the second person or in the plural number, and all verbs referring to an action as not really taking place: *were, had, ate, sang, loved, danced,* — homonymous in all instances except *were* with e).

Within each of these six classes there are, as among the nouns, sub-classes by phonetic and semantic parallelism. To take only one instance, class e) has one largest sub-class within which all words have a final [d] (*loved, trudged*), [t] (*danced, passed*), or [əd] (*rested, waited*), — these suffixes vary automatically, — as opposed to the corresponding forms of a), b), d). Other sub-classes show other forms of dental-addition, e. g. *sent, lent,* etc. or *should, would, could,* where each also stands in a smaller class by itself. Still other classes lack the dental, differing from the present-tense forms usually by change of vowel; e. g. such a class as *sang, rang, drank, sank,* etc. (present: *sing, ring, drink, sink*). Another class is formed by the few instances of homonymy with the present (*let, hit, beat, cost,* etc.). The two past verbs which bear no relation whatever, formally, to the corresponding presents also each form a class: *was* and *went.* The present-forms corresponding to each of these classes again form a class.

6. Difference between morphologic classification and non-linguistic association. The ways in which a morphologic word-classification may express itself, then, are various. Nevertheless, it is always possible to recognize a morphologic class, as opposed to a non-linguistic psychologic connection. If *sew* closely associates *needle*, the connection is not linguistic, for the two words belong in English to no one morphologic class, not even to the same part of speech. On the other hand, if *go* is closely associated with *went*, this association receives linguistic expression, for the semantic relation between these two words so habitually receives expression by phonetic similarity (*dance: danced; sing: sang*) that in this one instance the lack of phonetic similarity does not disturb the usual feeling of coherence of past-form and present-form: *go: went* fall into a morphologic class by their parallelism, semantically, with *dance: danced, sing: sang*, etc. If the English language possessed no other pair of words that stood to each other in the same semantic relation as *go: went*, or if there were other such pairs, but phonetic resemblance between them were everywhere as totally out of the question as in this instance, — then, to be sure, *go* and *went* would not fall into a common morphologic class beyond that of verbs.

7. Classes by composition. The most explicit expression of a classification of words is the likeness of compounds to simple words and to each other, as when *bed, bedsheet, bed-cover, bedpost, bedroom, bedridden*, etc., or *bedroom, dining-room, room*, etc., fall into a class. Of this type of word-classification we shall speak later.

8. Derivation and inflection. From the survey which we have just made of the principal types of morphologic classes, it appears that most commonly, when a number of words fall into a morphologic class, they present some phonetic resemblance to one another, and, of course, some phonetic divergence. That is, they differ formationally, e. g. *flame: flash: flare* or *boys: stones: fathers* or *boy: boys: boyish*.

In grammatical writings about English and the languages possessing a similar morphology it has become usual to distinguish two kinds of formational differences, according to the semantic nature of the classification. If the words have in common an element expressing material meaning and differ only in an element of relational content such as is categoric in the language (e. g., in English, number or tense), it is customary to speak of them as different 'forms' of one 'word' and of the relation between them as *inflection*. Thus *boy: boy's: boys* or *eat:*

eats: eating: ate: eaten are examples of inflection. If the words have in common an element expressing material meaning, but differ also in such an element, the relation between them is called *derivation*. Examples are *flash: flare: flame* or *flash: crash: dash* or *boy: boyish* or *eat: eater: eatable*, and so on, provided always that the relation between the words shall be not merely a difference of categoric function. If the words have in common only a relational element, as *boys, fathers, stones*, etc., it is common to call them 'parallel forms' of different words.

In the habits of speakers words related by inflection are very closely associated with each other. For the naive speaker, taking the categories of his language for granted as the natural and inevitable forms of expression, feels the inflectionally different words (or 'forms'), e. g. *boy: boys*, as necessary variations in the expression of a material content. The inflectionally related words are for him really 'forms' of one 'word', — 'forms' made necessary by the exigencies of expression.

9. The semantic nature of inflection: the commonest categories. Inflection, therefore, could be defined as variation between words to express relational differences which involve appurtenance to different categories. What is inflection in one language may, of course, be nothing of the sort in another, where the categories are different.

It will be worth while, then, to mention some of the relations which are expressed by inflection in different languages, — that is, to mention some of the commoner morphologic categories. Some of these we met in the third and fourth chapters, where, however, we were interested in the general rationale of relational expression, rather than in the ground covered by the individual categories.

Number. Among the English parts of speech the nouns have the categories of singular and plural number. Nearly every noun must express whether one object or a plurality is meant: we may say that each of these 'words' has two inflectional 'forms', a singular and a plural.

Some languages distinguish three numbers, singular, dual (for two objects), and plural, an instance being the Sanskrit *devaḥ* 'a god, the god, god', *devāu* 'the two gods, two gods', *devāḥ* 'the gods, gods (more than two)'. Ancient Greek also had inflection for these three numbers, and the singular-plural distinction was categoric, as in English. The distinction between dual and plural, however, was not categoric; the dual, in the writings that have come down to us, is used only of such objects as usually exist in pairs (*ósse* 'eyes', *kheîre* 'hands', etc.) and even there is not obligatory, occurring, indeed, less often than the plural. The contrast, in this respect, between Sanskrit and Greek is instructive: the categories represent obligatory forms of expression, the element which the different forms express being always associatively perceived in the experience; a non-categoric distinction receives expression only where the element involved (here, in Greek, duality) is vivid enough to enter into the analysis in spite of the lack of a regular habit in this direction. It accordingly can serve logical or esthetic impulses of the speaker; the dual of Ancient Greek, as lovers of Greek literature will testify, appears as one of the many graces of that tongue, while in a Sanskrit utterance the use of the dual is esthetically a matter of indifference. We have seen (p. 108) that in Chinese, for instance, the expression of the number of an object-idea is by no means obligatory, the category of number being absent.

Gender. It has already been mentioned that English has no categories of noun-gender. The genders of German appear in the congruence of the adjectives and pronouns. Like German Latin, Greek, Sanskrit, and the Slavic languages have three genders. The Romance and the Scandinavian languages have two, and some of the Bantu languages of Africa go as high as twenty-one, e. g. the Subiya: here relations of number and person are viewed as coordinate with the purely emotional gender-distinctions, there being a category for the speaker, one for the speaker and those with him, one for the person addressed, one for the person addressed and those with him, one for a single person, one for several persons, one for one small thing, one for several small things, one for abstracts, and so on.

Case. Case appears as a category in English especially in the personal and anaphoric pronouns, which vary according to the function of the object in the sentence: as actors appear *I, he, she, they,* as objects affected by the action of a verb or as objects with regard to which a prepositional relation is expressed, *me, him, her, them,* and as attributive possessors *my, his, her, their.* In the nouns there is inflection for the first and third of these relations only, and the possessive form is limited in occurrence almost entirely to nouns denoting living beings (*John: John's; father: father's*); nevertheless, the obligatory inflection of the pronouns forces the speaker to make a constant (categoric) distinction between these three relations.

German has four cases, the objects affected by a verb being divided into two categories, that of objects fully affected and that of objects less fully affected: e. g. *Er gab mir das Buch* 'He gave me the book', where *mir*, as object less fully affected, is in the 'dative' case, *das Buch*, as object fully affected, in the 'accusative' and *Er schlug mich* 'He beat me', where *mich* is in the accusative. The prepositions in German also vary as to the case they demand: *Er legte das Buch auf den Tisch* 'He laid the book on the table', *den Tisch* accusative: *Es liegt auf dem Tische* 'It is lying on the table', *dem Tische,* dative.

The local relations of objects which English or German analyze fully out of the experience and express by independent words (prepositions), are in many languages inflectionally included in the object-word, which thus varies categorically according to them, — so that there may be a great number of cases. Thus, in Sanskrit, *devaḥ* 'god' corresponds to our 'nominative' (*I, he*), *devam* to the German accusative, expressing the object as fully affected, *devāya* to the German dative, expressing the object as less fully affected by the action, *devasya* to our possessive, 'the god's'; but there are also a number of further cases: the 'instrumental' *devena* expressing the object as a means or an accompaniment ('by means of the god' or 'with the god'), the 'ablative' *devāt* expressing it as that from which ('from the god'), the 'locative' *deve*, as that in or near which ('by the god' or 'in the god'); and to these comes also a special form, the 'vocative', for interjectional use, as in calling, *deva* 'O god'. (See also pages 76, 92). The Latin cases have already been mentioned (p. 108). The number of cases in some languages, especially some of the Uralic, such as Finnish (cf. p. 108), is greater, but the principle is everywhere the same.

Tense. We have in English two tenses of verbs, past and present. Some European languages add a third tense, a future, e. g. Latin *canto* 'I sing', *cantābam* 'I sang', *cantābo* 'I shall sing' (cf. p. 68). Future action is in English, as the translation shows, analyzed into the independent words *shall* or *will*, which express futurity with a suggestion, respectively, of obligation or intention (in the present time), or, else, the present tense is used: *Tomorrow we die*. The category of tense is in many languages, as, for instance, in Chinese, entirely absent as such, time-relations being expressed by independent words (p. 68).

Manner (*Aspect*). A much commoner basis of categories than tense is manner of action. It does not exist as a morphologic category in English, where we either ignore the manner of an action or else analytically express it. Thus *I am writing, I was writing* are expressive of 'durative' action, *I have written, I had written* of 'perfectic' (completed) action, *I often write, I used to write* of 'iterative' action, *I wrote it down* of 'final terminative', *He burst out weeping* of 'inceptive terminative' action, and *I once wrote* of 'punctual' action. Many languages, however, express the manner of action in the same word with the action itself, making categoric distinctions between the different manners. Thus the Slavic languages distinguish categorically between, on the one hand, durative and iterative (in Slavic grammar called, together, 'imperfective') action, e. g. Russian [p′i ′sa·t′] 'to write' and [′p′i· sī vet′] 'to be wont to write, to write repeatedly', and, on the other hand, punctual and terminative action (in Slavic grammar, together, 'perfective'), e. g. Russian [nə p′i ′sa·t′] 'to write (once), to write down', [sp′i ′sa·t′] 'to write off', i. e. 'to copy', [pr′i p′i ′sa·t′] 'to write over', i. e. 'to sign away'.

Voice. Another set of categories not found in English are the voices or conjugations, such as 'active', 'middle', 'passive', 'causative', 'applicative', and the like. Thus, in Latin *amat*, active voice, is 'he loves', *amātur* passive voice, 'he is loved, is being loved', or in Greek *élȳse* 'he freed' is active, *elýthē* 'he was freed' is passive (actor as suffering the action), and *elýsato* 'he freed himself' or 'he freed for himself' (e. g. *elýsato tèn thygatéra* 'He-freed-for-himself the daughter', i. e. 'He freed his — own — daughter') is middle (actor as acting upon himself or for himself). In Sanskrit the active voice shows the following 'conjugations': *pátati*, normal, 'he falls'; *pātáyati*, causative, 'he causes to fall, fells'; *pāpatīti*, intensive, 'he falls hard' or 'he falls repeatedly'; *pipatiṣati*, desiderative, 'he wishes to fall' or 'he is about to fall'. Middle and passive forms run parallel to the active; thus the passive of the above causative is *pātyate* 'he is being felled, he is felled'; cf. further, *yájati* 'he sacrifices' (used of the priest who sacrifices in another's behalf) active, *yájate* 'he sacrifices (for himself)' middle, and *ijyáte* 'he (it) is being sacrificed' passive, all three being of normal conjugation. In both Greek and Sanskrit middle and passive are in a large part of the forms homonymous; in Modern Greek there is no middle voice.

The applicative conjugation is frequent in American languages; it expresses the action as applying to some person or thing that would not be involved, were the action-word used in normal conjugation. Thus in Nahwatl the normal *ni-petla-tšiwa* 'I-mat-make', i. e. 'I make mats' or *ni-k-tšiwa* 'I-it-make', i. e. 'I make it' (as in *ni-k-tšiwa se kaλi* 'I-it-make one house', i. e. 'I build a house') has by its side an applicative *ni-k-tšiwi-lia*, as in *ni-k-tšiwi-lia in no-piltsin se kaλi* 'I-it-make-for the my-son one house', i. e. 'I build a house for my son', with two objects affected instead of one. The applicative, in applying an action normally without objects affected to such an object, often coincides in meaning with the causative of Sanskrit, as in *ni-miki* 'I-die', *ni-k-mik-tia* 'I make him die, kill him'. As the English translations show, we lack these categories, looking upon the various forms of action either as upon totally different experiences (*die: kill*), giving them an indifferent derivational expression (*fall: fell*), or analyzing the relation (*sacrifices: sacrifices for himself: is sacrificed*, etc.).

Mode. One verb keeps alive in standard English a categoric distinction of mode, namely the verb *to be*. In *he were*, as opposed to the actual or 'indicative' *he is*, *he was*, we have an 'unreal' mode, and, as it is not standard English to say, for instance, *If he was here, he would help us*, we may call the distinction of mode categoric. Those dialectic ('illiterate') forms of English which do not use the form *he were* have lost this category: in them the 'past' tense-forms are expressive not specifically of action in the past, but of any action not present, be it past or viewed as unreal; they have a present and a past-unreal form, merging what are in standard English the categories of mode and tense. In older and still to some extent in literary English a third mode, an 'optative', also exists, and is used to express action as possible. It is homonymous with the infinitive, from which it differs by the precedence of a subject-actor: *If he be there, Be he live or be he dead*, as opposed to *he is, he were*.

In Ancient Greek three modes were categorically distinguished. An action viewed as really occurring was in the indicative: *phérei* 'he carries', *toũto gígnetai* 'this happens', while actions not so viewed fell, by a categoric distinction, which, however, was in part merged with congruence-relations of tense, into the 'subjunctive': *hína phérēi* 'so-that he-may-carry', *phobeĩtai mḕ toũto génētai* 'he-fears that this may-happen', or into the optative: *phéroi án* 'he might carry', *ei toũto génoito* 'if this should-happen'. The English translation shows how we analyze such modal relations by means of words like *may, can, should*. German also has three modes, an indicative: *Er ist krank* 'He is sick', an optative: *Er gehe* 'Let him go', *Man sagte, er sei krank* 'They said he was sick', and an unreal: *Wenn er krank wäre* 'If he were sick'; German grammars call the last two the 'first' or 'present' and 'second' or 'past' subjunctive.

Both Ancient Greek and German have, like many other languages, a special set of imperative forms for interjectional use of the verb in commands: German *geh!* 'go', Ancient Greek *phére* 'carry', *pheréto* 'let him carry', where the English equivalent is either the infinitive form or, for the third person, the infinitive of the verb *let* which directs the command, by an analysis of the situation, at the person spoken to.

Actor. We have seen that the English verb varies in form according to the person and number of the actor. The variation according to number (*The boy skates, The boys skate*) is properly a phenomenon of congruence with the number-category of the noun or pronoun expressing the subject-actor. The same may be said of the variation according to person (*I am, you are, he is*), although there can hardly be said to exist a categoric system of 'persons' in nouns and pronouns, since there is only one first-person pronoun (*I, we*), and only one for the second person (*you*): the 'person' of these words is simply their content as words.

In some other languages, as we have seen (p. 107), words expressing action really include personal-anaphoric mention of the actor. Thus Latin verb-forms such as *edo* 'I-eat', *edis* 'you-eat', *edit* 'he (she, it)-eats', *edimus* 'we-eat', etc., do not vary in mere congruence with categories of an actor, but actually include mention of the actor, who may not in any other way be expressed. The Latin verb, then, expresses not only an action, but an actor and an action, and just as it has categoric variation according to tense, mode, and voice of the action, it also varies categorically according to number and person of the actor.

Goal (Object affected). In other languages the action-word includes the objects or object affected by an action, or these together with an actor. This phenomenon is known as 'incorporation'. Here the action-word may, of course, be inflected for person and number of the object affected. We have already seen such forms from Greenlandish (p. 104) and from Nahwatl (p. 135). The following forms from the latter language will further illustrate this inflection:

ni-mits-matštia 'I-thee-teach', 'I teach thee',
n-amets̈-matštia 'I-ye-teach', 'I teach ye',
ni-k-matštia 'I-him-teach', 'I teach him',
ni-kin-matštia 'I-them-teach', 'I teach them',
ti-nets̈-matštia 'thou-me-teachest', 'thou teachest me',
ti-tets̈-matštia 'thou-us-teachest', 'thou teachest us',
ti-k-matštia 'thou-him-teachest', 'thou teachest him',
ti-kin-matštia 'thou-them-teachest', 'thou teachest them',
nets̈-matštia 'me-teaches', 'he teaches me',

and so on. Two objects affected are seen in *ni-te-tla-maka* 'I-someone-something-give', 'I give someone something', *ni-k-tla-maka* 'I-him-something-give', 'I give him something', *ni-k-maka* 'I give it to him'. Here we see a threefold inflection: for actor and for two objects affected.

Possessor. With object-words the person, number, and even gender of another attributive object may be expressed (p. 107, with example from modern Arabic), and this expression may be categoric. In Nahwatl, for instance, one cannot say 'mother' or 'hand' without expressing an attributive (possessing) object, as in *no-nan* 'my-mother' or *to-ma* 'our-hand'; one can also say *te-nan* 'someone's, an uncertain person's mother'. In some languages this applies to every object-word, so that one cannot say, for instance, 'house', but only 'my-house', 'his-house', 'an-uncertain-person's-house', or the like.

An interesting phenomenon found in some languages is the fusion of the categories of possessor of an object with those of performer of an action. In the language of the extinct Lules in South America, for instance, the following showed parallel inflection:

umue-s my mother   *amaitsi-s* I love
umue-tse thy mother   *amaitsi-tse* thou lovest
umue-p his mother   *amaitsi-p* he loves.

No English translation, of course, could do justice to this complete merging of what we analyze as two entirely different relations. In other languages the possessor of an object is fused with the object affected by an action; thus in Greenlandish these and the actor also are in part expressed alike: [iḷ:u-a] 'house-his', 'his house', [iḷ:u-t] 'thy house' show the same inflectional endings as [tusaʀp-a-t] 'sounding-his-thine', i. e. 'thou hearest him'. All this illustrates the vast divergence as to the semantic character of inflection.

10. The semantic nature of derivation. When the relation between words of a phonetic-semantic class is not a difference of category, we call it derivation (p. 141); thus the relation between *flame, flash, flare*, etc. or between *bull, bullock*, we have seen, is derivation. In such instances as the latter it is frequently said that the longer word is 'derived' from the shorter, or a 'derivative' of it. This mode of expression is permissible, as long as one does not allow it to affect one's view as to the historical priority: historically it is quite possible in such cases that the longer word existed before the shorter one, which then, in reality, may have been derived from the longer.

As to the semantic values of derivation, it is impossible to set limits, or even to quote, as in the case of inflection, some of the commoner relations expressed. Almost any material relation may be expressed by it. The following sets of derivatives may illustrate this multiplicity:

English *flame, flash, flare, flimmer, flicker.*
English *drip, drop, droop, dribble, drabble.*
English *clash, crash, dash, flash, gash, gnash, hash, lash, mash, plash, slash, splash.*
English *dribble, nibble, quibble.*
English *tend, tense, tension, tensity, tenseness, intense, intensive, intensity, intend, intent, attend, attention, inattention, attentive, inattentive,* etc. No doubt *tend* is moreover associated, for most of us, with *trend.*

From the Nass dialect of Tsimshian (British Columbia): [haḷíe:] 'to walk along the edge of the water', [wi:tsʼənïe:] 'to walk back through the house', [aḷdaïe:] 'to walk in the dark', and so on.

Crossing this class: [aḷdawa:ç] 'to paddle in the night', [aḷdaïe:] 'to walk in the dark'.

11. The phonetic character of the morphologic processes. The formal phase of morphology includes every conceivable phonetic variation.

This phonetic variation is to be sharply distinguished from automatic sound-variation. Whether we say [ju] as in *Will you?* or [ʃu] as in *Won't you?* [wilju, wowntʃu], has nothing to do with our meaning (and is therefore of no grammatical significance) but depends entirely on the nature of the sound we have been uttering when we come to the *you.* The same is true, for instance, of the Sanskrit sandhi-variations (p. 102). On the other hand, whether we say *dash* or *mash* or *plash* or *splash,* and whether a German says *der, die,* or *das,* and an Irishman *bó, vó,* or *mó,* is of decided significance. In these English words the material content varies with the difference of form; in the German and the Irish the morphologic category of other words is involved.

Pitch-variation. Pitch-variation for derivation can occur, of course, only where the pitch-relations within a word are fixed. It is found, for instance in Norwegian and Swedish; thus in the former language: ['skriː vər/] 'write, writes' (present-tense form of verb): ['skriːˌ vər/] 'writer'. In Chinese there are a great many words distinguished only by their pitch-relations, and in some instances such words are derivationally connected in the feeling of the speakers, e. g. [ˈnan/] 'difficult' and [ˌnan\] 'suffer', [ˌmaš/] 'buy' and [ˌmaš\] 'sell'.

Stress-variation. The place of the stress in a word is in English significant and consequently can be used for morphologic sound-variation. As the quality of certain vowels further depends automatically in English on the place of the stress, the following examples illustrate both morphologic and automatic sound-variation: *accent*, noun [ˈæksn̩t]: verb [əkˈsent]; — *address*, noun [ˈædɹes] or [ˈædɹs]: verb [əˈdɹes]; — *overthrow*, noun [ˈowvɹ̩Θɹo]: verb [ovɹ̩ˈΘɹow]. Similarly, in Russian: [ˈruˑki] 'the hands': [ruˈkiˑ] 'of the hand'; — [u znɑˈjuˑ] 'I recognize': [uˈznɑˑ ju] 'I shall recognize'. Place of stress is interesting in Ancient Greek: in the verb it varies automatically and cannot, therefore, be of morphologic significance; in the other parts of speech it is free and receives morphologic employment, e. g. in *tómos* 'slice': *tomós* 'cutter'.

Variation of articulations. Vowel-variation is common in English morphologic expression: *goose: geese; man: men; foot: feet; mouse: mice; woman* [wumən]: *women* [wimen]; *eat: ate; see: saw; sing: sang: sung: song; ride: rode; read*, present tense [ɹijd]: *read*, past tense [ɹed]; *sip: sop: sup: seep: sap; drip: drop: droop; sniff: snuff; snip: snap*, — and so on. The terms 'umlaut' and 'ablaut' are used in the grammar of English and the related languages as designations for certain cases of vowel-variation: 'umlaut' for our vowel-variation for number in the noun (*mouse:*

mice), 'ablaut' for that in the tense-inflection of the verb (*sing: sang*).

Consonant variation also is common in English; we have seen it in our example of *clash: crash: dash: flash*, etc.; also in the Irish *bó: vó: mó* and the like. Further English examples are *have: has: had; crash: crack; squeak: squeal; squawk: squall; bend: bent; send: sent*. Another example is the Kafir word for 'all' which varies in congruence with the gender — the Kafir is a Bantu language, cf. p. 143, — of the word it modifies: *bonke: lonke: yonke: zonke: wonke: konke*.

It is common to find sound-variation in both consonants and vowels, as in *flame: flash; crash: creak; was: were; will: would* [wud]; *can: could;* German *schneiden* 'to cut' ['ʃnaědṇ]: *schnitten* 'were cutting' ['ʃnitṇ], and the like.

Affixation. Somewhat different from sound-variation is the plus or minus of sounds seen in such groups of words as *sing: sings: singer: singing* or *man: manly* or *bull: bullock*. This kind of word-variation is called *affixation*, the phonetic element that is common to a set of words related by affixation being spoken of as the *kernel*, the elements present or absent in the different words, as the *affixes*. Thus in the first group among our instances *sing-* is the kernel and *-s* [z], *-er*, and *-ing* are affixes. Here again our terminology is metaphoric: there is no reason to believe that the longer words of a group related by affixation necessarily arose from the shortest word by any actual process of 'affixing' or adding phonetic elements: that is a question of historic fact which is not answered by our use of the terms 'affix' and 'affixation'. Instead of 'affix' the terms 'determinative', 'formative', and 'formans' are current in certain branches of grammar; and the kernels of certain word-groups in certain languages are called 'bases', 'stems', and 'roots'[1]).

The difference between sound-variation and affixation is not an absolute one, but depends frequently on our point of view. We might call Latin *amās* 'thou lovest': *amat* 'he loves' an example of sound-variation; if, however, we take into view some other forms of this verb, such as *amo* 'I love', *amāvit* 'he loved', *amētur* 'he may be loved', it is possible to call them all related by affixation, the kernel being *am-*, the affixes in the quoted forms, *-ās, -at, -o, -āvit, -ētur*. In this instance the group does not contain a word that equals the kernel, or, as we might say, has 'affix zero', — a condition fulfilled by the first of the quoted forms in the example of English *sing: sings*, etc. An English group like *flash: flame: flare: flicker* might be regarded as an example either of sound-variation or of affixation to a kernel *fl-*.

In all these examples the affix appears at the end of the word and is, specifically, a *suffix* or *ending*. Other examples of suffixation are the German article-forms *der: die: das* (with kernel *d-*), English *bull: bullock; man: man's: manly: mannish; boy: boys: boyish*, and so on.

Prefixation borders, like suffixation, on sound-variation: thus the forms of the Kafir word for 'all', *bonke: lonke:*

---

1) As to the last of these terms, it may be well to warn the reader against attributing to it any mystical character. Fifty years ago most students of language believed that the kernels they had abstracted from some of the ancient languages possessed a unique validity and age: that, in fact, they or their like were the original elements with which language had begun and out of which its more elaborate forms were pieced together. Today we mean by all the above terms simply certain phonetic elements common to sets of formationally related words, and do not allow our terminology to commit us to any view as to the historic origin of these related words.

yonke: sonke: wonke: konke are often spoken of as a kernel *-nke* with different prefixes, — owing to certain morphologic features which prevail in the language. Other examples of prefixation are, from the English, *kind: unkind; speak: bespeak; septic: aseptic,* and the like. *Plash: splash; mash: smash; lash: slash,* and the like may be viewed as sound-variation or as prefixation, — the former because the initial group of *s* plus consonant is exceedingly frequent in the language.

Infixation is affixation within the word. We may view Latin *amat* 'he, she, it loves': *amant* 'they love' as infixation, the kernel being *ama-t,* the infix, *-n-;* on the other hand, if we include in consideration the above-quoted forms *amo* 'I love', *amāvit* 'he loved', *amētur* 'he may be loved', and so on, we shall speak rather of suffixation of *-at, -ant, -o,* etc. to a kernel *am-*. Less pliable examples of infixation are English *clap: clamp* and Latin *fidit* 'he split': *findit* 'he splits', *scidit* 'he rent': *scindit* 'he rends'. Another example of affixation may be seen in Sanskrit, e. g. in *yuktáḥ* 'yoked, bound': *yuñktáḥ* 'they-two yoke, bind': *yunákti* 'he (she, it) yokes, binds'; the kernel of the word-group to which these forms belong is here seen as *yu-k-,* with the suffixes *-taḥ* and *-ti* and the infix *-na-: -n-*.

These Sanskrit forms illustrate also the phenomenon of automatic sound-variation in affixes. The infix is here *-na-* when accented, but *-n-* when unaccented, — a variation by no means universal in the Sanskrit language. We have a few similar instances in English, where, for instance, our plural-suffix of nouns, our possessive suffix of nouns, and our third-person singular congruence-suffix of verbs all have a homonymous form which appears as [ez] after sibilants, as [z] after non-sibilant voiced sounds, and as [s] after non-sibilant unvoiced sounds:

plurals: *watches, peaches,* — *boys, fathers,* — *hats, cliffs;*

possessives: *boss's, Madge's, — John's, father's, — count's, Pete's;*

third-person verbs: *watches, dances, — loves, hears, — waits, counts.*

Yet the language as a whole cannot be said to have such an automatic sound-variation as this: the automatic variation is peculiar to these suffixes.

Affixation may of course be accompanied by morphologic sound-variation; instances are the German *will* 'wants to': *wollen* 'want to' (suffix *-en*, with vowel-variation *i: o*); English *child: children* (suffix *-ren* with vowel-variation [aɛ̆]: [i]); or the different affixational processes may occur together, as in Ancient Greek *lambánō* 'I take': *élabon* 'I took' (kernel *-la-b-*, prefix *e-*, infix *-m-*, suffixes *-anō* and *-on;* the shifting of the accent is here automatic).

Reduplication. A peculiar kind of affixation is *reduplication*, which consists of the repetition of the whole word or some part of it. Examples are Malay *tuwan* 'master': *tuwun-tuwan* 'masters'; Latin *quis* 'who?': *quisquis* 'whoever'; Sanskrit *bharti* 'he carries': *bharībharti* 'he carries hither and thither' (reduplication with infixed *-ī-*); Latin *tendit* 'he stretches': *tetendit* 'he stretched'. Reduplication is often irregular, approaching the other forms of affixation, e. g., connected with the above Sanskrit *bharti* a form *jabhāra* [ɟabhɑːra] 'he carried' (kernel *-bh-r-*, prefix or irregular reduplication *ja-*, vowel-variation *a: ā*, suffixes *-ti* and *-a*); Latin *pello* 'I drive': *pepulī* 'I drove' (reduplication with sound-variation and different suffixes). The boundary between reduplication and the other forms of affixation is thus not a sharp one: English *do: did* could be looked upon as an example of either process.

It is noteworthy that reduplication is confined to certain narrow spheres of meaning. It often denotes increase, changing, for instance, words in the singular number to plurals of different kinds, as in our instance of the Malay *tuwan-tuwan* 'masters'. Other examples are Japanese *jama-jama* 'mountains' (*jama* 'mountain'); Nahwatl *in tšatšan o-jajake* '(into) the his-houses they-each-went', i. e. 'They went each into his house', as opposed to *in tšan o-jake* 'they went (together) into their (one) house'; *okitš-pil* 'little man', plural *okitš-pipil* 'little men'; Tsimshian [aļix] 'to speak', [əl'aļix] 'to speak, of several people'; [Gan] 'tree', [GanGan] 'trees'. It may further denote repetition, continuity, or intensity: Latin *quisquis* 'who-who', i. e. 'everytime who', 'whoever'; Sanskrit *dame-dame* 'in every house', as opposed to *dame* 'in the house'; Greek *ébēn* 'I stepped': *ebíbēn* 'I made repeated steps, walked'; Sanskrit *bharībharti* 'he carries hither and thither'; Nahwatl *kotōna* 'cut': *kōkotōna* 'cut in many pieces': *kokotōna* 'cut many things'; English *snip-snap, fiddle-faddle, slip-slop, flip-flop*. Occasionally it has diminutive sense, as in these English examples, where, for instance, *flip-flop* expresses a less violent movement than *flop;* the same is true in Dayak (a Malayan language of Borneo) of *hai* 'large': *hahai* 'fairly large'; *handang* 'red': *hahandang* 'reddish'. Desire for an action as opposed to the action itself we see in Sanskrit *jīvāmi* 'I live': *jijīviṣāmi* 'I desire to live'; *vidmaḥ* 'we know': *vivitsati* or *vividiṣati* 'he wishes to learn', compare also page 146. Finally, it expresses perfectic action, as in the Greek *léloipa* 'I have left' as opposed to the durative *leípo* 'I am leaving', and, rarely, but in this use familiar to us from Latin, it expresses past tense: Sanskrit *jabhāra* 'he carried', Latin *tetendit* 'he stretched', *pepulit* 'he drove'.

Homomorphy and suppletion. One and the same semantic relation between two words, — such as in English the difference of present and past tense, — may find expression in the most various formal processes. Thus in the present-past inflection of the English verb we find suffixation (*dance: danced*), vowel-variation (*sing: sang*), consonant-variation (*send: sent*), and so on. We saw in paragraph 5 that all words making a given inflection in the same formal way fall into a class by phonetic-semantic parallelism. Thus our 'regular' verbs with the suffix *-ed* for the past form a large class, as do also our different groups of 'irregular' verbs. The same can be said of the plural-inflection of our nouns.

Among the small 'irregular' classes so singled off, the formal relation between inflections may be that of identity. This phenomenon is called homonymy or, more specifically, *homomorphy*. For instance, among the English verbs there are a few which are alike in the two tenses: *cost, hit, beat, put, let*. These unchanging verbs are, however, so much in the minority that we do not ordinarily realize that their present and past tenses are alike. The identity of the two forms constitutes simply an irregular kind of inflection, owing to the vast preponderance of verbs that do vary. In the noun-inflection homomorphy is seen in *deer, sheep, fish*.

The opposite of homomorphy is *suppletion*, which consists of the entire absence of phonetic relation in some few members of a large class by semantic parallelism; that is, where the whole class is so numerous that in the few cases where the 'forms' are not formally related, we still feel that they belong together. Among the English verbs, for instance, we find the inflectional forms *be, am, are, is, was, were* which in spite of complete dissimilarity belong together by parallelism with the other verbs. Another example is *go: went* (p. 139, f.). In the forms of the adjective we have, beside the regular type, *kind: kinder: kindest*, the suppletive sets *good: better: best, bad: worse: worst*. Similarly, in the relation between adjective and derived adverb, beside the regular *kind: kindly, rapid: rapidly*, etc., the suppletive *good: well*, and in that between cardinal numeral and ordinal numeral, beside the regular *four: fourth, six: sixth*, etc., and the irregular *three: third, five: fifth*, also the suppletive *one: first, two: second*. Suppletion is found, as a rule, in very common words, and irregularity also, though in a far less degree, tends to confine itself to these.

12. Word-composition: semantic value. In paragraph 7 I mentioned the relation of compounds to each other and to simple words as the most explicit expression of morphologic classification.

Word-composition consists of the use of two or more words in a combination that has a different meaning from that of the simple words in syntactic collocation. This may be illustrated by a few transparent English examples. Our word *long-nose*, as in *I can't stand that long-nose* (meaning a person) differs from a *long nose*, for it means not a nose of this shape, but a person having such a nose. *Shorthand* does not mean what the words *short hand* as separate successive words in syntactic collocation would mean, but, instead, is used of a certain kind of writing. A different kind of deviation from the meaning of independent words appears in *bulldog*. This compound, to be sure, does designate a *dog*: but *bull*, a noun, could not in English syntactic collocation, modify another following noun, such as *dog* (p. 96).

The problem of in any way classifying compounds is an exceedingly difficult one, because the material and logical relations between the 'members' of compounds are, even within one and the same language, often well-nigh endless in variety. Perhaps the most justifiable basis of classification is that which distinguishes compounds which in form resemble a syntactic word-group and those which do not. By this classification *long-nose, shorthand, crows-foot, man-of-war,* for instance, would belong to the former class, for, though diverging in meaning, these compounds externally resemble such collocations as *long nose, short hand, crow's foot, man of war* (as opposed to *man of peace*). To the second class would belong *bulldog, apple-tree, sofa-cushion,* and the like, which do not resemble syntactic groups. The compounds of the latter class can further be divided according to whether they describe an actually present feature of the experience, like *apple-tree,* or, like *bulldog,* express merely an associative element entering from past experiences: the apples are perhaps visible on the tree, but the dog merely reminds one of a bull.

While the specific values of compounds as opposed to collocations of simple words vary greatly even within a single language, yet, when we look at other languages, we find that each one has certain limitations. As an instance of a kind of composition not found in English, the following Nahwatl examples may serve: simple words, *nakatl* 'meat' (or 'It is meat') and *nikkwa* 'I eat it': compound, *ni-naka-kwa* 'I-meat-eat'; in English we form no verbal compounds of this type, though we freely parallel them in our nouns, such as *meat-eater.* A further example from Nahwatl is *ni-šotši-temoa* 'I seek flowers': simple words, *šotšitl* 'flower' and *niktemoa* 'I seek it'. These Nahwatl compounds differ from simple words, in that the simple words can always express a predication a-piece: *nikkwa nakatl* can mean 'I eat it. It is meat'.

The following Sanskrit compounds, called in the grammar of that language 'copulative', would also be impossible in English: *vrīhiḥ* 'rice', *yavaḥ* 'barley' (both in the nominative case, singular number): *vrīhiyavāu* 'rice and barley' (nominative case, dual number), as though we should say 'rice-barleys' for 'rice and barley'. This Sanskrit compound differs from a syntactic collocation in that the case and number are expressed not for each member separately, but only once, at the end, as in any simple word; this gives a tone of unity to the whole. Other examples of this type are: *brāhmana-kṣatriya-viṭ-śūdrāḥ*, nominative plural, 'brahmans, kshatriyas, vaiçyas, and çudras' (men of the four castes); or *vṛttaḥ* 'round', *pīnaḥ* 'plump': *vṛttapīnaḥ* 'round and plump'.

In Chinese [ˈçĭuŋˀ ˌti\], as we have seen (p. 86), means 'brother, brothers'; a syntactic collocation of the two words [ˈçĭuŋˀ] 'older brother' and [ˌti\] 'younger brother', if it occurred at all, could mean only 'younger brother of an older brother'. This differs from anything we have in English; it would correspond to a compound *brothersister* in the meaning of 'brother or sister', 'child of the same parents'. Similarly [ˈʃə/ˌsze\], as a syntactic collocation would mean 'ten fours' (compare, for instance [ˌszeˡ ˈʃə/] 'four tens', 'forty'), but it is really a compound, 'ten-four', meaning 'fourteen'.

We may illustrate now some of the varieties of compounds used in English. Most strikingly different from the simple words in syntactic succession are the so-called 'exocentric' compounds, which denote an object *having* the thing named in the compound, as *long-nose, shorthorn, swallow-tail*. Similar to these are the forms *long-nosed, short-horned, swallow-tailed, rough-shod;* these are in total effect nearer the simple words (compare, for instance, *tailed monkeys*), but still, in their use of adjective modifying adjective differ from a collocation of words, where we use adverbs to modify adjectives (*roughly shod*). The compounds consisting of two nouns have already been mentioned. We may name such further examples as *dog-pound, dust-rag, schoolroom, headache, summerhouse, man-nurse*. The semantic relation between the parts is, it appears, of practically unlimited variety. We have mentioned also the type in which an object affected by an action and the actor or instrument (in the form of a verbal noun) are joined together: *meat-eater, lion-tamer, tennis-player, screw-driver, coat-hanger*.

13. Word-composition not a phonetic process. It will be noticed that nothing has here been said about any formal difference between compounds and syntactic collocations. If we recall the fact that the word, — and, therefore, by inclusion, also the compound word, — is not a phonetic unit (p. 99), it will be clear that there need not necessarily be a phonetic difference between a compound and a succession of words. The difference between a single word, simple or compound, and a succession of words lies in the semantic value and not in the sounds. Not even the stress-accent of a language like English or German necessarily distinguishes a compound from a succession of words. This is especially clear in German, where such compounds as *durchmessen* 'to measure through, to cross' [durç 'mɛsn̩] do not differ in accent from such collocations as *sich messen* 'to vie, to measure oneself' [ziç 'mɛsn̩]. In English we have the same similarity under certain conditions of stress, thus *my mother* with an emphatic *my*, resembles in stress-relations the compounds *godmother, grandmother*, and similarly *mother of mine* resembles *mother-in-law*.

Furthermore, a compound need not be phonetically continuous. In Latin *nē quidem* 'not even' is a compound word which may be separated, as in *nē Caesar quidem* 'not even Caesar'. Similarly, in German, *wenngleich* 'even if', as in *Wenn ich gleich schreie* 'Even if I cry', and a great many compound verbs like *vorlesen* 'to read aloud', as in *Ich les' ihm jeden Abend vor* 'I read to him every evening'. In French we find such compound words as *ne pas* 'not' in *Je ne lui donne pas*... 'I don't give him..' In English we have such verb-compounds as *bring out* in the sense of 'emphasize, make clear' (the simple words appear in collocation in *Bring out your golf-sticks*), which are separated in such sentences as *You don't bring that out very clearly*.

All this shows us that the concept of a compound, like that of a word is not absolutely definable. Is *stand off* in *Stand off, there!* a compound? It differs from the ordinary use of *stand*, which excludes the idea of movement; on the other hand, in view of *stand up* and *stand aside* we might say that *stand* means not only 'to be in an upright position' but also 'to assume an upright position'. (Cf. p. 97, f.). That is to say, then, the difference between compounds and sets of simple words is, like that between derivationally formed words and compounds (p. 96), a matter of the speaker's associative disposition which may vary from person to person and from hour to hour.

While phonetic differences between compounds and simple words are thus by no means necessary, they are, on the other hand, not uncommon. A number of examples deserve mention.

In English compounds usually differ in stress from successions of simple words. In general, our syntactic groups of simple words tend to be evenly stressed, with a highest stress on each word, while our compounds, like all other single words, have a high stress on one syllable, usually the first. Thus, for instance, we distinguish phonetically between ˈ*bulldog* and the simple words in ˈ*bull*, ˈ*dog, and* ˈ*cat*, between a ˈ*crowsfoot* and a ˈ*crow's* ˈ*foot*, between a ˈ*longnose* and a ˈ*long* ˈ*nose*, and between ˈ*bloodshed* and ˈ*all the* ˈ*blood* ˈ*shed in the* ˈ*Civil* ˈ*War*.

It is evident that in languages that have a regulated

pitch within the word, difference of pitch may figure in phonetic divergence between compound and simple word. Thus in Norwegian we find *land* [lɑn/] 'country', *mand* [mɑn/] 'man': *landmand* ['lɑn˳mɑn/] 'farmer, peasant, countryman'.

It is common also to find compounds differing in vowel and consonant articulations from the simple words, e. g. *fore* and *head*, but *forehead*, — [fɔːɹ], [hed] : ['fɑɹəd]; German *die Sonne* 'the sun', genitive case *der Sonne* 'the sun's', *das Licht* 'the light': *das Sonnenlicht* 'the sunlight', with an added -*n*-. Thus Sanskrit *vrīhiyavāu* 'rice and barley' is in the genitive *vrīhiyavayoḥ* 'of rice and barley', where the lack of inflection of *vrīhi*-'rice', — a form which, moreover, never occurs as a separate word, — distinguishes it both semantically and in form from *vrīhiḥ* 'rice', genitive *vrīheḥ*. So *mahādhanam* as opposed to *mahad dhanam* (p. 106). Likewise, in Ancient Greek *hȳlotómos* means 'wood-cutting (adjective)' and is inflected, for instance in the accusative, for congruence with a noun, *hȳlotómon:* the first element is here uninflected: as an independent word, moreover, it is in the nominative *hȳlē*, in the accusative *hȳlēn*, and in no form *hȳlo-*.

The greatest divergence between simple words and compounds appears in those languages which, owing to an objective habit of expression, compounds are in most frequent use (p. 104). Thus the Nahwatl compound above quoted *ni-naka-kwa* 'I eat meat' corresponds to the simple words *nakatl* 'meat, it is meat', and *nikkwa* 'I eat it'. Thus, aside from the semantic divergences, there are the following in form alone: -*tl* in simple word is left off in compound; *ni*- at beginning of simple word appears at the beginning of the compound; -*k*- (semantically 'it') left off in compound.

Like the English *forehead* (where the spelling preserves

our feeling of connection with simple words), such Nahwatl compounds approach the boundary where the compound would cease to be felt by the speaker to resemble any simple words, and, consequently, would no longer be a compound. This line is, of course, not sharply traceable. Those who know the word [ˈhʌzəf] 'sewing-bag' from speech alone will scarcely feel it to be a compound, as will those who know it from its written form *housewife* or in its 'spelling pronunciation' [ˈhaŏswaĕf].

14. Simple word: compound: phrase. This, then, is the second direction in which compounds approach simple words. On the one hand, we have seen instances where it was doubtful whether a certain element was merely an affix or a member of a compound word: In *fourteen, sixteen, seventeen*, etc. (p. 96) the element *-teen* may be a suffix: in that case the words are simple; if, however, in view of the usage in *She is in her teens*, *teen* is an independent word, then *fourteen*, etc. are compounds. Similarly, in Italian there are a number of words with a suffix *-accio, -accia*, expressing the idea of unpleasantness, e. g. *roba* 'stuff, goods': *robaccia* 'trash', *tempo* 'weather': *tempaccio* 'nasty weather', *Alfredo* 'Alfred': *Alfredaccio* 'naughty Alfred', *vecchio* 'old', 'old man': *vecchiaccio* 'unpleasant old man', etc. In view of the locution *Quanto siete accio!* 'How unpleasant you are!' all these may, however, be looked upon as compounds. On the other hand, we now find compounds departing so widely in form from the corresponding simple words, that the compositional or merely formational structure is again questionable. It is, of course, really in both cases the same phenomenon seen from a different point of view: in cases like *fourteen* our feeling inclines to take the word as simple, in those like *housewife* to recognize a compound of two members: both approach the boundary between simple words and compounds.

We have seen, also, that compounds may approach the value of syntactic collocations, until, in cases like *bulldog* (p. 97) and *stand off* (p. 163), we may hesitate before the alternative of speaking of composition or of setting up the apparent first members as independent words.

Thus we see, in our survey of morphology, the most varied types of expression: first, the unit word, which, if classed at all with any other, must be suppletively classed, in the manner of *go: went;* then the inflected word, grouping itself with others that express the same material content with a difference of category, such as *eat, eats, ate, eaten, eating;* then again, the derived word, bordering on a compound, such as *unkind, fourteen;* and finally, the compound, bordering, in its turn, on a syntactic collocation of words.

It is with this syntactic collocation that we shall have to do in the next chapter.

CHAPTER VI.
SYNTAX.

1. The field of syntax. Syntax studies the interrelations of words in the sentence. These interrelations are primarily the discursive ones of predication and attribution (pp. 61, 110, f.), to which may be added the serial relation (p. 113). These are modified by the emotional dominance of individual words (p. 113, f.) and specialized into set forms designating material relations of objects (p. 114, f.).

Syntax cannot be sharply separated from morphology. This is apparent when we find that it is not always possible to determine what is one word, what a combination of words. There is, however, another more essential point of contact. To the extent in which the words of a language include relational content, to that extent the morphology of a language involves questions of syntax. In an objective language, where relations are included with the material content of every word, there is comparatively little left to say of the syntax. The sentence, indeed, is often a single word, as in the Nahwatl *ninakakwa* 'I-meat-eat': the syntax of such a sentence is, of course, the morphology of a word. When we come to languages like Latin or Sanskrit, in which the noun, for instance, appears in a number of case-forms with each its relational content (pp. 108, 143, f.), it is the task of morphology to define the values of these cases. These relational values must be carefully studied, before syntax, in the strict sense, can be begun: but in defining them we are already entering upon the interrelations of words. The value, for example, of the dative case in Latin (p. 115) involves the use of dative-case nouns in the sentence. In English the syntax is more extended, for relations are here more frequently expressed by independent words: the dative case of Latin, for instance, often by the prepositions *for* or *to* (p. 115). Chinese has no inflection and scarcely any derivation: its grammar is almost entirely a matter of syntax.

The forms of syntax are less fixed than those of morphology, because the utterance of a sentence is a more complex process and one more easily displaced than that of a word. In exclamation, especially, the usual syntactic habit is often disturbed, the elements of the experience effecting expression in other than the accustomed form. Thus we may exclaim *A rabbit — white!* instead of *A white rabbit!* 'Anacolouthon', the breaking off one's construction, is common where the emotional charge is considerable: *I wonder if he — but of course he has not done it!*

2. The discursive relations. The substratum of the interrelation of words in a sentence is formed by the binary discursive groupings of predication and attribution (p. 61) and by the serial grouping (p. 113). We saw in the fourth chapter (p. 111) that these relations are not always expressed, that in Latin, for instance, *Māgna culpa* could express a predication 'Great is the fault' or an attribution 'Great fault'. The discursive relations may, as a matter of constant habit, fail to receive syntactic expression. In a Latin sentence such as *Cantat* 'He (she) sings' we have an actor-subject and an action-predicate, but, as both are included in one word, the predication does not receive syntactic expression, but only morphologic. In other languages there is no distinct expression of predication at all. In Nahwatl *piltsin* means, from the English point of view, either 'He is a son' or 'a son'. Almost every word here can be used to express a predication or, especially within a larger utterance, as part of a predication. The utterance *nikmaka tlaškalli in nopiltsin* can be looked upon as 'I give it him. It is bread. It is that one. It is my son.' or as 'I give my son bread'. The difficulty of interpretation is due entirely to the English idiom; from the Nahwatl point of view there is no difference between the two forms of expression. This is true of many American languages: their words are 'sentence-words' (p. 64) with the power of expressing a predication, and there is no formal indication in any utterance as to whether a given word is or is not expressing predication. This sentence-word quality, indeed, is what gives to the Latin verb, such as *cantat*, the power of expressing an entire predication, both subject and predicate. In Latin this quality is confined, however, to the verb. In contrast with this is English, in which no word can, by itself, express a whole predication: not even our verb, for it, unlike the Latin verb, does not include an actor-subject; we cannot say *Sings*, but only *He sings, She sings*.

Thus we may, by contrasting two such languages as Nahwatl and English, see the different degrees of recognition which the discursive relations may receive. In Nahwatl predication is formally a matter of indifference: any word may express it or not, and the Aztec speaker does not need to decide whether it is doing so or not. In English at least two words are needed to express a predication: a subject and a predicate. The subject must be a word of the noun or pronoun class, and the predicate must be a verb. Verbs, moreover, except for one special form, the infinitive, always constitute a predicate, and such a predicate is not permitted to appear without a subject. In short, predication is precisely defined and serves as the basis of our word-classification (parts of speech) and of our sentence-structure.

In viewing such phenomena as these one must guard against confusing a sentence-equivalent with a sentence. If one asks, in English, *Did he bring it?* and gets the answer *Yes*, this answer is in communicative value equal to a predication, *He brought it.* Linguistically, however, it is not a sentence, but only a sentence-equivalent. If one asks *What are you doing?* and receives the answer *Writing*, this is in communicative content equal to a sentence, *I am writing*, but as language it is only a word, not an utterance presenting discursive relations.

3. The emotional relations. The emotional substratum of sentences is to some extent independent of these discursive relations. The different elements in a sentence usually vary as to the place they hold in the emotional interest of the speaker; in the whole sentence there is often unity in that some one element markedly exceeds the others in emotional value. The natural expression for these relations seems to be greater stress (loudness) for the more highly charged words (p. 50); this seems to be a universal habit among languages, though the exact degree of stress-differences varies. We can imagine a sequence of words spoken with varying distribution of emotional value, for instance in opposition to a series of contrary propositions: the dominant element will in each case receive highest stress (pp. 50, 113) e. g.: *To'day is my birthday, Today 'is my birthday, Today is 'my birthday, Today is my 'birthday*. There may be two dominant elements: *To'day is 'my birthday (and tomorrow is my mother's)*. In languages that express more than one semantic element in one word, different parts of a word may be thus stressed. Even in English, with our rigid stress-accent on certain syllables, we can speak not only of *'bulldogs and 'lapdogs*, but also of *bull'dogs and bull'frogs*. This may be more pronounced where more semantic elements are included in one word, thus in Mesquaki (one of the Algonquian languages) ['wɔ ba mi nu] '*Look* at me', [wɔ ba 'mi nu] 'Look at *me*', [wɔ ba mi 'nu] '*You* look at me'.

Differences of word-order, also, may be used to express the emotional relations. 'Julius loves Julia' is in Latin *Jūlius Jūliam amat*, but 'Julius loves *Julia*' is *Jūliam amat Jūlius*. This appears to some extent also in English, as in the contrast between *I bought a hat yesterday* and *Yesterday I bought a hat*, *He came last* and *Last came he*. Where the word-order is not free, a similar effect can be obtained by altering the logical structure of the sentence (p. 114), e. g. *It is Julia whom Julius loves*. In the Celtic languages and in French this mode of expression is very common; we may recall its use in Irish English.

4. Material relations. Another factor entering into the syntactic structure of the sentence is the perceptual content. Certain word-sequences or types of word-sequences become habitual as the expression for certain relations of the objects of the perceptual world; thus in English we have studied the peculiar construction of words designating spatial relations (prepositions) with words denoting the object with regard to which the relation holds true (p. 116). I shall not here recall the instances that have been given of such syntactic forms (pp. 114, ff.), but shall speak in greater detail of only one of these, the relation of actor and action, which in English has been identified with that of subject and predicate.

This generalization is not in accord with experience, for actually a sentence may not express an action, as does *He ate an apple*, but an equation, e. g.: *That tall man is my father*, a subsumption: *The whale is a mammal*, the assigning of a quality: *The peasant is poor*, a condition: *He is sleeping*, or the process of undergoing something: *He sees; He is getting drenched*, and so on. These differences of material content are not given expression in the English sentence: in English and many of the related languages the sentence-type of action has been generalized. As a French scholar has said, these languages present the sentence in the form of a little drama in which the subject is always acting.[1])

In Russian the sentence-structure is in part the same as in English, but the action-type has not been so completely generalized; the assignment of a quality still has a different form: [mu ′ʒĭ·k ′b′e· d′in] 'peasant poor', 'The peasant is poor'. This form of locution would be impossible in English, because we cannot express predication except as an action, by means of a verb, — in this case the abstract verb *is*, whose actual content is only that of predication, put into the form of an action, and by the speaker felt as such. Latin allows in these cases of both types expression: *Māgna culpa* or *Māgna est culpa*.

All three of these languages, English, Russian, and Latin, express as an action by the subject sentence-contents in which the subject is actually undergoing something. They view the undergoing process directly as an

---

1) M. Bréal, *Essai de Sémantique*⁴, p. 86.

action, as, for instance, in saying *He sees* instead of 'Light-vibrations strike him'. In part they use special expressions which reverse the occurrence; for this Latin has a special voice, the passive (p. 145). *Amātur* 'He is being loved, is loved', for instance, represents the subject as actor of a verb, the content of which is 'to be the object of affection'. Russian uses for such sentences a manner of expression frequent in languages of our type; it represents the subject as acting upon itself, when, really, other actors are acting upon it, e. g. [gɑ ′zɛ· tɑ tʃ'i 'tɑ·ji tsɑ] 'The newspaper reads-itself', 'The newspaper is being read, is read'. Similarly in French: *Cela se raconte partout* 'That itself tells everywhere', 'That is being told everywhere'. In English we use a circumlocution which represents the actor as being (cf. above) in the condition of being acted upon: *It is being read, It is read, He is getting drenched,* exactly like *He is being impudent, He is poor, He is getting old.* This form of expression occurs also in French: *Il est aimé de tous* 'He is loved by all', like *Il est bon* 'He is good'. German uses a circumlocution with the word 'becomes', e. g. *Das Lied wurde gesungen* 'The song became sung', i. e. 'The song was sung', exactly like *Es wurde kalt* 'It became cold'; so also in Scandinavian (which also has a real passive, comparable to the Latin, in restricted use). e. g. Norwegian *Sangen blev sunget* 'The song was sung', like *Det blev koldt* 'It grew cold'.

The distinction between an action performed by the subject and a sensational process undergone by it finds expression, inconsistently, — as is always the case in linguistic expression of such distinctions, — in Georgian. There, as we have seen (p. 110), we find the contrast of [v-t'ser] 'I-write' and [m-e-smi-s] 'me-to-sound-is', i. e. 'I hear'.

Just as in English we generalize the type of occurrence in which the subject is performing an action, so some languages generalize that in which there is assigned to the subject some quality or condition. So, for instance, in the language of the Wolof in western Africa one says *sopa-na* 'loving-he', 'He loves' just as one says *baxe-na* 'good-he', 'He is good': the action of loving is expressed as a predicate of exactly the same kind as the quality of goodness.

In still other languages the occurrence in which the subject undergoes an action is generalized (p. 110), and one says, for instance, not 'I kill him' but 'He dies for me'; so in Greenlandish, not only [tusaRpa:] 'Sounding-its-his', i. e. 'There is sounding of it to him', 'He hears it', but also [tikip:a:] 'Reaching-its-his', 'There is reaching of it to him', 'He reaches it' or [qaja-toR-ḷu-ne] 'Boat-using-in-his', that is 'It was when he used his boat'.

As these translations show, Greenlandish illustrates another generalization as well: it expresses all these occurrences as statements of possession. Thus [tusaRpa:] 'sounding-its-his' and [tikip:a:] 'reaching-its-his' are parallel to [iḷ:u-a] 'house-his', 'his house'; and [qaja-toR-ḷu-ne] is parallel to [iḷ:u-ne] 'house-his (own)', 'his (own) house'. The same generalization of a possessive sentence-type we saw (p. 150) in the language of the Lules, where one said *amaitsi-s* 'love-my', 'I love', *amaitsi-p* 'love-his', 'he loves', exactly as one said *umue-s* 'mother-my', *umue-p* 'mother-his'.

5. **Syntactic categories.** We may thus contrast several languages as to the freedom or rigidness of their sentence-structure. As opposed to English, for instance, Russian and Georgian are comparatively liberal, in allowing of two sentence-types. In English the emotional re-

lations receive free expression: one may, without altering anything else, speak with greater stress any part of the sentence that happens to be emotionally dominant. To some extent in French and completely in Old Irish, the emotional relations of the sentence also are forced into set form: the dominant element must stand as the predicate of an abstract deictic subject (p. 171). Thus in French the regular way of saying '*I* did that' is *C'est moi qui ai fait cela* 'It's I that have done that', and in Old Irish glosses we find always such expressions as *is oc precept sosceli attó* 'It's at preaching of-the-gospel I-am'.

In short, just as there are morphologic, there are also syntactic categories (p. 68), and the existence of the two is often involved in one and the same mental habit: so with the English parts of speech and the English action-sentence. The English language has the syntactic categories of actor and action; that is, it has identified subject with actor and predicate with action. Our parts of speech serve these syntactic demands: the verbs, for instance, express an action (or some other content viewed as such) and must therefore be present as the central element of the predicate in every sentence. Old Irish has the dominant-category: the emotionally dominant element has to be the central element of the predicate

Other syntactic categories affect single word-classes. We have in English three syntactic categories affecting the noun. An object (or several objects) must be explicitly described as either (1) definite, (2) indefinite but individual, or (3) collective or unindividual (p. 118). In the first case some deictic pronoun must modify the noun, in the second case some indefinite pronoun, and only in the third case, that of collective or unindividual use, may the noun be unmodified. We can speak of *man* or of *men* only if we mean either all men: *Man needs but little...*, *Men are easily moved by such things*, or men, regardless of identity: *Men were shouting*. If we do not mean this, we must say either (2) 'an indefinite man', 'a number of indefinite men', e. g. *some man, any man, one man, some men, six men, several men*, or else, (1) deictically, *this man, that man, your man, Smith's man, these men, those men*, etc. This formal demand is so insistent that we have two pronominal words of abstract meaning which serve no other purpose than, with the least possible amount of incrimination, to provide this description: (1) the 'definite article' *the* and (2) the 'indefinite article' *a, an*. These categories are absent, for instance, in Latin, where one could say *homo*, whether one meant 'man', 'the man', or 'a man', and only when such elements were actually vivid needed to say *ille homo* 'that man' or *homo aliquis* 'some man'.

Another syntactic category in English is that of strictly transitive verbs, that is, of verbs which demand expression of an object affected. Thus one cannot say *He broke* without adding an object affected: *He broke the bowl, He broke it*, or, at the very least, *He broke something*. This peculiarity is shared by the verbal nouns and adjectives derived form such verbs, e. g. *Breaking stone is hard work; Breaking the shell, he examined the contents*.

6. The expression of syntactic relations: modulation in the sentence. We may now turn to the formal means of expressing syntactic relation. At the basis of all such expression lies the fact that the words of a sentence are spoken consecutively, in an uninterrupted sequence. Although within this sequence there may be pauses, these cannot be extended at liberty.

The unity and the word-interrelations of the sentence may be further expressed by modulations of pitch and of stress. This modulation is limited by the habitual word-accent and the habitual syllable-accent. In a language like ours, where certain syllables of words are habitually pronounced with greater stress than others, the stress-modulation of the sentence is not entirely free, but will always be a compromise between these habitual stressings and the 'ideal' sentence-stress, — that is, the stress-relations that we might conceivably use, were we not bound to stress certain syllables. Thus in *Today is 'my birthday*, where *my*, the emotionally dominant element, receives highest stress, we are also bound by the convention of our language, to give the syllables *-day* in *today* and *birth-* in *birthday* higher stress than we give *to-* and *-day*. When we speak of *bull'dogs and bull'frogs*, or of *'aseptic and 'antiseptic*, the sentence-modulation of stress is at odds with the conventional word-accent and carries off the victory.

In languages with fixed pitch-relations for certain syllables, words, or groups, the ideal sentence-pitch is forced similarly to compromise with the syllable-pitch and group-pitch. Thus, in Norwegian, the three words *han* 'he', *heter* 'is called', and the name *Hjalmar* all have, when spoken alone, simple rising accent, e. g. [hɑn/]. In the sentence *Han heter Hjalmar*, however, the pitch-modulation of the sentence overcomes that of the first two words, and one says [ˌhɑn heːtər jɑl/ˈmɑr/]. In other languages with word-pitch, such as Chinese, the conditions are similar. In contrast with this, English sentence-modulation of pitch has almost no obstacles to overcome, for, beyond the circumstance that we pronounce the stressed syllables with higher pitch, this factor is left entirely to syntactic employment. Consequently we can maintain such habits as the use of even and then falling pitch in statements (*He came back*), rising pitch in sentence-questions (*Did you say that?*), and rising-falling pitch in word-questions (*What was he doing?*), not to speak of a number of modulations for more delicate emotional shadings. In our ears such a language as Norwegian sounds, accordingly, like a monotonous series of questions or enlivening exhortations.

Such modulations, then, are of decided significance. In English words of less material content receive weaker stress, so especially abstract and purely formal words: *the 'man, a 'man, It is 'cold, He 'ate it, He 'gave the 'book to his 'brother*. These words receive greater stress only when they are used in more than mere satisfying of syntactic requirements: *It 'is cold*. The sequence of attribute and subject shows in English even stress: *the 'young 'man;* in *He 'failed com'pletely to make his meaning clear*, the adverb *completely*, in even stress with *failed*, modifies it, but in *He 'failed completely to make his meaning clear*, it modifies the less stressed *make*.

7. Cross-referring constructions. In general, however, these sentence-modulations of pause, pitch, and stress express the emotional rather than the discursive or the material relations between the words. These are expressed in various other ways.

Most obvious and most cumbersome among these means is the double expression of an element, first relationally in connection with another word and then explicitly in a separate word expressing the material content. Speakers of English can best feel the value of such double expression by calling to mind dialectal locutions like *John his knife* or *John he went home*. Here *John* gives the material content of the element which in *he, his* is expressed anaphorically over again in relation with the other elements of the sentence; — the use of *John* here is called 'absolutive'. These constructions are unnecessarily cumbersome, for in English *John* can figure as subject-actor, or, in possessive inflection, as attribute-possessor (*John went home, John's knife*); and it is safe to suppose that educated writers' and speakers' disuse of this construction is due to the feeling that the added word is superfluous. Supposing, however, that it were impossible in English to say *went home* without an anaphoric actor *he*, and impossible to say *knife* without an anaphorically expressed possessor: then such constructions as *John he-went* and *John his-knife* would be unavoidable.

These conditions are fulfilled in numerous languages. In Latin, for instance, where the verb always includes personal-anaphoric mention of the actor, and a form such as *cantat* means 'he-sings' or 'she-sings', one cannot say 'The girl sings' but only *puella cantat* literally, then, '(The) girl she-sings'.

The same may be true of objects affected. In Nahwatl *nikmaka* means 'I-it-him-give'. To express concretely the objects affected one may form a compound with one of them, e. g. *niktlaškalmaka* 'I-him-bread-give'. For the second of the objects affected, however, and most commonly also for the first, one adds specific mention of the object in an absolutive form: *nikmaka tlaškalli in nopiltsin* 'I-him-it-give, bread, (the) my-son'. Just so in Greenlandish: [qaĭne tukaʀpa:] 'His-boat he-tramples-it' (more literally, — cf. above, — 'It is his boat. There is trampling of it of him').

The parallel to *John his knife* is seen in the Greenlandish [qim:ip neqa:] '(The) dog his-meat'.

This method of syntactic expression is subject to some ambiguity. The relation of the words for 'bread' and 'my-son' in the Nahwatl example above can be deduced from their content, but it is not expressed otherwise than by the material absurdity of the subject's giving his son to some bread. When we learn, further, that the word expressing the actor may also in absolutive form follow the action-word, we see that this method of syntactic expression, with all its explicitness, is far from being proportionately exact or clear.

8. Congruence. Another expression of syntactic relations is the phenomenon of congruence, which we have several times met (pp. 128, ff.). Congruence is syntactically expressive because it is limited to words in certain relations with each other, — such as subject and verb in English. When we say *I am; you, we, they are; he, she, it is*, the form of the verb shows in the first case, for instance, that the verb has as its actor the speaker. To be sure, the congruence is not needed, for even without it, as in *I, you, he, she, it, we, they can (shall, will, did, gave*, etc.), the position of the actor-word immediately before the verb expresses the relation between the words: our congruence of verb with person and number of actor is logically superfluous.

This, however, is not true of most cases of congruence. In those European languages which divide their nouns categorically into gender-classes and express this classification by congruence of attributive, anaphoric, and relative words, locutions constantly occur in which congruence alone expresses the syntactic relations. In German such expressions as *das Fremden unzugängliche Haus*, literally 'the to-strangers unapproachable house', are clear because *das*, the article, is in congruence ('agrees') only with *Haus*, not with *Fremden*, which would require, by congruence, another form of an article attributive to it. So in relative reference, *Die Maus im Keller, welche naß war,*... (literally 'The mouse in the cellar, which wet was,...') is clear: the form *welche* shows that the relative pronoun refers to the 'feminine' noun *Maus;* if it is the cellar which was wet, one says *Die Maus im Keller, welcher naß war,*..., with the 'masculine' congruence-form of the relative pronoun.

Such congruence of attributive words with gender, number, and case of their subject nouns may serve to relate words in what would seem to us the most puzzling jumble. This is true, especially, in the older stages of the European languages. Thus, in Latin, Horace was able to write:

... Mē tabulā sacer
vōtīvā pariēs indicat ūvida
suspendisse potentī
vestimenta maris deō.

'By a votive tablet the sacred wall shows me to have hung up drenched garments (as an offering) to the mighty god of the sea', — word for word: 'Me by-a-tablet sacred votive wall shows wet to-have-hung-up powerful clothes of-the-sea to-the-god'. The sentence includes four adjectives and five nouns, which are grouped, adjective with noun, only by the congruence of the former with the latter as to gender number, and case. That is, *sacer* 'sacred' agrees only with *pariēs* 'wall', *vōtīvā* 'votive' only with *tabulā* 'tablet', *ūvida* 'wet' with *vestimenta* 'clothes', and *potentī* 'powerful' agrees only with *deō* 'god', leaving *maris* 'the sea's' without an adjective. In short, the application of the adjectives is expressed entirely by their congruence.

To be sure, not every instance is as clear as this one. Suppose that instead of 'sacred wall' a Roman had said 'sacred temple', *sacra aedēs*. Now, owing to homonymy between the adjective forms for the nominative singular feminine (*sacra*) and the accusative (and nominative) plural neuter (*ūvida*), *sacra* could belong with *vestimenta* ('sacred garments') and *ūvida* with *aedēs* ('drenched temple'), and only the material content or the order in which the words were presented to the hearer could determine the syntactic relations between these adjectives and nouns.

But even when there is no homonymy congruence can never be unambiguous. For, if ambiguity is to be avoided in every instance, the number of categories according to which there is congruence must approach infinity. In the Bantu languages of southern and central Africa congruence plays a very large role in syntactic expression, and we find, accordingly, a large number of categories of the object-expressions with which other words must agree. The Subiya language, as above mentioned, (p. 143), so distinguishes in all twenty-one categories. In the Kafir, which is closely related to this dialect, one says, for instance (p. 154):

bonke abazalwana 'all the brothers',
lonke ilizwe 'all the land',
yonke indlu 'all the house',
sonke isilo 'all the creatures',
wonke umhlaba 'all the earth',
konke ukutya 'all the food',

where the attributive 'all' varies in congruence with the noun-genders. Similarly, an attributive noun varies in congruence with that modified, which precedes it:

umfazi gowomtu 'the wife of the man',
ihaše lelomtu 'the horse of the man',
umfazi gowenkosi 'the wife of the chief',
ihaše lelenkosi 'the horse of the chief'.

The numeral words similarly agree:

immini zamašumi mane 'days tens four, fourty days',
ubusuke bamašumi mane 'nights tens four, forty nights'.

So also the action-word:

umntu uyadla innyama 'the man goes to eat meat',
abantu bayadla innyama 'the men go to eat meat'.

9. Government. Another means of expressing syntactic relations is word-variation according to the relation the word bears to some other word. With such word-variation we are familiar from the discussion of morphology, where we saw (pp. 104, ff., 143, f.) how relational elements are in most languages included in the same word with concrete elements to which they pertain. In so far as such inflection includes relations to other words of the same sentence, it is of syntactic force. When the English verb includes in its form an indication of time, this indication is, generally, of no syntactic importance. In the sentence *He bought many clothes* the form *bought* expresses the time, relative to the speaker's present, of the occurrence, but not the relation of the verb to the other parts of the sentence: this relation is no different when the other tense-form, *He buys many clothes,* is used. In the noun, on the other hand, we have a special form, the possessive, which indicates that the noun in this form is an attribute (possessor) of some other noun. As opposed to *Father has a new hat, Who has seen my father?, with my father,* the form *father's* in *Where is father's new hat?* shows the experience-element *father* to be neither actor nor object affected nor point of view of a local relation, but attribute of another noun. In our pronouns, where we have a third case-form, this goes farther. The forms *I, he, she, we, they, who* are used only as subject of a verb or in the predicate of a sentence expressing equation, e. g. *It is he.* The forms *my, his, her, our, their, whose* are attributive, and the third set of forms, *me, him, her, us, them, whom,* show the content of the pronoun to stand in the relation of object affected to a verb, or of point of view to a preposition: *He saw me, I know him, Come to us.* As between *It is he* and *It hurts him,* for instance, the variation in the form of the pronoun shows the relation to the verb: *him* is object affected, *he* not so, but 'complement', that is, genuine predicate following the abstract equation-verb *is. He loves her* shows by the form of the pronouns who is the actor, who the object affected. *Rection* or *government,* then, is the process by which a word has a different form according to its relation to other words in the sentence.¹)

Government is in very active use in such languages as German, Latin, Greek, or Sanskrit, where the nouns (or words modifying them) have different case-forms for different relations. In Latin *Pater filiō librum dat* in any order of the words is equally clear, for *pater* is in the nominative form, as actor, *filiō* in the dative, as object less fully affected, *librum* in the accusative, as object fully affected: 'The father gives the son a book'; the case-forms of the words express the syntactic relations.²) In the quotation from Horace,

> ... *Mē tabulā sacer*
> *vōtīvā pariēs indicat ūvida*
> *suspendisse potentī*
> *vestimenta maris deō,*

we have seen how congruence shows the grouping of adjectives with nouns, to wit: *vōtīvā tabulā* 'votive tablet', *sacer pariēs* 'sacred wall', *ūvida vestimenta* 'drenched garments', *potentī deō* 'powerful god'. Government lays clear the syntactic relations of these nouns. Namely, (*sacer*) *pariēs*, in the nominative case, must figure as subject of the verb (*indicat* 'shows'); *mē*, as accusative form, is object fully affected by this verb; *tabulā* (*vōtīvā*), an ablative form of instrumental value, expresses the means

---

1) Those dialectal speakers who say *It is me, him, her, us, them*, using the accusative form wherever a pronoun appears after a verb, make no use of government, but instead use the nominative and accusative forms merely in congruence with the position of the pronoun: in position before the verb, one set of forms; in position after it or after a preposition, another.

2) Between *pater* 'father' and *dat*, literally 'he-gives', the relation is, however, really expressed by cross-reference, cf. above.

of the action ('by means of a votive tablet'); (*ūvida*) *vestimenta*, again accusative, is the object fully affected by the infinitive *suspendisse* 'to have hung up'; *maris* is in the genitive case, expressing, somewhat like the English possessive, an attributive relation, 'the sea's'; (*potentī*) *deō*, finally, in the dative case, is the object less fully affected by *suspendisse*, 'to the mighty god'. The meaning is, accordingly, as we have seen, 'The sacred wall, by a votive tablet, shows me to have hung up drenched garments to the mighty god of the sea'.

But, as a matter of fact, some of these forms are by no means unambiguous. Partly this is due to homonymy: *mē* could be ablative ('by means of me') as well as accusative, and the accusative *ūvida vestimenta* could also be nominative (subject of a verb). The ambiguity is removed only by the fact that *indicat*, the verb, must have an object affected, for which *mē*, in the beginning the only form available, is accordingly taken, as an accusative: and later, when *ūvida vestimenta* appears, the indubitable nominative, *sacer pariēs* has already occupied the place of subject-actor.

Moreover, even aside from homonymy, the sentence, so far as government is concerned, is left ambiguous, for government tells us neither which accusative, *mē* or *ūvida vestimenta*, is the object affected by *indicat* and which by *suspendisse*, nor does it show which noun *maris* 'of the sea' modifies. Like the ambiguities already mentioned, these also are removed by that very natural means, the order of the words: when we hear *indicat*, *mē* alone is available as object affected, and the position of *maris* between *potentī* and *deō* suggests the concretely obvious connection. In other sentences the material content alone can remove the ambiguity: *Ūvida vestimenta mē suspendisse indicat,* — a good Latin sentence, — could mean either 'It shows me to have hung up wet garments' or 'It shows wet garments to have hung me up'.

Government may extend to all kinds of relational expression. Thus in German one says *Er ging in den Wald* 'He walked into the woods', but *Er ging in dem Walde* 'He walked in the woods'. The two relations which we express in English as *into* and *in* are expressed in German by the same word *in*, government alone distinguishing: the object with regard to which the relation is viewed stands in the former instance in the accusative, in the latter in the dative case.

10. Word-order. In the discussion of our quotation from Horace it appeared that some of the ambiguity left by government as a syntactic method was naturally removed by the order in which the words were presented to the hearer. This function of the word-order was by no means due to any convention of the Latin language, but entirely to the natural reproductive processes of the listener, who would, for instance, at once take up *mē* as the object fully affected by *indicat*, because, when he heard the latter word, no other accusative had yet reached him. The speaker analytically expressing his total experience will naturally follow some connected order, except for such emotionally dominant elements as thrust themselves, regardless of logical or material connection, at once into expression. The hearer, for his part, reproduces as he hears and uses each element as it comes, unless habitual processes of the language force him to hold them apart, as when the Roman, hearing *tabulā sacer*, is kept by the congruence-habits of his speech, from even tentatively applying the adjective to this noun, but waits for another with which *sacer* will agree. In short, quite independently of any fixed habit, the order of words in a sentence cannot but be to some extent indicative of their syntactic relations, just as all the words of a sentence, to begin with, form an uninterrupted sequence.

In many languages, such as our own, the order of words has a habitual syntactic significance. Where a Latin, for example, could pronounce in any one of the six mathematically possible orders the words *Jūlius* (nominative), *Jūliam* (accusative), and *amat* ('he, she loves', verb), expressing by cross-reference and goverment that *Jūlius* is the actor, by government that *Jūlia* is the object affected, there we can say only *Julius loves Julia*. The noun preceding the verb is in English the actor, that following it, the object affected.

This use of word-order as a syntactic method is doubly significant. From a logical, post factum point of view, it makes use of what is inevitably present, for in some order the words must be spoken, and dispenses with any further encumbrance for the expression of relations. Psychologically, it involves a fixed habit as to the order with which one in speaking analyzes and in hearing reproduces a total experience. The fixing of this habit cannot but save energy: the English sentence can be understood, — that is, the experience reproduced by the hearer, — with less effort of the attention than the Latin.

In English word-order is the prevailing method of syntactic expression. We have already seen that the actor-subject precedes the verb. The objects affected follow it, the object less fully affected preceding that fully affected (*He gave John a book*), unless, indeed, the former relation is analyzed into a separate word (*He gave a book to John*), when it falls under the head of preposition with its noun, which always follows the objects affected. The abstract verb *is* precedes the true predicate (*This man is my brother, You are good*). Attributive modifiers precede nouns (*a good friend, father's hat*), and prepositions precede the noun with regard to which they are used (*in the house*). Only as to the attributive modifiers of verbs is there some freedom (*Quickly he ran, He quickly ran, He ran quickly*). Thus not only the discursive but also material and emotional relations are expressed by word-order.

In Chinese word-order is even more exclusively the expression of syntactic relations. The subject precedes the predicate, as in [⌈t'a⌉ ˌxaδ/] 'He (is) good' or [⌈t'a⌉ ˌcç'y\] 'He goes', and attributes precede their subject: [ˌxaδ/⌈ʒʌn/] 'good man, good people', [ˌman\ ˌcç'y\] 'Slowly go', 'Go slowly'. The material relation of objects affected is also recognized: they follow the transitive word, e. g. [ˌwo/ ˌp'a\ ⌈t'a⌉] 'I fear him', [⌈t'a⌉ ˌp'a\ ˌwo/] 'He fears me'. Other examples have been explained on pages 115, ff. and 126, f.

11. Set phrases: the transition from syntax to style.
In spite of this simplicity of Chinese syntactic expression, an English-speaking person who had access to information as to the meaning of every individual Chinese word and knew these rules of word-order, would still fail to understand many sentences of this language. He would be baffled by set combinations of words, 'idioms', deviating from the meaning of the simple words and thus approaching the value of compounds. In such idiomatic phrases Chinese is very rich. They exist, however, in every speech-community and not least in English and its various local forms. A stranger would have no success, if he attempted, word by word, to understand such usage as that of *at* in *We sat at the table, He threw it at me, He is at work, Don't be angry at me, Not at all,* and so on, or of *do* in *He did it, Did he go?, Did he do it?, Do to death, It does him credit, He did me a service, How do you do?, Do the roast well, I have done six copies, You would do wisely to go,* of

THE TRANSITION FROM SYNTAX TO STYLE 189

have in *I have your hat, I have written, I have to do it, You had better go,* of *about* in *We walked about the garden, We talked about you, About three miles,* and so on.

When the idiomatic set phrase deviates too considerably from the individual meanings of the words, we have, of course, a compound word: the boundary is by no means clearly traceable. Is *at all* a compound? In Chinese we have seen [ˈɕiuŋˈ ˌti\] in which the first word means 'older brother' and the second 'younger brother'; together the two, were this not an idiomatic phrase, would mean 'younger brother of an older brother'. The phrase, however, may be looked upon, from the English standpoint as meaning 'older brother(s) and (or) younger brother(s)', i. e. often 'brothers, brother'. Shall we call the Chinese expression a compound or a two-word phrase?

On the other hand, the boundary between set phrase and syntactic expression is never clearly traceable. What is one of a number of equally favored possibilities of expression in one generation, may in the next become a habitual phrase, and a few generations later be the only correct expression. Some time ago one said indifferently in English *He gave me it, He gave it me,* or *He gave it to me*. Today we use, in America at least, the last of these far more frequently than the first two; tomorrow it alone may be correct, — or else an idiomatic use here prevalent in the sense of 'He scolded me, punished me' may specialize it. In such a sentence as *He sees me* the syntactic relations are expressed by congruence (*he sees*), government (*he sees, sees me*), and word-order. The expression was therefore just as intelligible in times when the third factor was absent and one could say *Me he sees, He me sees,* and the like. The order *He sees me* here became, successively, the favorite phraseologic order and then the only correct one.

12. The complex sentence. This crystallization of word-groups is psychologically most natural. Once a certain expression has been heard and used, it is, by the principle of habituation, more likely to be called up and used in the future than some other less familiar form. Ultimately, if enough used, it becomes mechanized, in the sense that a single initial impulse is sufficient to start off the utterance of the entire word-group, so that the relations between the single words, like the single articulatory movements, need no longer be conscious. Most of our speaking, in fact, is done in this way. We speak by whole phrases, even by whole sentences, and, at the very least, by certain well-practised schemes, — sentence-skeletons that require but the variation of a few words from utterance to utterance. If we stop to analyze even a moderately long sentence of ordinary speech into single words and stop to determine the relations between them, the result is a very complex structure and the process always strikes us as unnatural: we are certain that in speaking the casual sentence we built up no such maze of variously interwoven attributions, serial groups, and predications. Our feeling is justified, for most of the word-groups within which such relations ultimately subsist are in actuality so practised that no analytic activity of the attention is necessary for their utterance. Unless this were the case, it would require a master mind to construct any but the briefest and baldest utterances.

The utterance of longer, more complex sentences is due, therefore, to the mechanization of greater and greater groups of words. The most typical illustration of this is the attributive subordination of one predication to another. In languages that have no specific expression of predication this subordination does not formally appear. When a Greenlander says [tuawioʀtoʀsːʽuoḷːune aneʀḷaʀ- .

poq] we may interpret it as 'It-is-in-his-hurrying-very-much. He-goes-home' or as 'Hurrying very much, he goes home'. Which interpretation is the juster depends on the mental process of the speaker in each instance, unless it happens that the expression is known to be a very common one, when we may be sure of subordination. This simple succession of two predications one of which is psychologically, but not in expression, subordinate (i. e. attributive) to the other, is called *parataxis*. Another example of it is the locution so frequent in German fairy tales: *Es war einmal ein Mann, der hatte drei Töchter* 'There was once a man. He had three daughters' or 'There was once a man who had three daughters'; exactly as in the Greenlandish example, both English renderings are wrong: the German expression could, formally, be two sentences, but in the feeling of every German speaker the second predication is subordinate to the first. An English example is *He writes me he is sick*. Modulations of stress, pitch, and duration (pause) may, of course, enter as expression of the subordination.

If, however, the expression of subordination goes beyond this, we have no longer parataxis, but *hypotaxis*. Such a phenomenon as hypotaxis is conceivable only when large word-groups constituting parts of the whole utterance have become specifically or in plan mechanized. Hypotaxis is attained by means of special attributive forms for larger subordinate elements. Such a form is the English verbal adjective (participle) in -*ing* followed, like the verb, by expression of objects affected: *Giving his friend the letter, he turned to go*. This form of expression is in some languages so great a favorite that, of a number, say, of occurrences, only a few receive independent predicative expression. In English the participle is generally used only where it may be taken as an attribute of the subject of the sentence: in other languages the subordinate elements may modify various parts of the sentence. In Turkish, for instance, there occur such constructions as [xodʒa ɯnanmaz, biri daxɯ gelip, ⌀ɪle s⌀ɪler, xodʒa gertʃek sanɯp, kuzuju bogazlar], literally: 'Master believing-not, one-of-them again coming, similarly speaking, master true believing, the lamb slaughters', i. e. 'When the master did not believe this, another of them came and spoke similarly; whereupon the master, now believing it, slaughtered the lamb'. In Sanskrit, which has generally a structure similar to that of Latin, we find in certain writings, perhaps owing to the influence of other languages of India, which construct very much on the Turkish principle, an extended use of such participial expression. For instance, *Ity ālocya, tena, grāmą gatvā, Dadhikarṇa-nāma biḍālo, mąs-ādy-āhāreṇa sątoṣya, prayatnād ānīya, sva-kandare dhŗtaḥ*, literally: 'So having-reflected, by-him, to-the-village having-gone, Dadhikarna-by-name (a) cat (nom.), by-means-of-meat-and-other-food having-satisfied, carefully having-brought, in-his-cave was-kept'. All the participial expressions (ending in *-ya* and *-tvā*) here apply not to the subject (the cat), but to the instrumental ('by-him'); here, as above in the Turkish example, these expressions are really attributes not of any object-word or other element, but of the predication as a whole. Hence we may here translate: 'After he had so reflected, by him, when he had gone to the village, a cat, Dadhikarna by name, when he had given it its fill of meat and other food and led it carefully home, was kept in his cave', or, changing to the active and coordinating construction favored in English: 'After these reflections he went to the village, and, having satisfied a certain cat named Dadhikarna with meat and other food, brought it carefully home and kept it in his cave'.

In these examples the subordinated elements deviate considerably in form from independent predications. In English, however, we may, by means of a subordinating conjunction express one predication, word for word, as attributive to another. Thus, paratactic: *It looks like rain; he had better carry an umbrella;* hypotactic: *As it looks like rain, he had better carry an umbrella*, where *as*, the subordinating conjunction, expresses the attributive character of the first predication. Beside using such subordinating conjunctions as *as, when, if, how, since, because, while, after, although,* and the like, we express hypotaxis also by our relative pronouns, e. g.: *I don't know the man whom you mention*, where the peculiar word-order (*whom you mention*, as opposed, for instance, to *you mention him*) and the double function of the relative pronoun *whom* as both member (in this case, object affected) of the subordinate sentence and expression of the subordination, carry the hypotaxis. A peculiar form of hypotaxis is the English construction in which a noun figures as predicate or as object affected in the principal sentence and at the same time as object affected in the second; the subordination is expressed by this double function of the word and by a word-order differing from the normal: thus the last sentence could be put: *I don't know the man you mention* or *He isn't the man I mean*. This type of hypotaxis, is called, by its Greek name, the construction *apò koinoũ*. In German subordination is expressed by subordinating conjunctions or relative pronouns and, most strikingly, by the word-order: the verb stands second among the elements of the declarative sentence, except in case of subordination, when it stands last. Consequently, although German has much homonymy between adverbs and subordinating conjunctions and between relative and demonstrative pronouns, hypotaxis is always clearly distinguished.

Thus in *Da kam er*, 'Then he came', *da* is adverb and we have an independent sentence, but in *Da er kam, konnten wir ihn fragen* 'Since he came, we were able to ask him', *da* is a subordinating conjunction and *da er kam*, a 'dependent clause'. The paratactic *Es war einmal ein Mann, der hatte drei Töchter* 'There was once a man; he had three daughters' (*der* anaphoric pronoun) is distinguished by word-order only from the hypotactic *Es war einmal ein Mann, der drei Töchter hatte* 'There was once a man who had three daughters' (*der* relative pronoun). By such means the sentence may in literary languages like Sanskrit, Latin, German, or English be expanded until it is simply a kind of logical puzzle. In natural speech, however, no matter how complex a sentence may be from the logical point of view, it really never consists of more than a very few elements, each of which, even if discursively divisible, is in the mind of the speaker nevertheless a single associatively mechanized element, which he is not compelled to analyze, unless some circumstance should particularly draw his attention to it.

Here again, the actual conditions of language are not mathematically definable. It is impossible to determine exactly how far every speaker goes in the analysis of the total experience and how much of what he says is a matter of practised combinations. Here again, moreover, the constant change in language makes itself apparent: new phrases and methods of construction come into favor and old ones lapse into oblivion.

CHAPTER VII.
INTERNAL CHANGE IN LANGUAGE.

1. Language constantly changing. The speech of former times, wherever history has given us records of it, differs from that of the present. When we read Shakspere, for example, we are disturbed by subtle deviations from our own habit in the use of words and in construction; if our actors pronounced the lines as Shakspere and his contemporaries did, we should say that they had an Irish or German brogue. Chaucer we cannot read without some grammatical explanation and a glossary; correctly pronounced his language would sound to us more like Low German than like our English. If we go back only about forty generations from our time to that of Alfred the Great, we come to English as strange to us as modern German, and quite unintelligible, unless we study carefully both grammar and lexicon.

2. Causes of the instability of language. It is by no means surprising that language changes. As a physical phenomenon it consists of certain finely graded habitual movements, which, we know, cannot always be performed in exactly the same way. There must be endless infinitesimal variations, smaller even than those which scientific observation unmistakably reveals, — not to speak of such as can be heard by anyone who listens for them. Thus, such a sentence as *Going to the university?* is often pronounced [ˈgowɪ tðjɛ ˈvɪ̩sti]. To be sure, we are so much in memory of the sound that these words have in more deliberate speech (and, in our state of culture, of their form in writing) that we ordinarily fail to notice what sounds we or our acquaintances have actually uttered; yet, as the language is spoken by generation after generation, such tendencies cannot but have their lasting effect.

The same is true, mutatis mutandis, of the other phases of language. The experience itself is always new: shall the speaker class it under this particular word or that? A member of a happy family points to his house and says: 'This is our little home.' What more natural than that, just as his interlocutor might now tell people that 'N. has a beautiful little home,' other people should gradually come to speak of any house intended for dwelling purposes as a *home*, until we read in our newspapers that there is for sale 'a fine new ten-room *home*,' and realize that for many English speaking people the word *home* has no longer the meaning which it used to have.

In the morphologic word-classes we need only look at the assimilative process by which inflection takes place (p. 59, f.), to see how unstable it must be, from its very nature. Preterite tense and unreal mode are expressed by only one form in every English verb except *was: were*. It is a natural consequence that many speakers use *was* for *were*, saying, for instance, 'If he *was* here, he wouldn't allow it.' Owing to the identity of form of other verbs (*came, said, had, thought*) such a speaker, without consciousness of innovation, says *was* where *were* is in our feeling alone correct.

Gradual change in the manner of performing articulation-movements, the inclusion of new experiences under new words, and the occurrence of a few unprecedented morphologic assimilations among the many previously usual ones, — these are inevitable attendant occurrences of all language. On the other side are the no less inevitable conservative forces. The speaker hears others who are not making the same innovation and either realizes that he spoke in violation of custom and perhaps unintelligibly, or, far more commonly, has the correct form reawakened or strengthened in his speech-predisposition without ever growing aware of the temporary divergence. His interlocutor's answer, for instance, contains the forms [juni ɩ 'vɪsi ti], *house*, *If he were here*, and, inadvertently, these instead of the new associations are uppermost when next he speaks. But when our interlocutors, too, have formed the new association, so that it is in them strengthened by our use of the new form, they will notice nothing unusual in our words and will utter the like. Finally the new association may become practised and vigorous, and the old fall into such desuetude that, when we hear its forms, they seem strange and unusual.

It is evident, then, that an innovation, in order to spread, and not to lapse into oblivion as a once-made slip of the tongue, must be such as to fall in readily with the other habits and associations of the speakers. The use of *was* for *were* has spread because one form for all the numbers and persons of preterite and unreal, — that is, the absence of these distinctions, — is customary in all other verbs. No change takes place in a language unless there is a predisposition for it in a large number of speakers. Fashion, to be sure, and the conscious desire to be like some admired person or class of people, may help to spread or to check the spreading of an innovation. The young boy who wants to seem virile imitates the speech of the 'tough', and the snob affects the manner of speech that happens to be natural to the aristocrat. More legitimately, the public speaker, the teacher, and, above all, the writer, exert a wide influence over the speech of others. In spite of all this, however, every innovation, in its beginnings, is the result of a psychic predisposition not only on the part of those speakers who independently originate it, but also on the part of those who unconsciously take it up. It would, indeed, be impossible to determine who first spoke a given innovation, who spoke it only after hearing it from others. Neither speaker is conscious of saying anything novel. If the innovation fails to find acceptance, both kinds of speakers lapse back to the old forms of speech, without ever realizing that they once or a few times spoke differently, and if the innovation spreads, it remains usually for scholars who long afterward look back at an earlier form of speech, to realize that a change has taken place. No London-English mother, in the forty generations from Alfred's time to ours, has realized that her children were not learning exactly the same English that she had learned in her infancy; and, indeed, had she been able to hear the two forms of speech in close succession, she could not have detected any difference, unless she were an extremely careful observer. It is only under the most favorable conditions that linguistic study has been able to perceive the deviation of speech from generation to generation in a small community. It is evident that we are, all of us, contributing, through all our lives, to the change of our language, but neither do we from any direct consciousness of the process know this, nor could we, though our lives were at stake, tell how or in what respects we are altering the language we learned from our parents.

To say all this, is, of course, only to repeat that the facts of language are facts of social, not of individual psychology. Could we definitely mark out the speaker who first spoke a given innovation, trace the forces which

CAUSES OF THE INSTABILITY OF LANGUAGE 199

impelled him to make it to certain features of his mental situation at the time, and similarly lay clear the motives of all the other speakers who propagated the new form, then we should be accomplishing the interpretation of a social development into terms of individual psychology. This, of course, could be done only by an omniscient observer. It is, for that matter, immaterial who first spoke a given innovation. Both he and those others who, independently, produced the same form, as well as those who spoke the new form only after hearing it, were unconscious of any change. The expressive habits of the community as a whole were ready for the innovation, — or rather, were in such a form that what was, physically, an innovation, was psychologically no change at all.

Here lies, of course, the great difficulty of historical language study. In descriptive study we can, in the worst case, confine ourselves to the phenomena in a limited number of utterances or speakers. To tell with historical correctness the story of a single change, however, we should need not only an exact knowlege of when, where, by whom, and under what circumstances the change was first made, and of exactly how, occurrence by occurrence, hour by hour, speaker by speaker, house by house, village by village, it spread, but also an insight into the entire mentality of each speaker, so as to see what favorable predispositions the change met, and what obstacles, how it became strengthened by hearing and speaking, and weakened and strengthened again, — and all these occurrences, we must remember, belong to a phase of activity so mechanized that the details of it are never, except in the rarest instances, sufficiently focused by the attention to come into vivid consciousness.

Another difficulty lies in the fact that our records of past speech are always, in the face of such an ideal, extremely scanty, and that they are representative of writing, an activity in which the single actions are performed much more slowly and much more under the spotlight of the attention than are those of ordinary speech, and, finally, that writing is capable of but a very imperfect representation of the phonetic facts.

Historical language study is thus at best imperfect. Its imperfections can be partly repaired by certain technical means, which enable us to correct and supplement our records of past speech, especially as to phonetic form, and also to ascertain facts about the speech of certain periods from which no records have come down to us. Of these technical means, called the 'comparative method', I shall be able to speak more fully in the next chapter; for the present a single instance may suffice. Although the orthography of Shakspere and of Chaucer's 'Middle English' does not materially differ from that current today, we can determine with considerable precision how the English of those times was pronounced. We are further able to interpret into phonetic terms the orthography of the 'Old English' of Alfred's time. Beyond all this, however, we can arrive at a great many facts and many more probabilities about the English that was spoken before the time of our written records, at the time, for instance, when the 'Angles, Saxons, and Jutes', the bearers of English speech, still lived on the European mainland. This prehistoric English, back to a certain time, we call 'pre-English'. Back of pre-English lies a point in time only relatively determinable, about which also we can state a good many linguistic facts: the language at this point is called 'Primitive West-Germanic'. Back of this point lies another period, which we call 'pre-West-Germanic'; and back of this period another point in time, where the language is called 'Primitive

Germanic'; then, through the 'pre-Germanic' period, we come, once more, to a specific though not absolutely determinable point in time, thousands of years ago, when 'Primitive Indo-European' was spoken. Beyond this stage of the language we cannot as yet penetrate. To return, however, from our example to our point: in spite of all this supplementation, our historic study cannot go beyond the crudest outlines as compared with the ideal demands of the situation. We can tell, at best, that a specific change, beginning at such and such a time, — often determinable only within a century, if at all otherwise than relatively, — and spreading in a certain general direction, had become, by the expiration of such and such a period, the universal form of speech. In very many cases we cannot determine what the predisposition was that made the innovation successful; at other times we can understand the predisposition (as in the case of *was* for *were*) but then, as a rule, we fail to see why the change succeeded in spreading at this and no other time, in this and no other place. This last is, indeed, the greatest difficulty we have to encounter. It is almost always left a mystery why a given change occurred where and when it did, even though the motives of the change, when it does occur, seem clear.[1])

---

1) This drawback is one that attends every phase of investigation neither amenable to experiment (as is, for instance, physics) nor of universal validity (mathematics). That determination of an event which the physicist or chemist can make in his laboratory is due to the artificial simplification of the conditions which is at his disposal. In language such experiment is impossible, because we cannot make and unmake communities, govern all essential factors, and observe through any length of time. No given occurrence, moreover, — not even in the domain of natural science, — could be fully accounted for by anything less than omniscience: the distinction between an immediate cause and

3. Change in articulation. *Phonetic change* consists of change in the articulatory habits, independently of the semantic content of speech. In Shakspere's time, for instance, one of the English vowels was a long open [ɔ:], which occurred in *stone* [stɔ:n], *bone* [bɔ:n], *rode* [rɔ:d], and a great many other words. By the eighteenth century the pronounciation of this sound had gradually changed, until it was a long closed [o:]. Today we further close the end of it, so that it has become a diphthong [ow], and we pronounce [stown, bown, ɹowd], and so on. In this instance, as in many others, the cause of the change of habit is unknown to us. What this statement means will appear, if we consider in detail how such changes take place.

The Elizabethan [ɔ:]-sound, like all other speech-sounds at all times, was pronounced in a great many variants. Even the same speaker would pronounce it now more open, now more closed, now longer, now shorter, in an infinity of unconscious, minute variations, — just as we today, and all people, cannot possibly perform a repeated action, no matter how habitual, with unfailing accuracy. So far as the variations of quantity were concerned, the equilibrium was maintained, and has been to this day. If a speaker at one time shortened the sound, he lengthened it at an-

---

an underlying condition is here forced upon us. If the physicist were asked to tell why a certain electric fuse 'burned out' at a certain time, he could tell us that such and such a current of electricity had passed through it, but how, ultimately, he had come to perform this experiment at this and no other time and place, he could not tell. Or, if a stroke of lightning had caused the destruction of the fuse, no meteorologist could tell why the lightning struck where and when it did. So in language, the immediate causes of phenomena are generally, except for sound-changes, known, but the underlying conditions are too complex for any known methods of investigation.

other, and if one speaker tended more often to shorten it, his neighbor counterbalanced him in the other direction. With the variations of closure, however, it was different. While in the speech of many individuals there may, in this respect also, have been an equilibrium; while with other individuals the more open variations may have predominated, the more closed variations, whenever they occurred, seem to have struck more fertile ground in the hearers, — to have better stimulated sound-memory and movement-memory. Gradually the more closed variants predominated, until the average of articulations was shifted to a more closed sound, let us say [ɔːᴧ]. By this time the most open variants of [ɔː] no longer occurred, and, on the other hand, more closed forms began to be spoken than had ever been pronounced when [ɔː] represented the mean. Why all this took place in this direction and not in the opposite (in which a similar change has, in fact, occurred at other times and in other places), and why equilibrium was not, as in the case of quantity, maintained, no one can say. Since then English pronunciation-habits have leaned toward the closed variants, until in the eighteenth century the mean of pronunciation, as we have seen, became [oː], and today we speak [ow]. Thus the same variations have been favored by eight to ten generations, if we do not look back of Shakspere's time; if we do, we shall find that the process had been going on since long before, as the sound in Old English times was [ɑː]. Although theories have been proposed, attributing such movements as these to influences of climate, food, occupation, and the like, none of them have been more than mere surmises, contradicted by the next best set of facts that presented itself. Thus, it has been suggested that phonetic change is due to increasing speed of the process of articulation, which, it is said, accompanies the increasing rapidity of the mental processes due to the advance of culture and the general development of man's intellectual powers. This explanation is in itself plausible, because, as we shall see, sound-change does tend to produce more and more rapidly pronounceable and psychologically more appropriate forms. It is true, moreover, that a prescribed complicated series of delicate movements to be rapidly performed will be incorrectly gone through. In sound-change, however, we see the movements being performed in approximately the same way sometimes for centuries, before certain variants come to be favored; and when the mean of articulation has been shifted, stability may again ensue. It has never been proved either that there is an increase in the rapidity of articulation or that an increase of rapidity would account for all such changes as have occurred; — the vowel change of English just described, for instance, does not seem referable, directly at least, to increased speed of articulation. So much we can safely say: that sound-change, altogether, is an evolutionary process, a phenomenon of the historic change of man's physical and mental organization and habits.

While the causes of sound-change, then, are obscure, its general manner of action and, in many cases, the trend of its results are plain.

The action of sound-change has often been described as a process suffering no exception and comparable, consequently, to the laws discovered in physics or chemistry. In reality sound-change is a change of habit in a community of people and is due, ultimately, to some change in the organization or environment of these people. And, as mankind is undoubtedly active in the shaping of environment, the description of 'phonetic laws' as 'natural laws' cannot be correct: a sound-change is not a law of nature, but a historic occurrence. Those who, otherwise than metaphorically, have subscribed to the above definition, have been misled by a certain salient feature of phonetic change, — namely, its unsemantic character. From the definition of phonetic change, it is clear, that, once certain variants are being favored, it matters not what the semantic content of the word or of the sentence may be, the result is the same. The speaker has, of course, no suspicion that he is making any variations at all or that he and his fellows are favoring one or the other type of variants. He is intent on expressing his meaning, and for all he knows, is expressing it in the same sounds, words, and constructions from one end of his life to the other. The favoring of phonetic variants in this or that direction, — that is, sound change, — has nothing to do with the meaning of the particular word or sentence that is being uttered. Owing to its uniformity, then, throughout words of the most various meaning, a historic change in the manner or place of a given articulation may be called a 'phonetic law'. There can be no objection to this term, provided we do not allow it to mislead us. When we say, as is customary, that by a phonetic law 'Elizabethan [ɔ:] > modern [ow]', we mean that the average of articulation at the former time was [ɔ:], that the variants in the direction of [ow] were favored, unconsciously and regardless of the meanings of words, and that today, as a result, [ow] represents the average of pronunciation.

The metaphoric term 'phonetic law' is very useful, because it emphasizes the phonetic, articulatory character and the regularity, no matter what the semantic content, of the process of sound-change. Linguistically untrained observers will often claim that a possible sound-change did not take place because, if it had, it would have obliterated some important semantic distinction, or that a given sound-change did take place because a certain semantic distinction, which it obliterated, was no longer felt to be necessary. There is no need of referring to the concrete details of the process, to show the impossibility of such motives. For all we know, we are today in the act of making a sound-change that will obliterate the most clear-cut or the most universal distinctions in the English language. At least that is what has happened again and again in every language whose history we know. Thus, a categoric distinction in the oldest stages of English was that of the cases of the noun; yet, by the time of our earliest records the nominative and accusative of many nouns had come to be spoken alike: for instance, 'stone' in these two cases was in the singular *stān*, in the plural *stānas*, although many other words still had distinct forms: for instance, 'care', nominative singular *caru*, accusative singular *cara*. In primitive Germanic the nominative singular of *stān* had been *stainoz,[1]) the accusative *stainon, but a phonetic change had led to the dropping of these semantically important final syllables. Meanwhile the dative case was still distinct: e. g. singular *stāne*; likewise, the genitive singular *stānes* was different from the nominative-accusative plural *stānas*. We know how little phonetic change has spared these categoric distinctions: the dative case has been lost, coinciding today with the nominative-accusative in the form *stone* [stown]; *cara* and *caru* are now both *care* [kejɪ]; the genitive singular *stānes* and the nominative-accusative plural *stānas* are now *stone's stones* [stownz], only the written language making a distinction. As to

---

1) The asterisk means that the form does not occur in our historical records.

words, *knight* and *night* were in Chaucer's time different: [kniçt] and [niçt]; today they are indistinguishably [naĕt]. In present English [hiz'maĕt] may mean either 'his great power' (*might*) or 'his trifle' (*mite*), as in 'He contributed [hiz'maĕt] to the effort', but in Middle English the former meaning was pronounced [miçt], the latter [mi:tə]. If we wish to distinguish, we must do so by what we explicitly say, for instance by using the adjectives *great* and *little*. In Chinese there has been a great deal of such loss of distinctions through phonetic change; the language is consequently so full of homonyms that, though on paper the writing may, as with us, show which sense is meant, in speech phrases or compounds must be used whenever homonymy might otherwise make the meaning obscure. Thus [ˌfu\] 'father', as in [ˌfu\ˌmu/] 'father and mother', 'parents', cannot be used alone in speaking, owing to the homonymy with a number of other words; one must use the phrase [fu\ ⌈cç'in⌉] 'father-relative'. Similarly [⌈i⌉] 'garment, clothing' cannot be used alone: one says [⌈i⌉⌈fu⌉] 'clothing-utensil', for the word by itself is homonymous with a number of others, e. g. [⌈i⌉] 'physician'. A similar phenomenon appears in English dictionaries: our verbs have so largely become homonymous with nouns that they have to be quoted with the word *to*, e. g. in a French dictionary '*dormir*, to sleep', where in German, for instance, one could write '*dormir*, schlafen', — for in German the noun 'sleep' is *Schlaf*.

Not only does a sound-change always extend over all the occurrences of a single sound, but it may extend over several sounds. The sound-change by which Elizabethan [stɔ:n] became eighteenth-century [sto:n] was a closing to mid-position of the long open vowel which took effect regardless of the point of articulation; for the front-vowel counterpart of [ɔ:], namely [ɛ:] as in [nɛ:m] 'name' shared in the change, being in the eighteenth century [neːm]. Similarly, the diphthongization that followed affected both of these vowels: we say [stown] and [nejm]. In fact, the sound-change has gone even beyond this: we may say that there has been, since Chaucer's time, a constant closing and diphthongization of all long vowels, — as will appear from the following examples:

Middle English.	Early Modern English.	18th Century.	Present.
[naːmə]	[nɛːm]	[neːm]	[nejm] 'name'
[drɛːm]	[dreːm]	[dɹiːm]	[dɹijm] 'dream'
[stɔːn]	[stoːn]	[stoːn]	[stown] 'stone'
[moːd]	[moːd]	[müːd]	[muwd] 'mood'

A similar parallelism appears in:

[wiːn]	[wejn]	[wɛjn]	[waǒn] 'wine'
[huːs]	[hows]	[hɔws]	[haǒs] 'house'.

The reason for such parallelisms is plain, if we recall (p. 53, f.) that the various sounds of a language consist of a number of manners of articulation practised at a number of points of articulation. In phonetic change it is usually one of these factors rather than the production of any one sound that changes; this involves, of course, all sounds in which the changed factor occurs. Thus, if the articulation of fortis stops changes to spirant articulation, [p, t, k] will become, respectively, [f, θ, x], — a change that took place in the pre-Germanic period in the history of English. It was followed by another example in point: the voiced aspirate stops [bʻ, dʻ, gʻ] became, in complete parallelism, voiced spirants [v, ð, g]. Later the plain voiced stops [b, d, g] became unvoiced [p, t, k]. These three changes together are known, by the name of their discoverer, as 'Grimm's law'. So, much later, in German, [p, t, k] became, between vowels, [f, s, x], whence such correspondences as English *grope:* German *greifen,* English *water:* German *Wasser,* English *make:* German *machen.*

There are many phonetic changes which, though the causes that brought them about are no clearer than in other instances, allow at least of classification as to their immediate tendency. In speaking of sound-changes that obliterated semantic distinctions, we saw a sound-change by which *knight* and *night* became homonymous: early in the seventeenth century initial *k* before *n* was dropped. As this did not happen after vowel, as in *acknowledge,* it was probably after certain preceding final consonants that the new variants were first favored. These new variants involved a simplification of the required articulatory movements. To pronounce *kn-* one had to begin with voiceless, non-nasal, velar articulation [k] and then to change to voiced, nasal, dental articulation [n], — in other words, simultaneously (1) to start one's vocal chords into voice-vibration, (2) to lower the velum, and (3) to move the tongue from velar to dental articulation. It is evident that a variant which saved, for instance, the lowering of the velum (2), by beginning the word with nasal articulation (or retaining it after a final nasal of a preceding word, as in *yon knight*) simplified the whole performance by lessening the number of required simultaneous movements. Such a variant would be [ŋnejt]. A further variant which began at once with tongue-articulation at the *n*-position (or kept that position after a preceding dental consonant, as in *that knight*), namely [n̥nejt], brought another simplification by saving the necessity of a change of tongue-position (3). A variant that saved the adjustment of the vocal chords into voicing position during the *n*-sound, was to voice the initial sound (or to continue voicing after a preceding voiced sound, as in *the knight*), giving [nːejt] and [nejt], present-day [nɑĕt]. The variants that were favored resulted, thus, in a simplification of the movements necessary to produce the word. They may be said to have resulted, further, in a lessening of the total number of different combinations of movement occurring in the language, — since [n̥n], for instance, did not otherwise occur. Thus, while we do not know the actual causes, we see here the typical results of many sound-changes. But we cannot follow the tempting course of arguing directly from these results to the causes, for the results do not indicate why the change took place where and when it did. Thus, if the simplification in the above instance were looked upon as the cause, it would be inexplicable why it did not take place earlier: by the seventeenth century people had been speaking initial *kn-* from time immemorial and always, it seems, maintaining an equilibrium of habit. Or, if we look to German, how does it come that the simpler variants have never gained ground there, *kn-* being still spoken, as in *Knecht* [knɛçt] 'servant', *Knie* [kniː] 'knee', *Knabe* [knɑːbə] 'boy'? We are face to face with the same difficulty that we met above, with regard to the closing and diphthongization of the English vowels. In this second case we can see that the favored variants brought a simplification, — involved a lessening of the labor of speech, but we still do not know why they were favored here and not elsewhere, now and not sooner.[1])

---

1) It seems possible that the new variants in the change of *kn-* tended to occur rather after non-syllabic than after syllabic sounds (cf. *acknowledge*), and that the increasing diphthongization of long vowels, which would often precede the *kn-* words, as in *I know; thou knowest* etc., led the *n-* variants to be favored at this particular time. If this explanation should prove correct,

Very many of the sound-changes known to have occurred in different languages show this same result of simplification of movements. In *knight, night, might*, etc. we have dropped the palatal spirant of Middle English [kniçt, niçt, miçt]. This was a simplification not only because it saved an articulation, but also because it lessened the number of different articulations in the language, which after the change contained no more [ç] 's.

In general, the successive sound-changes in a language often result in shortening the words. Where there is highest stress-accent on one syllable, we find sound-changes taking place, which shorten the unstressed syllables. For instance, in English, which has since prehistoric times had such an accent, the primitive Germanic **stainos* 'stone', nominative singular, and **stainon*, accusative singular, were shortened, by the historic time, to Old English *stān;* the Old English *stāne*, dative singular, is in modern English, like these other forms, monosyllabic *stone* [stown], and the Old English genitive singular *stānes* and nominative and accusative plural *stānas* also, are today monosyllables, *stone's, stones* [stownz]. The Old English *caru* 'care', nominative singular, and all the other forms of this word, in Old English disyllabic, are today limited to one syllable, that which was in Old English stressed, — a phenomenon so universal, in fact, that our language, which in earlier periods had almost no words of less than two syllables has now few uncompounded native words of more than one. So, to quote a classical example, pre-English **habēda* and **habēdun* became in Old English *hæfde* and *hæfdon* and are in present English (*I, we*) *had*

---

our sound-change would be due to the closing and diphthongization of the long vowels, which in turn, however, is unexplained as to motive.

In addition to the general facilitation involved in the reduction of words from several syllables to one, it is especially to be noticed, that, given a powerful stress-accent, indistinct, shortened articulation of the unstressed syllables represents an immediate simplification, because of the particular voice and breath conditions. The strong stress on the accented vowel means that during its production the vocal chords are vibrating under high tension (p. 25); after this tension is released there follows an outrush of the breath which was shut in under the vocal chords during voicing: it is easier, consequently, to pronounce them with shortened, weakened articulations and with murmur instead of voice, lessening as much as possible all interference with the breath-stream. Thus, in the history of English we find such Latin-French loanwords as *contemporaneous prohibition* changing from the full values of the vowels as written to the modern forms [kṇtempə'ɹejnjəs, pɹhə'biʃṇ], with the unstressed vowels often murmured. One might see in this weakening an immediate result of the stress-accent on one favored syllable, were it not that in Italian, for instance, the same words, with a similar accent, retain their full form *contemporaneo, proibizione*. The same change as in English has occurred in other languages with high word-stress. The contrast in Latin, for example, between *facio* 'I do, I make' and its compound *conficio* 'I finish' is due to the pre-Latin conditions, in which all words were spoken with stress on the first syllable: at this time the second syllable of *conficio* received its divergent weakened form. The stress-accent of Russian has similarly changed an older [po to ro 'p'i s'i] 'hurry up' to [pə tə ra 'p'i·s'], an older ['kła· n'aj t'e s'i] 'give greeting' to ['kła· n'i t'is'], and so on.

In other instances the simplification brought about by

a sound-change is apparent upon closer inspection. For instance, it has happened in the history of a number of languages that such combinations as *nr, lr* became *ndr, ldr*, and such as *mr, ml* became *mbr, mbl:* in Middle English, for instance, *þunres* 'thunder's' became *þundres*, *alre* 'alder-tree's' became *aldre*, *þymle* 'thimble' became *þymble*, and **getimre* 'carpentry' had in Old English already become *getimbre* (cf. modern *timber*). The apparent addition to the required series of articulations is really a simplification. In the transition from *n* to *r*, for instance, two changes had to be made simultaneously: (1) the velum raised, to stop nasalizing, and (2) the tongue moved from the contact of *n* to the position for *r*. The change consists in raising the velum a little before the tongue-movement, — an *n, m* with raised velum is of course a *d, b*, — so that only one movement need now be made at a time: addition to the number of movements there is none.

Some of the sound-changes so far discussed affected certain sounds wherever they occurred in the language; such, for instance, was the English vowel-shift, also the loss of [ç] in English. Other changes, called *conditioned sound-changes*, occur only in certain phonetic surroundings. Thus *kn* in English was not simplified to *n* between vowels, as in *acknowledge*, the English, pre-Latin, and Russian vowel-weakenings occurred only in unstressed syllables, and the pre-Germanic change of [p, t, k] to [f, θ, x] (p. 208) did not take place when these sounds were preceded by a spirant: *spoon* and *stone*, for example, have preserved their *p* and *t* since before this pre-Germanic change. The High German change of [p, t, k] to [f, s, x], similarly, did not occur after spirants: the German words *Spahn* 'splinter' and *Stein* 'stone', German representatives of *spoon* and *stone*, have retained the stops.

Initially the same sounds changed in German to [pf, ts, kx], the former two, for instance, in *Pfund* 'pound' and *zehn* 'ten', as opposed to the corresponding English words.

Such conditioned sound-changes are usually transparent as to the simplification they afford. We find, thus, that the velar spirant [x] in German became the palatal [ç] wherever it followed a front vowel, as in *ich* [ʔiç] 'I', from older [ʔix]. As in this case, the result is often an assimilation of one articulation to the other, and the term *assimilation* has come to be regularly used in this connection.

When, as in this German example, a sound is assimilated to one preceding, we speak of *progressive* assimilation. The modern English automatic sound-variation in the plural-suffix between [z] and [s] is the result of a progressive assimilation: when in Early Modern English, the unstressed vowel of forms like *stones* [stɔːnəz], *beasts* [beːstəz] was dropped, the [z] was assimilated, as to voicing, to a preceding unvoiced sound, whence modern [stownz] but [bijsts].

Regressive assimilation is in the history of most languages commoner. A widespread type of it is 'palatalization', the assimilation of a velar or dental to a following palatal. Thus pre-English [k, ɡ, g] became before front vowels Old English [c, ɟ, j]. The former two have since become [tʃ, dʒ]. Instances are our words *child, ridge, yield,* which were in Old English *cild, hrycg, gieldan*, pronounced [cild, hryɟ, jeldan], and go back to Primitive Germanic *kildis, *hrugjos, *geldonon. Latin *cinque* (with initial [k], a late form for *quinque* 'five') and *generum* (accusative, 'son-in-law') have had their initial sounds palatalized in the modern forms, such as Italian ['tʃiŋkwe, 'dʒenero] and French [sɛ̃ːk, ʒɑ̃ːdr]; in these languages we can see also the palatalization of dentals, as when Latin *pretium* 'price' and *radium* (accusative) 'ray' give in Italian ['prɛtso, 'radʒo]. The tendency to palatalization is especially active in the Slavic languages, where velar and dental stops have been repeatedly subjected to it, and all other consonants at least once; thus a pre-Slavic *kensti- 'part' gave in Čechish [tʃaˑst̚] in Russian [tʃaˑst'], and in Polish [tʃɛˑʃt'ʃ].

Another example of regressive assimilation is the vowel-change which took place during the first millenium of the Christian era in all the Germanic languages, assimilating stressed back vowels to following front vowels, probably through the medium of palatalization of the intervening consonants. Thus primitive Germanic *harjoz gave Old English *here* 'army', *fōtiz gave *fēt* 'feet', the loan-word (from Latin *uncia*) *uŋki- gave *ynce* 'inch', and *mūsiz gave *mȳs* 'mice'.

A total regressive assimilation is the development of Latin *pt* and *kt* into Italian *tt*, as in *septem* 'seven' > *sette*, *octo* 'eight' > *otto*.

Assimilation may be to both the preceding and the following sounds, as when in pre-Latin *s* between vowels became voiced, *z*; this *z* later changed to *r*, whence the inflection of *genus* 'race, kin, sex', genitive *generis*, from older *geneses.

The assimilative tendency may be counteracted in certain connections. In English there has been a strong tendency to voice unvoiced spirants; this tendency seems to be assimilative and due to contiguous voiced sounds. Thus in the early period of Modern English *stones* ['stɔːnəs] became ['stɔːnəz], *luxurious* [lukˈʃuːriʊs] became [lugˈʒuːriʊs], *with* [wiθ] became [wið], *is* [is] became [iz], *was* [was] became [waz], *of* [of] became [ov], and so on; but this tendency was counteracted, after an accented vowel, by some other factor, — perhaps by the outrush of breath after the stress. Hence in such words as *geese, pence, luxury* ['lʌkʃəɹi], and in the accented uses of *of*, now in such cases written *off*, the spirant remained unvoiced. Initially, also, it was kept, owing, no doubt, to the lack of preceding voicing, as in *select, forget*. At an earlier stage of the language, probably in pre-English, the older [θ] of *the, this, that, then*, etc. became in the same way, owing to unaccented use of these words, [ð]. At a still earlier period, in pre-Germanic, there was a change of exactly the same kind, by which for instance, *wása 'I was' remained unchanged, but *wēsumín 'we were' became *wēzumín, — which difference of consonant is preserved in the present *was: were*. This pre-Germanic voicing is known as 'Verner's law'.

It is customary to set off certain sound-changes as 'sudden' in opposition to the majority which, like all our examples so far, are called 'gradual'. These so-called sudden sound-changes are changes in pronunciation which, in part, could not have been arrived at through a series of variants. Two types are comparatively common, *metathesis* and *dissimilation*.

There are but few indisputable cases of metathesis in the known history of languages. Part of the supposed cases are really gradual sound-changes. Thus pre-English *rinnan (as in the Old English compound *gerinnan* 'to coagulate') gave Old English *iernan* 'to run', and pre-English *brinnan gave Old English *biernan* 'to burn'. In these examples the 'metathesis' was probably a gradual process, the *r* first becoming syllabic to the exclusion of the vowel, which left only a palatal affection: [r̩'nan, br̩'nan]; later a new vowel, determined by the palatal coloring, arose before the *r*. Other cases of metathesis, like the English dialectal *ax* for *ask* or the pre-German *atīk* 'vinegar' (modern *Essig*) for older *akīto* are probably not phonetic changes at all, as we shall see.

Dissimilation is due to the tendency which appears when one tries to articulate such series as *Peter Piper picked a peck of pickled peppers*. When the vocal organs are to be placed repeatedly into the same position, it is hard to keep in focus the exact part of the prospective movement-complex at which one has arrived: the tendency is to mistake the quicker movement of the attention for the slower one of actual articulation, — to confuse an earlier for a later stage of the series; thus one might say: *Peter Piked* ... for *Peter Pi(per pi)cked* ... Another tendency is to confuse the unwonted repetition of the same movement with some more practised succession of diverse articulations, — to say, for instance, *Peter Piper ticked* ... Both of these tendencies have in rare instances brought about permanent phonetic changes. To the former tendency are due the so-called *haplologies*, such as Latin *stipendium* 'stipend' for older *stipipendium* or Ancient Greek *amphoreús* 'amphora' for earlier *amphiphoreús*. As well as a repeated syllable a repeated sound may be omitted, as in the colloquial Latin *cinque* [kiŋkwe] 'five' for earlier *quinque* [kwiŋkwe]. The other phase of the dissimilative tendency appears in such changes as Late Latin *pelegrīnus* 'pilgrim' for earlier *peregrīnus*. Here again most of the quotable examples, including probably this, are really not cases of phonetic change in the strict sense, but rather of assimilative mispronunciation of words of a foreign language: *pelegrīnus* was probably originated by people whose native language was not Latin, or at any rate did not contain this word. A genuine dissimilation occurred in pre-Greek, where two successive syllables beginning with aspirated stops were dissimilated, the former losing its aspiration: thus, *thé-

thnā́ke 'he has died, is dead' became *téthnēke*, **khékhēna* 'I have gaped' became *kékhēna*. The same dissimilation took place in pre-Indic, such forms as **dhadhāti* 'he puts' becoming in Sanskrit *dadhāti*.

A similar process may lead, on the other hand, to assimilative repetition of the same sound in the place of two articulations originally different, as when a pre-Latin **pibeti* 'he drinks' gives Latin *bibit*, with *b-* for *p-*. Such sudden changes as all these are, however, rare, compared to the gradual changes above described.

The specific change in the complex conditions of human existence which brought about a given sound-change is, then, as a rule, hidden from our view. We have reason to believe that, if we knew the underlying change in the conditions of life, we should find it affecting not the particular sounds which we see changing, but rather some more general factor of articulation, such as the rest-position of the vocal organs, or the manner of voicing and breathing. The preponderant tendency of sound-change to simplification of word-forms, and the harmony of various sound-changes in a language (such as change of stop-articulations in pre-Germanic, spirant-voicing, shifting of vowels, and weakening of unstressed syllables in English, palatalization in Slavic), all point in this direction. As a result of some such fundamental change there take place the various sound-changes found to occur in a given period. The individual sound-changes bear, each of them, accordingly, the character of lessening of the labor of speech by means of adaptation to the prevailing rest-position of the vocal organs or to the prevailing manner of speaking. We may suppose that every sound-change is assimilative in nature, changing some discordant element in the habits of pronunciation into an articulation harmonious with the total speech-activities of the time. Each change, however, probably in turn displaces this total habit-complex, so that further adjustments become necessary and an endless series of sound-changes results. Accordingly, when we establish that a given sound-change is simplification, we are not naming its cause, but merely describing, in part, the general nature of sound-change. The cause is probably in every case a change in the speech-habits as a whole, due, in turn, to a change in the underlying conditions of life. As soon as we try to determine these we are on the open sea of surmise.

Only under one set of circumstances do sound-changes bid fair to be thoroughly explained. We know that it is only under the most favorable pedagogic conditions that people ever learn to pronounce a foreign language correctly. As a result of a simultaneous association, one hears a resembling familiar sound where a foreign one has actually been uttered, and even when one hears the latter correctly, imitation is usually impossible (p. 19). We see this in the speech of the foreign people who learn English. In some parts of Wisconsin, for instance, a German 'accent' is audible even in the speech of the younger generation that does not speak German, but learned from its parents the English (with German sounds) which they spoke. In this case the growing intercommunication with people who speak purer English will no doubt in time efface the peculiarity. There have been however, instances where a comparatively small number of conquerors have forced their language on a people of alien language. In such a case we may expect to find substituted for the sounds of the new language the corresponding nearest sounds of the old. The clearest instance at present known of such sound-substitution is in the Indo-European languages of India. In prehistoric times the bearers of the Indo-European pre-Indic language entered the country and forced their speech upon certain sections of the inhabitants, from whom, in the course of time, it spread farther and farther. As some of the older languages, however, escaped and are spoken to this day, — for instance, in the Dravidian languages, — we know something about the phonetic habits of the people upon whom the pre-Indic language was forced. They had two series of tongue-tip stops, one purely dental, like the modern French series [t, d] and one pronounced even farther back than our alveolars, namely the cerebrals [ṭ, ḍ] (p. 30). The language of the Indo-European invaders had only the former series, but in all the historic languages that represent it, such as Sanskrit, we find the latter series also: it was substituted, evidently, for some sounds not familiar to the older inhabitants, probably for the dorsal articulations [c, ɉ] produced in the same place. The task of tracing such sound-changes has been barely undertaken by students of language; it may be expected that the phonetic change in the history of such dialects as South German, the Romance languages, and the Slavic languages will receive light from this treatment.

When a conditioned sound-change occurs a new multiformity of sounds may be created. Thus pre-English had no palatal stops until there occurred the change of velar stops to palatals before front vowels, as in the words *child, ridge*. Similarly, Old English had no z-sound, but, owing to changes in which s, under certain conditions, came to be voiced, we have now both s and z. As long as the conditions remain undisturbed the result of such a change is an automatic sound-variation. In forming the genitive of nouns, for instance, we use the suffix [əz] after sibilants, [s] after unvoiced sounds other than sibilants, and [z] after voiced sounds other than sibilants.

The variation is automatic in this suffix. The same is true of the preterite suffix of our regular verbs (*waited, waded, — passed, hoped, — turned, rowed*). The variation is automatic, further, in the sibilant plural suffix of our nouns, in so far as they are regular. In our colloquial pronunciation [j] varies automatically with [ʃ] after [t] and with [ʒ] after [d], for we say *have you, don't you, did you* with three different initials of *you*. There was a time when *of* [ɔv], *with* [wið] were used in unstressed, *off* [ɔf], *with* [wiθ] in stressed position (p. 215).

This automatic sound-variation may in several ways be disturbed. Further phonetic change may do it. The pre-Germanic spirant-voicing after unaccented vowel, for instance, left such automatic variations as **wása* 'I was': **wēsumún* 'we were' (p. 216); when, however, the stress was later shifted everywhere to the first syllable, the variation was of course no longer automatic, but purely traditional, as still in the modern forms, *was: were*. So, by a pre-English vowel-assimilation (p. 215) **fōtiz*, the nominative plural of **fōt* 'foot', became **fētiz*, a variation whose automatism was destroyed by the phonetic change which dropped the second syllable of **fētiz*, giving Old English *fēt*: here, as in the Modern English *foot: feet*, the variation is, of course, no longer automatic.

The other processes of change in language mentioned at the beginning of this chapter (p. 196), which we shall now discuss, may bring about the same result.

4. Analogic change. When change in the form of words is in any sense due to their meaning, we speak not of phonetic, but of *analogic change*.

We have seen that partial formal similarity between words, when it expresses a corresponding semantic similarity, is due to the psychic factor of assimilation (p. 59, f.). We have seen, further, that all such correspondence between meaning and form is maintained by repeated processes of assimilation in the mind of every speaker (p. 93, f.). If the same assimilations were always made, the form of words would, except for phonetic change (I use the word here, as always, in the strict sense), remain stable. There are, however, a number of factors which constantly displace the conditions under which the assimilations of speech take place.

Such factors are changes in mental organization, in culture, in surroundings. Not only changes in habitat and the progress of civilization, but also the vicissitudes of all the individual lives that go to make up the community, make it impossible that the same topics should always be spoken of, or be spoken of by the same people. The frequency, absolute and relative, with which any sentence or word recurs is constantly changing. As a result, words well practised a few centuries ago are now rare, and words then rare or unknown are today in constant use.

Another factor is the effect of phonetic change. Forms that where once nearly alike may become very different, owing to a conditioned sound-change. In pre-English there was a large group of nouns that formed their plural in *-as*, e. g. Old English *hring*, plural *hringas* (modern *ring, rings*); *stān, stānas* (modern *stone, stones*). When one spoke the plural of such a noun the others, of course, gave assimilative support. Among them was also **knīf* 'knife', plural **knīfas*. During this period, however, *f* between voiced sounds became voiced, so that we have to this day singular *knife*, plural *knives*, with change of consonant, and this plural is now, of course, irregular: when it is being spoken the regular plurals, such as *rings, stones, cliffs*, no longer lend their full support. In other words, the conditions of word-formation are altered.

Another highly potent factor is the change of speaking individuals. Every child has to learn all the habits of association which form the language, including of course the assimilative habits of inflection and derivation. Years elapse before the child's experience with speech is anything like that which may be called normal in the community. Insufficient practice, to take a common instance, in the preterite forms *brought, came* will allow an assimilation by the regular preterite forms, such as *lived, played* to become effective: the child says *bringed, comed*. The child is soon cured of the most striking of these false assimilations, but no speaker and no generation of speakers ever succeeds in reproducing entirely, in this respect, the speech of those who went before. Nowadays the great prevalence of printed speech lessens our divergence from earlier forms, especially as it allows of compendia (grammar and dictionary) of what is 'standard' speech; yet the obvious fact that we cannot and do not speak as we write is a confirmation of what has been said. The 'ungrammatical' speech of the classes less familiar with books, is a further witness. Thus we find that the plural of *cow* was formerly *kine*, of *book* a form that would now be *beech* (Old English *bēc*). These changes scarcely differ from those of the child when it says *bringed, comed*, — only, in fact, in that the conditions of the speech-community as a whole were such as to produce the innovation independently in many individual speakers and to make it so natural for their hearers, that these for the most part accepted the new forms without being aroused by their novelty. Where a hearer of an older generation, who had used and heard the older form of the word in question too much not to notice the innovation, would correct a speaker, there people might become conscious of the change, but for the most part the process is as unconscious as the child's innovation of *bringed*. Every one of us is taking part in such movements, unconsciously, unless corrected by someone of an older generation or someone more practised in the word concerned, — and even then, if the change is well under way among our fellow-speakers, we usually forget the correction or at least the direction which it took, — whether it was form A or form B which we were told was wrong. In communities without written records or with but little use of writing, — that is, in all but a few modern communities, — the authoritative force of literary usage, grammar, and dictionary is, of course, wanting on the conservative side.

This process, then, is called analogic change. We ought rather to speak of innovation due to the assimilative influencing of articulation by semantically associated words, — that is, of 'associative sound-assimilation'. The term 'analogic change' or 'analogy' is, in fact, retained only because it is conveniently brief. The modification 'false analogy' is better, because it conveys at least the idea of innovation, as opposed to the regular assimilative processes by which all speech is formed.

The term 'analogy' is most out of place in the simplest instances, those which most clearly show their character of assimilations; in speaking of these many scholars accordingly prefer the name 'contamination'. Contamination is said to occur when the articulation of a word is assimilatively modified by that of another single word of related meaning. Genuine cases of such contamination are hard to find; as a rule, when the conditions are minutely studied, it appears that some further factor beyond the single semantically associated word was active in inducing the change. The English pronoun *ye* is supposed to have been a contamination-form due to the influence of *we* upon *you*. The numeral *four* began in Primitive Indo-European with a velar or uvular consonant with lip-rounding, *qŭ*, and probably got its initial under the influence of *five*, but there may have been also an element of dissimilation in the change: the word seems to have been at one time **qŭeqŭor-*, where dissimilation to **peqŭor-* would be possible. Even aside from this possibility, the process of counting is so common that we might speak of a regressive assimilation, 'five' affecting 'four'. The initial of the Slavic word for 'nine', originally *no-*, seems to have been assimilated by the word for 'ten': Old Bulgarian *devęti* 'nine' (we should expect **novęti*), *desęti* 'ten'. The Latin *noctū* 'by night' is due to an assimilation of *nocte* (ablative of *nox* 'night') by *diū* 'by day'.

In most cases the assimilative effect is due not to a single word, but to a whole series of words in which the assimilating sound goes hand in hand with the common semantic element. Thus the word *squawk* may be looked upon as a contamination of *squeak* by *squall*, but *talk* and *caw* and even *maw* may also have been effective: in such cases the term 'adaptation' has been used. Latin *gravis* 'heavy' appears in Italian as *greve*. The change of *a* to *e* may be looked upon as a contamination with *leve* 'light' (Latin *levis*), or as an adaptation, if one supposes *breve* 'short' (Latin *brevis*) also to have been effective. English *render* is a loan from the French *rendre*, which owes its nasal to an adaptation of Latin *reddere* to *prehendere* (French *prendre*) 'to take' and other words in Latin *-endere* (French *-endre*), such as *vendere* (French *vendre*) 'to sell'. English *egotism* is an adaptation of *egoism* to such words as *despotism*, *nepotism*. English *shimmer* appeared by the side of such words as Old English *scima* 'a light' and the verb *shine* primarily under the influence of *glimmer*, but other words in *-immer* were no doubt also involved. A certain case of adaptation it is, when, much later, the word *flimmer* appears by the side of *flame* and *glimmer, shimmer*. In this way arise such sets of words as *clash, crash, dash, flash*, etc. (p. 133, f.). For instance, *flash* is on the one hand due to *flame* and perhaps others of the *fl-* words, and on the other to those of the *-ash* group. *Jounce* is due to *jump, jolt* and to *bounce, trounce*.

The third and commonest kind of analogic change, to which the term best applies, is called also 'proportional analogy'. When, in normal speech, we wish to form the plural of *girl* and the number-element, owing to such associated words as *boys, curls*, and, in fact to all regular plurals, is at once presented as [z], the result may, metaphorically, be viewed as the solution of a proportional equation: '*boy: boys* as *girl*: x'. This way of stating the thing is, to be sure, misleading, — it is characteristic, in fact, of a post factum way of viewing linguistic occurrences as if they were results of deliberate individual action, — nevertheless, it makes possible a diagrammatic indication of the place a new form holds in the morphologic system. Thus when the form *cows* for *kine* arose it could be looked upon as the result of a similar equation to that which gave *girls*, e. g. *dog: dogs* as *cow*: x. Hence the name 'proportional analogy'; needless to say that in reality the result is due not to any such mathematical comparison, but to a number of complex and variously graded psychic forces in each of the many individuals that make up the community.

'Proportional analogy' is not separable from the processes of contamination and adaptation. The English dialectal *squench*, similar in meaning to *quench*, may be looked upon as a contamination of this word and *squelch*;

but, as the association of *squirt* and even of other words with initial *s-*, such as *splash, spout, souse*, etc., must also have contributed to the assimilation, we may also speak of an adaptation; finally, we may look upon the initial *s-* as an element entering into articulation because of its semantic tone, due to occurrence in *squash*, as opposed to *quash, splash* as opposed to *plash, smash* as opposed to *mash*, and even *souse* as opposed to *douse*: as this last was surely a phase in the psychic process resulting in *squench*, this word may be looked upon as a 'proportional' formation (*plash: splash* as *quench: x*). In short, any attempt at classifying assimilative formations by the number of inducing words is frustrated by the complexity of the processes involved.

There remains the classification of assimilative processes according to the semantic character of the elements involved. It appears at once that these elements may be, from the point of view of the language concerned, either conceptual or relational.

The conceptual elements are involved, for instance, in the origin of the English *ye* (p. 224), in the changes of initial which produced the English *four* and the Slavic word for 'nine' (p. 226); further, in the origin of *squawk*, of *squench*, and of the Italian *greve*. The same may perhaps be said of *shimmer, flimmer*, and *flash*, above; as long as we can not with any freedom add *-immer* or *-ash* to other elements, we can hardly call these formational sound-sequences anything but material. Let us suppose, however, that these phonetic elements *-immer* and *-ash* should become extended to more and more words, until it became customary to use them in a given signification with any initial-element, then they would have become freely usable derivational elements. It is, thus, analogic change which gradually gives 'life' — i. e. morphologic mobility — to derivational and inflectional elements.

A few more examples of analogic change in the conceptual parts of words may be cited. The Latin word for 'your' was *vester*: in the course of time its vowel became assimilated to that of *noster* 'our', under the additional influence, no doubt, of the parallelism of *vos* 'you' and *nos* 'we': the word in the modern forms of Latin corresponds phonetically to a *voster*, e. g. French *votre*, Italian *vostro*. The German verb *lügen* 'to lie, tell falsehoods' was formerly *liegen* and owes its vowel to the association of *Lüge* 'a lie', with the parallelism of *fliegen* 'to fly': *Fliege* 'a fly', *peitschen* 'to whip': *Peitsche* 'a whip', and the like. English *neither*, instead of older *nawther*, owes its form to the influence of *either* and the parallelism of *nor*: *or*, *never*: *ever*.

Analogic change in the grammatical elements of words is even commoner. If we recall that the partial phonetic similarity between the different inflectional forms of a word is due to assimilative development (p. 59), it will be apparent that this kind of analogic change is one of the chief shaping forces of language. The historical instances, as this leads us to expect, are frequent in which divergence between the forms of a word is thus obliterated. Psychologically, the closely associated forms of the same word are, of course, powerful factors in bringing about such assimilation. Of the examples of analogic change so far quoted the child's error of *bringed*, *comed* for *brought*, *came* belongs here: just such analogies as these transform suppletive and irregular into regular inflection. They have changed, for instance, the plural of *cow* from *kine* to *cows*, that of *book* from *beech* (i. e. Old English *bēc*) to *books* (p. 223). In these changes the other forms of the word are active together with the parallelism of the regularly inflected words. Here belongs, further, the change in dialectal English of the preterite and unreal of the verb *to be*. The form *was* entered into articulation instead of Standard English *were* because its assimilative influence was supported by the entire volume of habit represented by the remaining verbs of our language: *I had it, They had it, I wish I had it,* — *I saw it, They saw it, I wish I saw it,* and so on, all confirm the habit of articulating the same form in the plural and unreal as in the singular of the real preterite; hence *They was there, I wish I was there.* As the plural is commoner than the unreal, and in the present tense real partly distinguished from the singular (*he has: they have,* etc.) the form *were* is in this value better retained than in the unreal.

The forms *was* and *were* differ by vowel and consonant variation. The vowel-variation goes back to Primitive Indo-European time; it is known among linguistic students by the German name 'ablaut'. The consonant-variation arose in pre-Germanic time through the spirant-voicing after unstressed vowels, 'Verner's law' (p. 216). In pre-Germanic the two forms were at first *wása and *wēsumé; the spirant-voicing changed the *s* of the latter form to *z*: *wēzumé; later the accent came to fall in all words on the first syllable, whence Primitive Germanic *wézume; in pre-West-Germanic, finally, the *z* became *r*: *wǣrume; then, what with certain pre-English changes, we find Old English *wæs, wǣron*. Owing to these same causes a number of verbs in Old English had sound-variation in the preterite. Thus one said *rād* 'I rode' but *ridon* 'we rode', *wrāt* 'I wrote' but *writon* 'we wrote', *seah* 'I saw' but *sāwon* 'we saw', and so on. While phonetic change is responsible for the loss of the plural-ending in Modern English, the association of verbs that lacked the sound-variation, such as Old English *fēoll* 'I fell', plural *fēollon* 'we fell', *wōc* 'I awoke', plural *wōcon* 'we awoke', impelled the assimilation of the two stem-forms: *rode, wrote*, with vowel corresponding to that of *rād, wrāt*, are now used in the plural also; *saw* corresponds in form to the Old English plural. The same levelling has taken place in the other languages that are modern forms of Primitive Germanic. Of these the Scandinavian languages have gone farther than English, all verbs, including *var* 'was, were', having the same form for singular and plural. Dutch agrees with English, except for the retention of the plural-suffix, having assimilated everywhere except in *was* 'was', plural *waren* 'were'. German has regularized this verb (*war*, plural *waren*), but retains *ward* (more commonly, however, *wurde*), plural *wurden* 'became'. It is interesting, further, to see how some of the other languages which historically represent Primitive Indo-European have made the same levelling of the preterite ablaut. Thus the Latin 'perfect' tense, which is partly the same in origin as our preterite, has everywhere the same vowel for singular and plural, e. g. *tutudī* 'I beat', *tutudimus* 'we beat', where Primitive Indo-European had, respectively, *tetoud- and *tetud- (for instance, in Sanskrit still *tutóda* and *tutudimá*). So in Ancient Greek, beside the singular *pépoitha* 'I have placed confidence, I trust', we find the plural *pepoíthamen* instead of an older *pépithmen.[1])

Another example of the regularizing force of grammatical analogic change is the development of the English noun. In pre-English there occurred a sound-change which turned back vowels of accented syllables into front vowels, if there followed a front vowel in the next syllable (p. 215). The resulting sound-variation, as seen, for instance, in the Old English nominative singular *fōt*, but

---

[1]) Here the change in Latin is due chiefly to a substitution of old middle-voice forms for active, that in Greek to direct grammatical analogy.

plural *fēt* from older **fōtiz* (modern *foot: feet*), is called by linguists 'umlaut'. The inflection of the word 'foot' was in Old English as follows:

	Singular.	Plural.
Nominative-accusative:	*fōt*	*fēt* (older **fōtiz*)
Genitive:	*fōtes*	*fōta*
Dative:	*fēt* (older **fōti*)	*fōtum*.

In the singular the lack of vowel-variation in most nouns (e. g. 'stone': *stān, stānes, stāne*) led in time to a new dative form *fōte;* in the plural, where the nominative and accusative, the most-used cases, had *ē*, the same influence of regular nouns led to an analogic assimilation of the vowel *ō* to *ē* in the other forms, whence the modern inflection of singular *foot*, plural *feet*. In the case of *book*, modern plural *books* (p. 223), the plural form was assimilated to the singular in vowel and consonant and also to the regular plural inflection with sibilant.

This kind of grammatical analogy is called 'material' as opposed to the 'formal', in which the assimilation brings greater unity not to the forms of one word, but to the corresponding forms of different words. Thus the change in the vowel and consonant of the plural of *book*, by which this form became more like the singular was 'material' grammatical analogy, but the assumption by this plural of the regular sibilant suffix was 'formal'. The 'formal' process differs from the 'material' in that the inducing factor in the assimilation is not an element of the other forms of the same word, but the total impulse of elements of the desired meaning in numerous other words. In Old English, for instance, only a limited part of the nouns formed their genitive singular and nominative plural with *s*-suffixes. The nominative plural of *hūs* 'house', *word* 'word', *teoru* 'tar', *trēo* 'tree' was homonymous with the nominative singular: *hūs, word, teoru, trēo*; the genitive singular of *caru* 'care' was *care*, the nominative plural *cara*; *spere* 'spear' was in the nominative plural *speru*, *tunge* 'tongue', *mōna* 'moon' were in the genitive singular and nominative plural *tungan, mōnan*, and so on. When in these cases the corresponding forms of regular nouns, such as *stān* 'stone' (genitive singular *stānes*, nominative plural *stānas*) induced assimilation to the s-inflection, the different forms of any one word were often made less alike than they were before, but the total inflectional habits of the language gained in unity. The French ordinal numbers formerly differed extensively from the cardinals: 'one' was *un*, but 'first' *premier*; 'two' *deux*, 'second' *second*; 'three' *trois*, 'third' *tiers*; 'four' *quatre*, 'fourth' *quart*; 'five' *cinq*, 'fifth' *quint*; but above these numbers the ordinal was regularly derived from the cardinal by a suffix *-ième*, e. g. *six* 'six', *sixième* 'sixth', *sept* 'seven', *septième* 'seventh'. Both factors, the material and the formal, of grammatical analogy brought about a *cinquième, quatrième, troisième*, and although *second* is still heard, *deuxième* is commoner, *premier* alone being undisturbed.

While as a rule grammatical analogy is thus regularizing, this is not always the case. German feminine nouns have all their singular forms alike; the only exception is the genitive form *nachts* 'at night', influenced by the masculine genitive *tags* 'by day': the force of the usual feminine declension is, however, sufficient to retain, in all but this somewhat isolated adverbial use, the regular genitive *Nacht*; compare Latin *noctū* (p. 225).

It is needless to add that, just as old forms are assimilated, so new ones are created by the analogic process. The regular assimilations of all speech are no different from the creation of an analogic new form, such as *books* or the French *deuxième* when they first were spoken, and

ANALOGIC CHANGE

this process, in turn, is no different from that by which an entirely new form or word may arise. Thus, such nouns as *telephone, automobile, aeroplane* were used in the plural in English with the regular plural-suffix as soon as they were introduced, without the least consciousness of an innovation (p. 70). In short, the articulation of some new analogic form is, in the process, no different from that of an old form. The action of the speaker who first used the plural *automobiles* was no different from that by which on the same day he may have said *wagons* or *horses*.

Certain morphologic habits, like the English *s*-suffix for the plural, extend to an unlimited number of words and spread freely to new words, while others are limited to certain words and do not freely spread to others, — such, for instance, as our suffix *-hood* for derived nouns, as in *boyhood, manhood, motherhood, priesthood*, which cannot be extended, e. g. to form *unclehood* or *friendhood*. We speak, accordingly, of 'living' and 'dead' morphologic processes. Even a 'dead' morphologic process, as long as the formal-semantic relation between the words affected is still felt, — that is, as long as it is still really a morphologic process, — can occasionally be extended by analogy. The amount of 'life' in a morphologic process may be of any degree, and may constantly change. Most of our verbs form their past tense with a dental suffix; compared to this very living process vowel-variation for tense is dead: yet even it has, in certain cases been extended. The preterite of the verb *dive* in Standard English is *dived*, but is in dialectal speech frequently assimilated to that of *drive* (*strive*), becoming *dove*. In German there is a plural-suffix of nouns, *-er* accompanied in certain cases by vowel-variation (e. g. *Lamm* 'lamb', plural *Lämmer*), which has never been very living, yet, word by word, it has spread from use a thousand years ago in a dozen words (and in some of them not exclusive use) to exclusive use in about seventy-five today. The -*sh* of such English verbs as *clash, crash* was probably in Primitive Indo-European and perhaps even later a living suffix; from this time we have the verb *thrash* and perhaps also *mash*. By the Primitive Germanic time the suffix was dead. In the historical period of English, however, through assimilation due to the meaning especially of *thrash*, verbs in -*ash* have been multiplied (e. g. *flash* from *flame*) until -*ash* (not -*sh*) is today a fairly important morphologic element and may, for all we know, become living. At least, if it did, this would be precedented, to take one of many instances, by the development of our living suffix -*en* by which we derive verbs such as *fatten, shorten, moisten* from adjectives and occasionally from nouns (*hearten*). Just as there was in Primitive Indo-European a living suffix which today would give -*sh*, so in Old English there was a living suffix -*ian* (phonetically this gives today zero) by which verbs could be derived from nouns and adjectives, e. g. *wundian* (modern *to wound*) from *wund* 'a wound' (modern *wound*). From the adjective *fægen* 'glad' there was thus derived *fægenian* 'to rejoice' and from the adjective *open* 'open' the verb *openian* 'to open'. The influence of these words caused the innovation of deriving from *fæst* 'firm, fast' not only *fæstian* but also *fæstenian* (our *fasten*), and later, under the added impulse of this and each new formation, other verbs in -*enian*, modern -*en*, which at last made this suffixation a living one.

If we had as complete records of the history of languages as we could wish, it would thus be possible to see in detail not only how old forms changed phonetically, but also how new forms, whether inflectional or other, came by analogic change into the language. Only a small minority of English, German, or French words and forms, for instance, could be traced back by merely observing phonetic changes, to the earliest known stage of these languages. In by far the most instances we should find that our word or form ('phoneme') had been created by analogic change. As to the exact methods of this change the internal conditions in each language are of course decisive. Thus in French most morphologic classes are due to the use of suffixes, hence it is by shifting these, as in *deuxième*, that new words arise. In English we have some suffixation, and new words, for example in *-er*, such as *teacher, preacher, bicycler, advertiser* can always be formed, but since in English vowel and consonant variations also are used, these too can underly assimilations, so as to produce new words of the *squawk* or *squench* type. It is scarcely necessary to add that compound-words, too, in languages that have them, are formed on the analogy of others; if, today, we can form in English a compound like *automobile-driver*, in which the relation of the parts is peculiarly compositional and would not be allowed in syntactic collocation, that possibility is due only to the analogy of such older compounds as *carriage-driver, muledriver, giant-killer*, and so on.

It would be natural, had we not this knowledge of analogic change, to see in many phenomena, such as the rise of new words or the peculiar relations allowed between the members of compounds, some mysterious force which presided over the origin of speech and now in these instances bashfully shows itself to the degenerate present. This mistake, indeed, has often been made, and one may read in many places lists of 'primitive creations' (such words as *squawk, flash*) and references to a time when 'mere word-stems' could be joined, in any semantic relation to each other, to form compounds. But whenever the facts in a specific case are brought to light, it appears plainly that, apart from phonetic change, analogic change is the only power that shapes or creates the forms of language, — that we have no right to assume that there ever was a golden age when this was otherwise. To say this is only to say that the semantic value of language is always and exclusively dependent on the habits of expression of the community. If the associational habits of speech in the community are such as to call forth the utterance of a given form, that form will come, whether it has ever been spoken before or is an innovation, and will be explicable only on the basis of these habits and never on the strength of any ulterior connection, real or imagined, between the sound and the sense. The assumption, for instance, that words like *squeeze*, *squawk*, or *flap* are in some way inherently significant of the actions they designate and owe their origin to this significance, is unfounded. They are significant to English-speaking people because, in the first place, we use them in the sense that they have, and, secondly, because the sound-groups they contain (*squ-*, *fl-*, *-awk*, *-ap*) occur in other words of related meaning. These sound-groups have gradually come, in the history of the language, through a series of analogic formations, to carry their present meaning. Should it appear that they are in some other way than by mere custom representative of the experiences they designate, then we should know only one of the factors that contributed to their spreading from sporadic and innovational to regular use.

Even were a speaker consciously to set out to invent a word, he could not escape the influence of his earlier expressive habits, — that is, to keep to the accepted term, could not escape the process of linguistic analogy. In the actions of an individual there come into evidence unique factors of causation which in a communal process are subdued and compensated by the conflicting factors of other individuals, — where they are not, indeed, from the start overcome by the unquestioning submission to communal practice. Innumerable individual tendencies are suppressed in the speech, and, to a lesser extent, in the religious, artistic, cultural, political, economic, and other activities of every person. When an individual invents a word, these factors come into action and, though their complexity and singularity make the result harder to analyze than the result of a communal process, — often, in fact, with the data we have, impossible to analyze, — it is certain that the laws which produce it are ultimately the same. The most famous individual formation is the word *gas*, invented about 1600 by the Dutch chemist Van Helmont. He believed that gas was a phenomenon related to the idea which the Greeks expressed by *chaos*, which in Dutch receives nearly the same pronunciation as *gas*, and he used also a term *blas* (a fairly regular derivative from the Dutch verb *blazen* 'to blow') for an aerial radiation from the stars. 'Lewis Carroll's' famous poem of *The Jabberwocky* in *Through the Looking-Glass* contains a number of individual creations, together with the author's explanation. In most cases even words known to have been invented by individuals are regular derivatives, e. g. *radium*.

5. Semantic change. The third process of change in language alters not the form of words, but only the semantic content with which they are associated. This process is called *semantic change*. We have seen that, as no two experiences are ever really identical, no word can ever be used twice in exactly the same meaning. When our attention analyzes a total experience into elements, we constantly assimilate these elements to earlier experiences and express them by words used for these earlier experiences. The assimilation is due to a partial similarity between the earlier experiences and the present one, a similarity inhering in some uniform component of both experiences. This component common to all of the experiences designated by the same word is called the dominant element (p. 57, f.). When we say *John bumped his head,* for instance, we assimilate the experience of John's head to that of the other heads we have seen and known, even though as to size, shape, color of hair, and many other features, his head is by no means identical with these other heads or with any one of them. In fact, as to certain details, both objective and subjective, the present experience of this very head is different from any earlier experience of the same head. In short, the experience is assimilated, by virtue of certain dominant features, to a host of past experiences, and is designated by the same word. If we take into consideration the points of individuality of the present experience, it is clear that even here the word has been used in a new meaning, that there has been here a semantic change. From this to other changes more striking to an observer after the fact there is a gradual and by no means definable transition. The speaker, for instance, who first spoke of a *head* of cabbage was no more conscious of having made an innovation than the utterer of *John bumped his head.* At the time of this new utterance the dominant elements that brought about the new use of the word, were only very general ones of shape and size: the cabbage-head was to the speaker as much a head, — it called up the word *head* as immediately, — as any human or animal head. By far the most semantic changes, that is to say, are unconscious shiftings of meaning directly resulting from the earlier uses

SEMANTIC CHANGE 239

of the word and the dominant element with which it is associated, and are made independently and simultaneously by numerous speakers. It is only the observer afterwards looking back over history who sees that a change has taken place.

Our example of a *head* of cabbage illustrates a 'partial' semantic change: one in which the older meanings have so far remained in use side by side with the newer. As long as this is the case and no intermediate meanings have been lost, the normal speaker is not usually conscious of any extension. Not only were the people who first spoke of the *head* or the *wing* of an army, the *leg* of a table, the *foot* of a mountain, the *nose* of a cliff, the *heart* of a cabbage or of a country, of books *lying*, glasses *standing*, and rivers *running*, unconscious of making any innovation, but we also are normally unconscious of any deviation from what, upon deliberation, seems to us the more original use of these words.

When we speak at different times of John's *head*, the *head* of an army, and a *head* of cabbage, the different momentary associations in which the word appears may, however, involve a difference of dominant elements, even if there was no such difference when these uses first arose. In the first case, let us say, if we stood behind John, the dominant element may have been the vision of a shock of hair, in the second case of soldiers riding at the front, and in the last case of a cluster of green cabbage-leaves. The same mobility of dominant element appears, for example, in the successive uses of *law* in *law and medicine, law and order, law and chance, law of gravity*, and so on. If it should occur, now, that some of these uses should lapse, — if, let us suppose, people stopped speaking of a person's *head* and instead used some other word, such as *occiput*, and stopped speaking of the study of *law* and said in this connection only *jurisprudence*, — then the dominant element could be said to have definitely and permanently changed: — 'total' semantic change.

This, in fact, is a frequent occurrence. Thus *disease* (*dis-ease*) once meant discomfort of any kind; but, as the uses of the word aside from that represented, say, by *health and disease*, were forgotten, the dominant element has taken permanently one of the forms among which it wavered in the earlier use. If, as is probable, the word *ness* for 'cliff' once meant 'nose', it is an example of the same process: the lapse of certain uses has left the dominant element changed. So *meat* once meant 'food' (cf. *sweetmeat*), but the value of the word in such uses as *meat and bone*, *meat and hide*, where 'meat', as the edible part of something, was contrasted with the inedible part, has alone survived, so that the dominant element ('flesh') of these uses has become fixed. To *spill* was once to 'destroy'; the uses other than that in *spill the milk* and the like lapsing, the dominant element changed to that of pouring out a liquid. The adverb *hardly* (*hard-ly*) once meant 'firmly, vigorously'. *They hardly followed the enemy* then meant that they followed close upon them. The other uses lapsed until only this of 'closely' remained, and of this use the locutions where 'closely' had the sense of 'just, barely' alone remained to fix the dominant element of present speakers. The history of *nearly* (*near-ly*) is similar. In all these instances the change is at root a change in the habits of association. In the case of the word *meat*, for example, what has happened is really that English-speaking people in such experiences as that of someone's having enough to eat and to drink have ceased to associate the experience-element in question with the sounds *meat* and associate it instead with the word *food*; the sounds *meat*, on the other hand, they have come to associate with the experience of edible flesh. In some cases formal causes prompt these changes of association. Thus *mash* originally meant 'to mix', — cf. *sour mash, bran mash*, — but owing to the association of the phonetic element *-ash* with violent action (*clash, crash, dash*, etc.) and of the whole word with *smash* (cf. *plash: splash, lash: slash*, etc.), the present meaning of 'to crush' became associated with it.

In the examples so far given the change in habits of association was due to the prevalence, for reasons mostly too complex to allow of our tracing, of certain semantic connections. A few examples can be cited where the prevalence was due to connection with actually uttered words of a sentence rather than with semantically related words. The French word for 'nothing' *rien* originally meant 'a thing, something' (Latin *rem*); it came to be used, however, so prevalently in the connection *ne...rien* 'not...a thing', e. g. *Il ne dit rien* 'He says not a thing, He says nothing' that it came to be associated with a dominant element that included the negative idea, until now a Frenchman answering a question 'What did he say?' can answer *Rien* 'Nothing'. The same is true of *jamais* 'never': formerly it meant 'any more, ever' (Latin *jam magis*); the negative element has come to be associated with it owing to prevalence of the usage in *Il ne vient jamais* 'He does not ever come, He never comes'. The commonest French negative is *ne....pas*, originally 'not...a step' (Latin *passum*), but today one can say, for instance *Pas moi* 'Not I', for *pas* has come to be associated with negation as its dominant element. Meanwhile the word *pas* in the older sense of 'step' is still in use, but the normal speaker of French is not conscious of the historical connection between the two words. The same cannot be said of *personne*, used in both the negative sense of 'nobody' (due, of course, to *ne...personne*) and the original of 'person'. The use of *but* in such sentences as *He had but one child* is an example of the same process. *But* here used to have the usual meaning of 'except' (as in *All but John went*) and the sentence was *He had not but one child;* only after the association of the negative element with *but* was the *not*, now superfluous, omitted. This, indeed, is the process by which cross-referring constructions become simplified. In Latin *amat* meant 'He (she, it) loves', but, owing to the necessary frequency of such sentences as *Pater amat* '(The) father he-loves', the dominant element associated with *amat* ceased to include an actor: today in French one cannot say *aime*, but only *il aime, elle aime* 'he (it) loves, she (it) loves'.

The adjective *capital* was used so frequently in the connection *capital city* that it came to be associated, in spite of the conflict of its other uses (cf. *capital punishment, a capital story*), with the object-idea of 'chief city', and is today so used. The same is true of *general* for *general officer*, of *glass* for *glass tumbler*, of *lyric* for *lyric poem*, and so on: the other uses have in these examples continued by the side of the new 'condensed' meaning. The change in morphologic and syntactic value of the words is apparent: adjectives become nouns. Similarly our conjunction *while* used to be the accusative case of the noun *while*, as still appears in the archaic *the while*, — the accusative expressing extent of time. Today, owing to the loss of such case-constructions, the connection is lost, the value of the conjunction *while* being totally distinct from that of the noun. In expressions such as *He was frightfully angry* the value of *frightfully* may come to be felt as merely intensifying, until people say *I am frightfully glad;* the German word for 'very' *sehr* is the result of such a process, for it originally meant 'sorely, painfully'.

Our prepositions are an instance of an entire word-class that has received its present value from this process of 'condensation'. In an earlier stage of the language the relations of nouns were shown by their case-endings only, — not only relations of actor and object affected, but also the local relations now expressed by prepositions. At this time there were also a number of common adverbs which came to be used regularly with nouns in certain cases. This state of things was illustrated above (p. 116, f.) from the Ancient Greek by such a sentence as *Kephalēs ápo phāros héleske.* The first word is here the genitive of the word for 'head', this case being used to express separation: 'from the head'; *ápo* is an adverb, meaning 'off', 'away': 'He-drew (the) cloak off from-the-head', 'He drew the cloak from the head'. The constant occurrence of *ápo* with genitives of separation finally gave rise to a semantic change by which the genitive forms were no longer felt to express the idea of separation, but to stand simply in government or congruence with the adverb. So, in Old and Middle English, expressions like *Hē heom stōd wið* 'He them stood against, He withstood them' show the transition: is the case of *heom* in itself expressive of the relation, or is it merely the habitual accompaniment (congruence, rection) of *wið* 'against'? In the modern form *He stood against them* the case-form of *them* is of course purely in syntactic government of *against* and by itself expresses no local relation. Originally, however, our prepositions were adverbs like the Greek *ápo* in its early stage, and the form of the noun by itself directly expressed the local relation.

There are a number of instances in which the change of mental habit underlying a semantic change is a tangible alteration in the external conditions of life. The ancient Romans were originally an agricultural and cattle-raising people; the standard and also, no doubt, the medium of exchange for larger values was among them cattle. Hence *pecūnia*, the Latin word for 'money', and *pecūlium*, that for 'property', are nouns originally meaning 'that pertaining to cattle'. Under the dominant element 'medium of exchange', the former word was later applied to the coined metal money used in historic times. The English word *fee* also once meant 'cattle' (cf. the German *Vieh*) and has passed through a change similar to that of the Latin word. *Pen* originally meant 'feather', including the quills used for writing; then, when the latter were being superseded by steel points, the dominant element of 'writing-implement' mediated the present use. German *Feder* and French *plume* have still both meanings, 'feather' and 'pen'. The same is true of such words as *marshall* which meant 'horse-servant' (of the king), *constable* which meant 'attendant of the stable', and similar words in many languages: the conditions of court life changing, these offices gradually lost their old significance and attained to higher dignity, until the old dominant elements in the words faded. The history of such words as *arrive*, which once meant 'come to shore', and *equip*, which meant 'fit with a ship', is probably due to similar changes in the conditions of life. At bottom all this is no different from the changes of meaning in such words as *house, street, carriage, car, light, hat, coat, shoe, gun,* and so on, which every advance in civilization and shift in fashion brings about.

Thus the history of words, *etymology*, is interesting to the student of civilization and culture. Often the only trace of changes in a nation's mode of life is in semantic changes; for instance, no better testimony for the use of cattle as a medium of exchange in ancient Rome and ancient England exists than the 'etymology' of *pecunia* and of *fee*. Often, on the other hand, the history of a word can be understood only if one knows the cultural or material history that underlies it. The German *Wand* 'wall' for a long time puzzled etymologists; its obvious connection in the language seemed to be as a derivative of the verb *winden* 'to wind', but this seemed semantically improbable, — until it was pointed out that houses with basket-work walls are still to be found in parts of Europe.

The development of expressive material which keeps pace with the general mental progress of a community, — or rather, which forms an integral and vital part of this progress, — is largely mediated by semantic change. The processes most favorable to this growth are semantic changes transferring a word into a new sphere of experience, especially, of course, from a sensational to an intellectual value.

Leading up to this process are those instances in which a word originally belonging to one sphere of sensation comes to be used for others also: this, of course, constitutes a subtilization of the value of the word. The transition is immediate: after speaking of a *clear* liquid one feels no 'transference' at all in speaking of a *clear* sound or tone. Thus we speak of *sharp* sounds, tastes, or smells, using a word that referred originally only to a touch-experience. We speak of *warm* and of *cold* colors; when we use the word *tone-color* we let the value of *color*, originally visual, apply to auditory sensations, — with no difficulty, for the dominant element of 'gradations of a peculiar emotional value' applies to one as well as the other. The opposite extension is, of course, equally natural: we speak of *tones* in a painting. In all these instances the emotional value of the word becomes dominant, allowing it to be applied to experiences of similar emotional, if very different perceptual value. The power, as instruments of thought, — in these instances of esthetic thought, — of such words is thereby greatly increased.

These sensation-words themselves, for that matter, seem universally to have developed, through a similar process, out of still more concrete words. Modern examples that point to such a conclusion are our color-words *orange* and *violet*: the quality is expressed in terms of the object with which it is associated. Thus *bitter* was once a derivative of *bite* and *sour* of a word meaning 'to scratch'; *salty* and *salt* are derivatives of the noun *salt; sweet*, however, has not been traced to any earlier meaning. The word *tone* in Ancient Greek (from which language it has come to us) was a derivative of a word meaning 'to stretch' and meant originally the stretched string of a musical instrument. To *feel* was originally a derivative of a word for 'palm of the hand'.

Purely subjective terms have often the same history of transference on the basis of an emotional dominant element. Thus we speak of a *cold* reception, *bitter* hatred, *burning* or *glowing* anger, and the like. *Anxiety* meant a 'narrow place', just as we speak of someone's being in a *pinch*, having a *close shave* or a *narrow escape*, or being in *straits* or *straitened* circumstances. *Distress*, similarly, was originally 'destriction', i. e. 'constriction'.

Finally, our words denoting intellectual processes lead back in their history, to physical actions. Thus to *understand* meant to 'stand in the midst of' (that is, to be in a position to judge), to *define* meant to 'give bounds to', to *conceive* meant to 'take up', just as we speak of *catching on* to a thing or *grasping* it. To *refute* once meant literally to *knock out* an argument. To *think* seems to have meant 'to handle'; *feel*, which we have seen meant to 'handle with the palm of the hand' and thence came to be used of the sense of touch, then of sensation generally, now is used also of emotion, subjectively.

In all these instances the transition was an immediate one, a psychic resultant: and at the time of its occurrence really no change at all. Yet, once the new meaning was current, it required no unusual analytic gift to realize that a transference had taken place.[1] Individuals recognize in the use of many words an original and a transferred meaning, and good speakers and poets have in all times, now more, now less consciously, refreshed and intensified these transferences, or imitated them. Thus poetic metaphor is an outgrowth of the natural transferences of normal speech. It was a general transition, no doubt, when people spoke of *ruffled* or of *deep* or of *stormy* feelings; this general usage was revived and deepened when, to quote a very well chosen example, Wordsworth wrote:

The gods approve
The depth and not the tumult of the soul.

The usual poetic metaphors, then, are individual creations on the model of the regular linguistic transference. The picturesque saying that 'Language is a book of faded metaphors' is exactly the reverse of reality, where poetry is rather a blazoned book of language.

Individual semantic change appears also in a great many namings. Most towns in the United States, for instance, are named after English and other places: *Boston, Lynn, Plymouth, New York, Cairo, Troy,* or after people: *St. Louis, Bismarck.* The *magnet* is named from a place in Asia Minor, and *copper* after the island of *Cyprus*. The word *money* meant originally the 'mint', which was named in

---

[1] It does not concern us here that such popular realization always distorts the process, looking upon it as a deliberate intellectual action, rather than an unconscious development.

Rome from the close-by temple of Juno *Monēta,* this last being perhaps the family name of some old Roman clan for whom the temple was named. So we speak of *Ohm's* or *Grimm's* law. Probably a great many other words are the result of individual transference: *electricity*, for instance, was derived from the Greek word for 'amber', a substance used in producing it, by some individual. This is true of most precise scientific terms. People's names furnish words, all probably by way of individual transference; thus, in English to *burke*, to *boycott:* Burke was a certain Edinburgh murderer, Boycott a hated Irish landlord who suffered this form of persecution. We speak, similarly, of a *Xanthippe*, of a *Quixotic* action, of *Homeric* laughter, of *tantalizing* a person (Tantalus), and so on.

It is not always easy to say, however, whether a given transference was originally individual or communal. The use of names of animals for people seems, for instance, to be a general tendency, but the individual cases are so characteristic that we must suspect individual mots to have started such locutions as calling a man an *ass*, a *hog*, a *fox*, or an *ox*, a child a *monkey*, a woman a *mouse* or a *goose* or *hen*. Similar are such expressions as *whitecaps* or, in French, *moutons* 'sheep' for the white crests of waves. The Romance languages have number of clever derivations of this kind that make the impression of individual creations: French (and English) *caprice* is derived from a word for 'goat', *se pavanner* 'to puff oneself up, to strut' from a word for 'peacock', the Spanish *moscardon* 'bore, insistent, bothersome person' from *moscarda* 'a gadfly' and *calabazada* 'a blow in the head' from *calabaza* 'a gourd, calabash'. Transferences embodied in metaphoric expressions extending over more than one word are equally common. The origin of *fighting windmills* is thus well known. *Tempering the wind to the shorn lamb,* often attributed to Sterne, though it seems to have occurred before him, is no doubt also an individual creation. Such expressions as to be *hand and (in) glove* seem also to be individual, for different languages differ in the metaphor employed; thus the German says 'to be one heart and soul', the French 'two heads under one cap', the Italian 'one soul in two bodies', Spanish 'nail and flesh'. We have seen how transferences that were never fully conscious and have become almost entirely mechanized may be revived by a poet who gives them a new turn. When Shakspere speaks of *taking up arms against a sea of troubles*, the violence of the expression rouses our appreciation of the more literal values of the words.

This more literal value of words, especially where the transfer is an individual one, may be obscured or forgotten. The transferred word is thus left in an inexplicable meaning and may come to be associated with some other that is historically not connected at all. We shall meet this process again as 'popular etymology'. Thus *Welsh rabbit*, a jocular individual creation, has failed to meet understanding and been assimilated by many speakers to *rare-bit*. In German there are a number of unintelligible proverbs due to popular etymologizing. *Sein Schäfchen ins Trockne bringen* 'to bring one's little sheep into the dry place' is used in the sense of our 'looking out for A number 1'. It is due to the failure to understand the dialectal form, in which the thing brought to the dry place is *Schepken* 'little ship'. Similarly *Maulaffen feilhalten*, used in the sense of 'to loaf around, to stand gaping', means literally 'to have for sale *Maulaffen*'; what these are no one knows: the word looks like a compound of *Maul* 'mouth, maw, snout' and *Affen* 'monkeys'. The expression is an assimilated form of a dialectal *Mul apen halden* 'to hold one's mouth open'.

Where phonetic change causes an automatic sound-variation, semantic change may destroy the automatism by transferring one or both forms to different or limited uses, — giving rise, thus, to two words or forms instead of one. The English spirant-voicing after unaccented vowels produced a by-form of the word *off* with voiced spirant, namely *of* (p. 215), which was used in unaccented position. The frequent use of the accented form as adverb and of the unaccented as preposition brought about an association in this sense. One came now to use *off* even where the adverb was unstressed (*He did not fall off, he jumped off*), and *of* even where the preposition was stressed (*of and for the people*). The same development may take place where the two forms are the result of analogic change. In an older stage of German there was a verb which today is in the infinitive *gedeihen* 'to thrive'; it had a participle which would be today *gedungen* 'thriven'. A more regular analogic participle *gediegen*, however usurped this use, and the old participle came to be used only in the transferred sense of 'excellent, strong'. It has since been lost in this meaning also. Today a still more regular analogic formation *gediehen* serves as participle of *gedeihen*, and *gediegen* has in its turn passed over into the meaning 'solid, excellent'. Further examples of such 'correlative' semantic change, as it has been called, are the English plurals *clothes* [klowz] with transferred meaning, and the analogic *cloths* [klɔðz] or [klɔθs] in meaning directly corresponding to the singular; or such formations as the analogic *unpractical* 'not practical', used where the shifted sense of the older negative form *impractical* is not intended; so also *unmoral* beside *immoral*.

Thus, as the cultural and intellectual life of a people grows, new experiences, assimilated at first to the old, are designated by the old words or analogic formations from them, until in time the word-stock that once expressed only the most concrete and simple experiences is available for philosophic and scientific discourse of any desired refinement.

6. The ultimate conditions of change in language. Change in language in thus due to the inevitable shifting of the conditions under which speech is carried on. This is most obvious in the case of semantic change: any new experience is assimilated to the old and expressed by the old word, which thus has changed its meaning, — a change which may become fixed by the lapse of the original use. Similarly, analogic change alters the form of a word by an assimilation to another word or set of words that is semantically associated, and the conditions underlying this process, — the weakening of the supplanted form and the strengthening of the inducing elements, — are again conditions which must constantly arise as the subjects of thought and discourse, the beliefs about the interrelations of phenomena, and the material interests of a people develop. Phonetic change is also, no doubt, the result of changes in the conditions of speech, even though here the alteration in the conditions is not, as a rule, traceable.

In accordance with all this, we are frequently able to recognize the outer conditions which bring about a semantic change, — a recognition which is one of the chief aims of etymologic study, — we are, further, able to see in analogic change a constant adaptation of the speech-habits to more and more harmonious relation with experience, and even in the little-understood processes of sound-change the total result, at any rate, is a lessening of the amount and complication of articulatory movement that is connected with a given element of experience. Two questions at once suggest themselves. To what extent does the history of languages, in accord with all this, show advance in mentality? And: Is it possible to trace in any language the mental characteristics of the nation which speaks it?

As to the former question, there is no doubt that the changes of language are not a chaos of haphazard and conflicting alteration, but an evolutionary process. Just as no individual, to the day of his death, ceases learning to speak, so mankind is ever altering its speech to more suitable forms. We have seen that phonetic change bears the appearance of a constant adaptation and re-adaptation, that analogic change tends to bring about the expression of similar semantic content by uniform instead of varied articulations, and that semantic change even more directly leads to the apt expression of what is at any time the content of thought. We must keep in mind, however, that language is traditional and social: tendencies toward alteration are constantly stifled by the conventional articulations, forms, words, and constructions which the speaker hears from others, — for the hearing of the conventional forms reawakens the older impressions, as opposed to the innovation. It is only when a tendency to alteration corresponds to the mental predisposition of a large part of the community that it gradually gains ground. Language is thus not extensively subject to conscious change: its development is by a gradual selective evolution, unconsciously made by the speakers, who merely use those forms of speech which present themselves most directly for articulation. As the correspondence of a new form of speech with the remaining speech-habits, and with the relations of experience, must, if the new form is to find acceptance, outweigh the mere habituation of an otherwise less adapted older form, the change, when it does take place, will usually be a step in advance. We may accordingly expect to see in every language a slow but certain progress in adaptation to the forms of experience.

This is clearly apparent in the broader outlines of the history of languages. The older stages show us complicated formations, by dint of which a fairly complex experience is without analysis or with but partial analysis expressed in a single word. An action with its actor, mode, manner, tense, circumstances, and objects affected may, for instance, appear in a single word. Such words as the already quoted Nahwatl *ninakakwa* 'I-meat-eat' or *okiketškotonke* 'They-him-neck-cut (past)', i. e. 'They cut his throat', or the Tsimshian [ḁdaïe:] 'to walk in the dark', or, for that matter, the Latin *amāvisset* 'he (she, it) would have loved', illustrate this. We may consider such words as indicative of an older state of language, in which the purely emotional responses of pre-linguistic times may be conceived as having barely developed into a repetition of the same sound-sequences under similar experiences. It is an advance when all but one of the more material elements receive only anaphoric-personal expression in the single word and are more explicitly mentioned by cross-reference, as in the Aztec *nikkwa in nakatl* 'I-it-eat, the meat' or in the quoted Latin word, e. g. *Pater amāvisset* 'The-father, he-would-have-loved'. It is a further step in advance when the value of the cross-reference elements is lost by semantic change ('condensation') and the words bear each a separate meaning, though the formerly cross-referring forms are still conventionally used together in congruence, as when in English we use *loves* with an actor in the third person singular, but with the other persons say *love*. When at last these habits also have been removed, we come to more unified words; thus we use a form like *may* without regard to person and number of the actor.

Even here the word expresses the tense as well as the action itself: we should, perhaps, call it a step in advance, if the tense also came to be expressed by a separate word, as in *I am writing, I was writing*. Word-composition may thus be an heirloom from the days when what we now call a compound represented the regular type of word, — that is, when words regularly contained two or more material semantic units. It is conceivable, under that condition, that some much-used member of compounds with a very general sense, like that of 'thing', could lose its specific meaning, until compounds of which it formed part represented but one material element, as opposed to others that still represented two or more. Thus the Nahwatl 'absolutive', as in *nakatl* 'meat' or 'It is meat', may originally have been a compound, the semantic fading of whose final member (*-tl*) first allowed people to express the idea of 'meat' outside of compounds, such as *ninakakwa* 'I-meat-eat'. The same may be true of the Primitive Indo-European nominative-suffix -*s*, which may have been originally a final member of compounds and, by losing its material value, have become the means of liberating an idea like *$*e\widehat{k}wo$-s* 'horse' from exclusive use in such compounds as *$*e\widehat{k}wo$-domo-s* 'horse-tamer'.

However all this may be, it is certain that we find in all languages a constant diminution of the unanalyzed content of single words, a lessening of cross-reference, congruence, and government in favor of explicit discursive expression, or, to look at the same thing from another point of view, a growing constancy in the form of words, as opposed to morphologic variation. In the older stages material elements are viewed either in connected groups (compound words) or, if alone, then only in some particular relation as to time, space, number, manner, and the like, and as to each other (inflected words); it is but gradually that the speech of man attains a fuller analysis of experience, an analysis into simpler independently recurring elements. Thus the earliest scientifically attainable stage of English shows us eight cases and three numbers of nouns in three genders, most variously and irregularly inflected, with adjectives agreeing in full congruence, a cross-referring verb containing mention of the actor and inflecting by cumbrous, complicated, and highly irregular prefixation, infixation, suffixation, and sound-variation in three persons and three numbers in two voices, all in a variety of modes and tenses, the latter based principally on manner of action, secondarily on relative time. If we contrast this with our modern brief forms and comparatively regular inflection and our simple sentence-structure, in which congruence and government play but a small part and cross-reference none, the advance is unmistakable.

As all such development is gradual and unconscious, we must not be surprised, on the other hand, when we see, alongside the progressive simplification, an occasional formation of the old kind arising, or a sound-change complicating what was formerly simpler. English has been rapidly losing derivational complexities, yet we find old compounds denoting manner by a second member Old English *-līce* 'in the manner of', becoming the regular means of deriving adverbs from adjectives, and this second element becoming phonetically reduced to an otherwise meaningless suffix *-ly*, as in *quickly, slowly, sharply*. The same thing has happened in the history of the Romance languages, where the Latin *mente* 'with a mind' came to be used as a suffix in the same sense, e. g. French *lent* 'slow' *lentement* 'slowly' (would be Latin *lentā mente* 'with a slow mind'). While in these instances the process may still be looked upon as a liberation of the single word from the compound through semantic fading of the other member, that is hardly possible when in the Romance languages we see a new tense-inflection arising from an older syntactic collocation: Late Latin *amāre habeo* 'I have to (am to, shall) love' became the modern Romance future, the second word being reduced to a suffix, e. g. French *j'aimerai* 'I shall love', — a counter-development which well illustrates the complexity of linguistic progress. It is only by dint of innumerable changes and readjustments and after the most various tendencies have conflicted and come into harmony, that simplification can occur, — and it is, in consequence, only by careful examination of the historical details that we can ever obtain a just idea of the growth of language.

To what extent languages are adapted to the national character of the speakers is a far more difficult question; but the difficulty lies in the vagueness of the latter term. At the present state of our knowledge the character of a nation is very much what our personal bias makes us wish to think it. The most completely known of national activities is language; it is very difficult, for instance, to decide what of a nation's art or religion is truly communal and what individual in origin.

It is possible, where we know that a nation has changed its language, to trace characteristics of the earlier language in the nation's peculiar use of the newer, and these stable characteristics, as it were, of a nation's speech, have the first right to be called national. Such a characteristic are the [ṭ, ḍ] sounds of the languages of India (p. 220). Another possible instance is the following. Irish is like English a modern form of Primitive Indo-European. Unlike this language and unlike English and the other sister-languages (with an exception to be noted), it has a few remarkable characteristics. One is the tolerance for phonetically divergent forms of the same word without corresponding semantic variation beyond what is implied in the mere existence of the forms (p. 102, f.), — as in the example *tà ba* 'There are cows' but *a va* 'his cows', and the like. In fact, there is a general lack of stability of the word-unit. Another peculiarity of Irish is the tendency to identify the emotionally dominant idea of the sentence with the central element of the predicate of an abstract subject and verb: *It's his brother he's cheating;* the latter feature appears also in the English spoken by Irish people. It is possible that the Indo-European speech of Ireland received these peculiarities from an earlier language which it superseded.

At any rate, it so happens that the Latin which replaced in France a sister-language of Irish and developed into Modern French, shows some of the same peculiarities. It gives little phonetic recognition to the word-boundary (p. 99, ff.), containing even such forms as *du* 'of the', *au* 'to the' (masculine) which, while plainly felt as two words, *de* (*à*) and *le* (compare, for instance the feminine *de la, à la* and the form used before vowels, *de l', à l'*), are phonetically indivisible, [dy, o]. French is tolerant of double forms of words, used, as in Irish, not automatically and yet without genuine semantic differentiation; such doublets, for instance, as [vu] and [vuz] 'you' or [a] and [at] 'has' are distributed not entirely by the occurrence of the longer form before vowel ([vu fɛt] 'you do' but [vuz ave] 'you have'; [ɛl a] 'she has' but [at ɛl] 'has she?'), for this form occurs only before words closely connected in certain relations of meaning. The identification of emotionally dominant element by peculiar syntactic position is also prevalent: *C'est eux qui l'ont fait* 'It's they who have done it', *C'est là que je l'ai vu*

'It's there that I saw him', *C'est moi qu'ils ont battu* 'It's me they beat'.

Thus future research in what may be called comparative phonology, morphology, and syntax may reveal national linguistic habits to which any language a people may come to speak is subjected. It will then remain to compare and relate these with such other characteristics of the nation as ethnologic study shall have ascertained.

All this, then, brings us to the question of the relation between language and race, to the question of what people speak alike and what differently, and to the consideration of the various changes in this distribution, — in short, to the external history of language.

CHAPTER VIII.
EXTERNAL CHANGE OF LANGUAGES.

1. Language never uniform. We have repeatedly seen that language, far from being an object or an independent organism of some kind, is merely a set of habits. Such similarity as there is between successive utterances is due, therefore, entirely to the psychic assimilative effects of earlier utterances upon later. The assimilative predisposition is in every individual constantly changing, for, if nothing else, then at least the utterance last spoken will alter the conditions of the next one. We may say, then, that the language even of a single individual is never exactly the same in any two utterances. What unity there is is due to the assimilative effect of earlier upon later actions.

In this regard the effect of the speech one has heard from others is the most important factor. In early childhood the individual's language is entirely in imitation of it, and even later, when one's own habits are reliable, one hears much more than one speaks. This, of course, is the link between the speech of different individuals which makes language a communal or social, not an individual phenomenon. Nevertheless, the predispositions of any two individuals will never be identical. They will differ more, as a rule, than the successive states of one and the same individual because, in addition to constitutional differences, the past language-experience of the two speakers is always different. Even more truly than the language of every utterance may be called unique, it may be said that every speaker has his own peculiar linguistic habits. These, in fact, are in everyday experience often noticed as idiosyncrasies of pronunciation, construction, and vocabulary: 'The style is the man'.

In spite of these individual divergences, the circumstance that language is our means of communication and, as such, is learned both in the beginning and all through life from our fellow-speakers, assures an extensive uniformity. The associative processes which produce an utterance are the effect of other people's utterances which we have heard from infancy to the present. Consequently a close-knit social group in which communication takes place frequently between all members possesses a relatively uniform set of speech-habits.

It would be very difficult, if not impossible, to find such a community. Everywhere there are groups of individuals among whom there is more communication than between members of the group and outsiders. One need think only of the family, the neighborhood, the trades and professions, the pleasures, games, vices, creeds, parties, and the social, economic, and educational strata. The result of the more lively communication within such groups is, of course, in every case, a relative uniformity which is at the same time a divergence from the speech of those outside the group. Even superficial observation shows us family dialects, neighborhood phrases, trade and professional·vocabularies, jargons such as those of the race-track or the base-ball field, speech of the slums, of the middle class, of the aristocrats, — and so on, without end. Any one speaker's habits present a combination of those different dialects which he has heard and spoken, a unique combination modified, further, by individual factors.

The most important of these dialect-divisions have always been the local. These are of various degrees. Where there are several local groups communicating freely with each other, each group will have its dialect, but the differences between these dialects will not be great enough to destroy mutual intelligibility. This condition is found, for example, in European countries, where often every village speaks its own dialect. When such connected groups cover a very large area and communication between members of those at the extreme ends is rare, these extreme dialects may be mutually unintelligible, although, as each dialect of the whole group understands those near it, they are connected by an unbroken chain of communication. Within what would otherwise be such a group there may, however, be some partial barrier, a political or tribal boundary, a river or a range of hills, and the like, — which lessens intercommunication of the two sides without preventing it. There we may find a decided break in resemblance, even though the dialects on the two sides are still intelligible to each other. Finally, a barrier of the kinds described, or one more impenetrable, may divide mutually unintelligible languages.

Where a barrier of the last kind exists, reflection and, especially, scientific research may discover some resemblance between the languages. A Norwegian and an English sailor who learned each others' languages would realize that they presented, in spite of being mutually unintelligible, considerable similarity, as opposed, for instance, to Greek or to Malay. Scientific study shows English and Greek to possess great morphologic and syntactic similarity and an original, though phonetically obscured resemblance of vocabulary, which mere reflection on the part of ordinary speakers of the languages would not discover; between these languages and Malay on the other hand, no such similarity has been discovered by science. We speak, then, of 'related' and 'unrelated' languages, according to our lights.

2. **Increase of uniformity.** Wherever history shows us anything of the past, we find barriers to intelligibility decreasing. Our continent, north of Mexico, once harbored a few million Indians speaking over a hundred, perhaps several hundreds, of mutually unintelligible languages; today this area contains more than a hundred million inhabitants, nearly all of whom speak English.

Such increase of uniformity occurs in various ways. Conquest may, as in America, partly annihilate the conquered und partly assimilate them to the language of the conquerors. Where the latter are less numerous the assimilating process is commoner, but seems to fail, if the vanquished are culturally superior. The Romans, who conquered Italy, Iberia, Gaul, Dacia, and Greece, were able to impose their language on the people of all these countries except the culturally superior Greeks. Differences of language may disappear, if one language is politically or culturally supreme: this is often the last phase of a preceding conquest, as in the gradual spread of English in Wales and Ireland, or of Russian in Siberia. Languages of large communicative value may spread as second languages of speakers for commercial and similar purposes: so English, French, Spanish, Hindustani, Malay, and others are spoken more or less inexactly by large numbers of people whose native language is less widely known. In this way arise trade jargons, the various forms of Lingua Franca, Pidgin English, 'Chinook' and the like.

3. Decrease of uniformity does not offset the increase. This growing uniformity is in part — and only in part — offset by a constant process of differentiation. A language spreading over a large area does not remain uniform. The various barriers to communication result gradually in a differentiation at first into dialects, then, often, into mutually unintelligible languages.

Thus, at the dawn of history we find Greece, many of the surrounding islands, and a strip of the coast of Asia Minor speaking numerous, in the main mutually intelligible dialects. The cultural and commercial supremacy of Athens and the districts of Asia Minor resulted in the spread of a uniform Greek speech, based chiefly on their dialects and called the *Koiné* ('common language'), over all of this territory except, it seems, a small district around Sparta. By the early centuries of our era this language was uniformly spoken, but dialect-differentiation soon set in, and by the nineteenth century the different communicative conditions had resulted in a set of dialects as unlike one another as were those of ancient Greece. It now seems that the speech of Athens will again become the common language of all Greece.

In Italy earliest history shows us a welter of the most various languages and dialects, many, so far as science can tell, wholly unrelated to others, some mutually unintelligible, though somewhat similar, and still others existing in groups of mutually intelligible dialects. Through military and political supremacy the Romans gradually extended their language, Latin, over all of Italy; their later conquests carried it over what is now Spain, Portugal, France, Latin Switzerland, and Roumania. It may be that the inhabitants of these countries who learned Latin spoke it from the first in a form so much assimilated to their earlier speech-habits that, say Portugal and Roumania never could have understood each other. At any rate, dialectal differentiation at once set in, and, as the Roman power decreased, the link of communication which had connected these dialects failed. Today we have five or six mutually unintelligible languages, each broken into a number of continuous dialects, such as those of Italy or France. These dialects correspond, often, to political, tribal, or geographic barriers: they are being superseded, at present, by languages of important centers, as, for instance, those of France by the speech of Paris, and those of Spain by Castilian. Spanish and Portuguese, in turn, have spread by conquest over the southern part of the Americas, where they have superseded numerous Indian languages. The unification has here vastly outweighed the differentiation, for the modern Romance languages, divisible into five or six mutually unintelligible groups, within each of which dialectal differentiation is limited and is rapidly disappearing, represent the extinction of dozens, probably hundreds, of languages of Europe and America. These old languages were spoken each by a few thousand people, the Romance languages are spoken by many millions.

At the time of our earliest records, from the seventh to the tenth century of our era, what is now Holland, Germany, and part of England was a territory of some dialectal differentiation; yet it appears that an Englishman could then understand a North German. The dialectal break that there was between the English dialects and those of the mainland was due, of course, to the emigration of the English tribes in the fifth century. This differentiation went on until English and the continental speech became mutually unintelligible. At the same time the differentiation within each of these groups became so great that the speakers of the different English dialects could often not understand each other, and the same was true of the dialects of the continent. Today all of these dialects are, however, disappearing before the spread of three favored forms of speech: Standard English, Dutch, and German. While the speakers of the old dialects are not succeeding in speaking these standardized dialects without some assimilation to the forms of their local speech, — Standard German as spoken in Bavaria differing much from that, say, of Mecklenburg, Standard English of Scotland from that of Kent, — yet they can understand one another's forms within each group. Meanwhile English, for instance, has superseded most of the Celtic speech of England, German much of the Baltic and Slavic of what is now Germany. We must not forget, also, the increase in population: the England of King Alfred's time had perhaps two million inhabitants, only part of whom spoke English. Meanwhile Standard English has spread to Ireland, North America, and Australia, and has become the uniform speech of many millions. The differentiation which there is in Standard English will probably never rise to the point of unintelligibility, for printing, rapid travel, and commercial intercourse are constituting communicative bonds more close, probably, than those which two-hundred years ago existed between the north and south of the little island of Britain.

4. Inferences from historic conditions. These historic instances allow of certain general conclusions. Where we find an area in which a number of mutually intelligible dialects are spoken, we infer that these are the result of differentiation of an older uniform speech. We do not hesitate to suppose, for instance, that the ancient Greek dialects were differentiated from a uniform prehistoric speech, which we call 'Primitive Greek', — just as the modern Greek dialects are divergent local forms of the Koiné. Similarly, we conclude that the earliest historic forms of English and the continental dialects of Holland and Germany were differentiated, during a period that we call 'pre-English', 'pre-Frisian', 'pre-Saxon', 'pre-Franconian', 'pre-Bavarian', etc., from a uniform prehistoric dialect, which we call 'Primitive West Germanic'.

Related languages we accordingly look upon as results of differentiation. Just as we see Portuguese, Spanish, French, Italian, and Roumanian diverging from Latin, we conclude, in every case where languages are, beyond the possibility of mere coincidence, alike, that their difference is due to gradual differentiation from a uniform speech. Among the Indians of North America we find, for instance, related languages spoken over three considerable pieces of territory. A large part of the northwestern interior from the Pacific coast to east of the Rocky Mountains; a few small bands in British Columbia and Washington and a strip of villages four-hundred miles long in Oregon and California; a large area of Arizona, New Mexico, western Texas, and Mexico; — these three districts, each embrace a number of mutually unintelligible languages, which, however, all present features of similarity that lead us to call them related (the 'Athapascan' family of languages) and to suppose that they are all divergent forms of a prehistoric uniform language ('Primitive Athapascan').

We have, of course, no right to suppose, in such cases, that the same number of people spoke the 'primitive' uniform language, or that it was spoken over the same area, as its later forms. It is possible, as mentioned, that the people of Portugal and those of Roumania could never have understood each other; it is certain that the people of these countries who learned Latin from the Romans never spoke it correctly enough to reach uniformity over the entire district. We can scarcely imagine a prehistoric Athapascan state of uniform language all over the West of our country: probably a comparatively large tribe broke up into parts which separated and then, after communication had ceased, became differentiated in speech, grew, linguistically assimilated other Indians, and again split into independent speech-communities.

It is very important, when we make these deductions, thus to keep in mind the exact meaning of our results. When we say that the West Germanic languages and dialects, — English, Frisian, Dutch, and German, — are differentiated forms of a uniform prehistoric language, which we call Primitive West Germanic, we have no right to assume anything about the exact manner in which the differentiation took place. For instance, Primitive West Germanic may have become differentiated by certain barriers in its territory, — by a religious confederation of certain of the clans, let us say, to which the other clans did not belong. A later splitting of the West Germanic group may not have coincided with this earlier division. Thus, before the emigration of the English there was a dialectal differentiation: some of the dialects changed an older [a] to [ε], saying, for instance, ðæt 'that' instead of ðat. The English who emigrated were part of those who had made this change; the Frisians, who had also made it, remained behind. There followed, of course, the great divergence of English from Frisian and all the other continental dialects, due to the overseas separation. Thus, in spite of the difference today between English on the one hand and the continental dialects on the other, we know that there was a time when English and Frisian belonged together, as opposed to all the others, — that the divergence of English from the mainland dialects was not the first differentiation to break the Primitive West Germanic unity. Had history not in this case favored us, we might be led to the wrong assumption that the first differentiation was the separation of English.

Primitive West Germanic, so far as its forms can be determined, and also the various historic West Germanic dialects, all show a decided resemblance to the languages of Iceland, Norway, Sweden, and Denmark. These languages, with their dialects, furnish another instance of differentiation from an earlier language. At present we find the dialect-division separating Iceland sharply from the rest. The remaining dialects are differentiated by lines running chiefly east and west, so that a dialect-belt will run, for instance, across a stretch of Norway and Sweden, regardless of present political boundaries. Had we no older records, we should, to be sure, deduce a Primitive Scandinavian or Primitive North Germanic parent-language, but the surmises which we might make on the basis of the modern dialects would be wrong. For our oldest records show us Norwegian and Icelandic almost alike: the divergence of the latter did not progress very far until some centuries after the settlement of Iceland by Norwegians a thousand years ago. Opposed to the almost uniform Icelandic-Norwegian or West-Scandinavian of the medieval records, we find Swedish and Danish closely alike: East-Scandinavian. This older division has, then, been superseded by developments in an entirely different direction. Thus, while it is safe to set up a uniform 'primitive' language, the process of differentiation itself may be obscured by repeated changes in various directions, as when more modern changes have crossed and in part obliterated the old division between West-Scandinavian and East-Scandinavian in favor of a new north-and-south division on the continent, opposed to a divergent Icelandic.

Of Primitive North Germanic (Primitive Norse, Primitive Scandinavian) a small amount is historically preserved in some of the runic inscriptions. Primitive West Germanic and Primitive North Germanic both closely resemble the language of a fourth-century Gothic Bible-translation used by the Goths in Italy. From this threefold relationship we deduce an older uniform language, Primitive Germanic, from which, in a period called pre-West-Germanic, pre-North-Germanic, and pre-East-Germanic ('pre-Gothic'), the three languages became differentiated. Here we must guard against the mistake into which we might in the other cases have fallen, had we lacked, — as here we do, — historic records. It is possible, for instance, that the threefold division which we know was preceded by an entirely different dialect-cleavage in Primitive Germanic. This would mean that such a division as Primitive West Germanic contains some dialectal differences dating from the Primitive Germanic time, and was therefore never wholly uniform after the original cleavage of Primitive Germanic. In so far as we insist that English, Dutch, Frisian, and German go back to an absolutely uniform older speech, that speech would then be Primitive Germanic; in so far as we considered only those features which today appear and ignored a possible but unauthenticated older dialect-cleavage, it would be Primitive West-Germanic.

The Germanic languages more distantly, though unmistakably resemble a number of languages of Europe and Asia. This resemblance is increased when we compare not the historic forms, but the various 'primitive' languages, such as Primitive Germanic and Primitive Greek, which we deduce from closely related groups. Thus the closely interrelated Baltic languages (Lithuanian, Lettish, and the now extinct Prussian) point to a Primitive Baltic, which, with Primitive Slavic, appearing historically differentiated in the modern Slavic languages (Russian, Polish, Bohemian or Čech, Servian, Bulgarian, etc.), points to a Primitive Balto-Slavic. The languages of Persia and Iran generally we derive from a Primitive Iranian, those of India that here come into consideration from a Primitive Indic; Primitive Iranian and Primitive Indic resemble each other so closely as to point unmistakably to Primitive Indo-Iranian ('Primitive Aryan') from which both are descended. Similarly we deduce a Primitive Armenian, Primitive Albanese, Primitive Italic (from Latin, Oscan, and Umbrian), and Primitive Celtic. All these 'primitive' languages, including Primitive Greek and Primitive Germanic, show so much similarity that we conclude that they are differentiated forms of a Primitive Indo-European, an ancient uniform language.

We must, however, again keep in mind all the limitations that require observation, if our conclusion is to have scientific value. In the first place, our conclusion does not justify us in supposing that the same number of people or the same districts that now speak the various Indo-European languages spoke Primitive Indo-European. We have, for instance, seen English spread from a million or less speakers to many millions, some of whom gave up another language for English, and, geographically, we have seen it spread from a part of England over almost all of the British Isles, most of North America, and Australia, not to speak of smaller colonies of English-speaking people all over the world. In so far as we insist upon Primitive Indo-European being a uniform state of speech, we must, in fact, assume that it was spoken by a homogeneous and therefore limited community, — a community of not more than a few thousand speakers.

Furthermore, we have no right to assume that Primitive Indo-European was carried bodily, as it were, into all the countries where Indo-European languages now exist. English, not Primitive Indo-European was carried to America. The branches of the Primitive Indo-European parent community surely altered their speech while migrating to those countries upon which they were to impose it. The people who in these countries had to learn the language of the dominant Indo-European-speaking immigrants surely spoke the new language in some approximation to their own, — of one such change at least we have good evidence (p. 220). These speakers of an implanted Indo-European may then have been instrumental in the further spread of the language. The deduction of a Primitive Indo-European speech does not, therefore, make probable any such improbabilities as that there was a time, say, when a man from the north of Europe could have understood a Greek or a Hindu.

Again, it is too common in history to see changes of language or culture in a people, to allow of our assuming that the present speakers of Indo-European languages are all descended, physically, from speakers of Primitive Indo-European. To all questions in this direction it can only be answered that anthropologists and ethnologists have found that language, culture, and physical descent are not coordinate in history. It even bids fair to appear that physical descent and physical characteristics are not coordinate. In other words, while we have knowledge of Indo-European languages, of a Primitive Indo-European language, and, to some extent, of the linguistic history which produced the former out of the latter, we know nothing about the people who spoke Primitive Indo-European, — nothing about their habitat, appearance, descent, or descendants, and of their culture only so much as is involved in our knowledge of their speech.

As to the process of cleavage of Primitive Indo-European also we must draw no hasty conclusions. There are certain phenomena in which the historic 'western' languages, namely, the Greek, Italic, Celtic, and Germanic, are apparently opposed to the 'eastern', Balto-Slavic, Indo-Iranian, Armenian, and Albanese. We find certain velar sounds in the former corresponding to sibilants in the latter, — in Primitive Indo-European they were probably palatals; — thus the word for 'hundred' is in Ancient Greek *he-katón*, in Latin *centum*, Old Irish *cēt*, Gothic *hund* (English *hund-red*; for the *h-* see Grimm's law, p. 208), but in Lithuanian *szimtas* (*sz* is [ʃ]), Avestan (an old Iranian language) *satəm*, Sanskrit *śatám*. It was supposed, accordingly, that this divergence represented the oldest dialectal cleavage of Primitive Indo-European into an eastern and a western dialect; the eastern languages were called the '*s-*' or '*satəm*' group, the western the '*k-*' or '*centum*' group. More careful observation, however, makes it probable that the cleavage into '*centum*' and '*satəm*' languages was not a dialectal cleavage of Primitive Indo-European, but that the languages have separately arrived at the historic forms. Aside from the peculiar position of Albanese between the Greek and Italic '*centum*' languages, there have recently been discovered in Central Asia (East Turkestan) manuscripts in an Indo-European language (to which has been given the name Tocharic) which has velar, not sibilant sounds in the corresponding words, (e. g. *känt* 'hundred'). Lithuanian, further, contains a number of words with velars

instead of the sibilants which such words as that for
'hundred' and the close resemblance of Baltic to Slavic
would lead us to expect. Finally, investigation has shown
that Indic, in spite of its close resemblance to Iranian,
never had sibilants in most of the words in question.
Thus it appears that the line of cleavage between velar
development and sibilant development of the Primitive
Indo-European palatals does not coincide with the other
lines of dialectal differentiation, and would perhaps still
less do so, had we records of intermediate dialects that
have been lost.

5. The process of differentiation. The uniformity
of linguistic habit in a community is maintained by the
common expressive predisposition of the speakers, due
to their having heard since infancy approximately the
same set of words, forms, and constructions. In so far as
this predisposition, owing to the necessarily divergent
experience of individuals, varies from speaker to speaker,
we find individual peculiarities of speech; in so far as it
varies for families, social strata, occupations, and the like,
we find the stratification of language mentioned at the
beginning of this chapter. The concurrence of the members of a community is known as *usage*. Usage, we know,
is constantly changing: sound-changes, analogic changes
and semantic development never cease; and the changes
of usage are never the same in any two separated communities. The differentiation of a uniform speech into dialects
and into separate languages takes place wherever there
is any interruption, absolute or relative, of communication.
Where geographic or social barriers have lessened communication we find the usage of the separated communities
diverging more and more, until at first well-defined dialects and then mutually unintelligible languages are found
to exist. This process of divergence is outweighed, as we

have seen, by the constant replacement of uniformity due to warlike, economic, or cultural domination of single communities.

6. Deduction of internal history from related forms. The case is frequent that we find historically a set of related dialects or languages but lack records of the uniform speech from which we must suppose that they have become differentiated. If we had no records, for instance, of Latin, we should speak of it as 'Primitive Romance', that is, as the uniform parent-speech of the Romance languages. The divergences of usage which differentiate these languages would have to be reconciled in this 'primitive' language. If we found, for instance, the word for 'father' in French *père* [pɛːr], in Spanish and in Italian *padre*, we might be doubtful as to what was the form in the common parent-speech, from which these forms by divergent phonetic and analogic changes had become differentiated. We might perhaps set up a 'Primitive Romance' **padre* or **pedre*. The Latin forms, accusative *patre(m)* and ablative *patre* show us that the *t* became *d* and was in French finally dropped, and that this language also changed the old *a* to *è;* furthermore, we find similar developments in many parallel forms.

Where the older uniform language is not accessible, our reconstructions are, correspondingly, most uncertain. Nevertheless, they have a great value as formulae. The word 'father' is in Old English *fæder* (for the *d* see p. 59, f.); in the oldest Frisian (eleventh century) we find *feder;* the north German dialects show the oldest form (ninth century) *fader;* the south German (ninth century) *fater*. As the common prehistoric form from which these were differentiated we set up a 'Primitive West Germanic' **fader*, supposing the English and Frisian to have changed *a* to *e*, and the South German *d* to *t.* The starred form thus set up is a formula in the sense that other words also show the same correspondences of sound. It means, therefore, that the word 'father' in the West Germanic speech-group is composed of the sounds indicated, to wit: (1) that which everywhere appears as *f*, (2) that which appears in English and Frisian as *e* and in the other dialects as *a*, — symbolized by *a* in our formula, (3) that which appears as *d* in all but the south German dialects, where it is *t*, — symbolized by *d*, (4) that which appears everywhere as an unaccented *e*, (5) that which appears everywhere in our group as *r*. Thus, to illustrate sound (3), we set up a Primitive West Germanic **daudo* for the Old English *deād* (modern *dead*), the Old Frisian *dād*, the Old Low (i. e. North) German *dōd*, and the Old High (i. e. South) German *tōt*. Here the symbol *d* recurs; the *au* is a similar token for Old English *ēa*, Old Frisian *ā*, north German *ŏ*, and south German *ō* before dentals or *h* (otherwise south German *au*); the final *-o* is due to considerations which we may here overlook. Our Primitive West Germanic forms, then, are mere formulae until they find some kind of corroboration. If they find this, it will appear that in the Primitive West Germanic speech-community *d* was spoken and that in the pre-South German development there was a change from this *d* to *t*. Or, if further facts were to appear showing that our Primitive West Germanic form was, in absolute phonetic value, wrong, then a Primitive West Germanic *t*, changing in all the dialects but South German to *d*, would be indicated.

The existence of North Germanic (Scandianavian) and East Germanic (Gothic) forms gives us the possibility of testing our West Germanic results. The Old Icelandic and, it is supposed, also the Primitive North Germanic form of our word 'father' is *faðer*, the Gothic *fadar* (with the *d* pronounced *ð*, as certain internal conditions in Gothic conclusively show). These forms indicate that our Primitive West Germanic *fader was in all probability (not with absolute certainty!) correct as to the a and the d: the latter because the voiced d is nearer to the ð of the other languages than the alternative of t. The comparison of the three Germanic branches is symbolized in the formula of a Primitive Germanic *fáðer, — with accent on the first syllable, as in all the historic dialects. This form, if literally correct, indicates a change of ð to d in pre-West Germanic and a change of e in the unaccented syllable (as other words show, only before r) to a in pre-East Germanic. If wrong, our formula would still express the general correspondence of d to ð, of -er to -ar in these languages.

Our Primitive Germanic form is again tested by the Primitive Indo-European correspondences. We find the word 'father' to be in Sanskrit *pitā́* (accusative *pitáram*), in Avestan *pita* (accusative *pitarəm*), in Ancient Greek *patḗr*, in Latin *pater*, in Old Irish *athair*, and in Armenian *hair*.

The correspondence of initial p of other languages in this and other words to Germanic f makes it extremely probable (but not certain!) that p was the older sound, changed in the pre-Germanic development to f; for a change of an older f to p independently in Sanskrit, Greek, Latin, and the other languages (which in other than initial position also in part show p) would be a very improbable coincidence; — as would also the origin of all these sounds from some sound not represented in any of the historic languages, e. g. an m. Nevertheless, should we in spite of this be wrong, the p in our Primitive Indo-European formula would still be a convenient symbol for the general correspondence of Germanic f, Sanskrit, Greek, and Latin p (Irish initial lost, Armenian initial h). This correspondence reappears in other words, such as that for 'cattle', where we set up, — on the basis of Gothic *faihu* (pronounced *fehu*), Old Icelandic *fē*, Old English *fēo* (modern *fee;* for the change of meaning see p. 244), Old Low German *fehu*, and Old High German *fihu*, — a Primitive Germanic *fehu, which stands beside Latin *pecu*, Sanskrit *paśu* (with sibilant, cf. p. 272), Lithuanian *pekus* (with velar stop, cf. p. 272, f.). Hence, be it with literal value, or, what is less probable but also possible, with only symbolic value, we set up the first sound of our Primitive Indo-European word as *p-*.

To return to the word 'father', the *a* of the different languages, as opposed to the *i* of Sanskrit and Avestan would appear as the more probable earlier form. We find, however, that in other cases an *a* of the other languages is found also in Sanskrit and Avestan, as in Old Icelandic *aka* 'to ride, drive', Primitive Germanic *akeđi 'he drives', Old Irish (*ad-*)*aig*, Latin *agit*, Ancient Greek *ágei*, Armenian *atsem* 'I lead, bring', corresponding to Sanskrit *ájati* 'he leads', Avestan *azaiti*. Consequently we suppose that Primitive Indo-European had two vowels, represented in most languages, owing to sound-change, by *a*, but distinct in Indo-Iranian as *a* and *i*. This supposition is by no means certain and has been disputed; it receives corroboration, however, from certain conditions of vowel-variation in the different languages. The Primitive Indo-European vowel which preceded the *i* of Indo-Iranian and the *a* of the other languages we represent by the symbol ə.

The third sound of our word has caused much trouble. After Grimm's law (see p. 208), by which the old *p-* of our word, for instance, became Germanic *f-*, had been established, it was expected that the *t* of the other languages should correspond to a Germanic *þ*[1]), not a *đ*, —

---

1) þ is the Germanic sign for [Θ].

as, for example, in the word 'brother': Sanskrit *bhrā́tā* (accusative *bhrā́taram*), Avestan *brāta* (accusative *brātarəm*), Ancient Greek *phrā́ter* ('fraternity brother'), Latin *frāter* Old Irish *brāthir*, Old Bulgarian *bratŭ*, *bratrŭ*, Lithuanian *broterė́lis* (with diminutive suffix), and Primitive Germanic *broþer (seen in Gothic *brōðar*, Old Icelandic *brōðer*, Old English *brōþor*, Old Frisian *brōther*, Old Low German *brōther*, Old High German *bruoder*). This difficulty was at last solved by Verner (p. 216): after the Primitive Indo-European unvoiced stops (e. g. *t*) had in pre-Germanic become spirants (þ) these spirants became voiced, if they followed an unaccented vowel (as in the Primitive Indo-European word for 'father', where the Sanskrit and Greek accent shows the second syllable to have been stressed). It was not till after this spirant-voicing that the accent in pre-Germanic was thrown universally on the first syllable; whence the Primitive Germanic *fáðer.

The next sound again causes difficulty. Sanskrit and Avestan show an *a*, the other languages an *e*, and for a long time it was believed that the former was the Primitive Indo-European sound. It was discovered, however, that the Indo-Iranian languages also once had an *e*. This appears in the fact that velar sounds are palatalized (p. 214) in these languages before those *a*'s to which *e* corresponds in the other languages. For instance, the Primitive Indo-European enclitic word for 'and' *$q^{u}e$, appearing in Latin as *que*, in Ancient Greek as *te* (from Primitive Greek *$q\breve{u}e$), in Gothic as *-h* (from Primitive Germanic *hwe), is in Sanskrit *ca* and in Avestan *ča*. Thus the *e* of the European languages is in such cases assured as the more original, Primitive Indo-European sound, which in pre-Indo-Iranian first palatalized a preceding velar and then changed to *a*, coinciding there with the Primitive Indo-European *a*. This probability of a Primitive Indo-European *e* corroborates our supposition that the vowel in Primitive Germanic was *e*, not the Gothic *a*. The long quantity of the vowel in Sanskrit and Greek in our word also appears original from a number of comparisons.

As to the final *r*, various considerations have led to the conclusion that in Primitive Indo-European there was an automatic sound-variation by which the *r* was kept before certain following sounds, especially vowels, and lost before others. In the different languages one or the other of the resulting forms was analogically generalized.

Hence we get, all in all, the formula of a Primitive Indo-European *pəté or *pətér. In part the absolute phonetic value of this formula may be doubtful, but it serves none the less well as a brief symbol for the various correspondences between the Indo-European languages: correspondences which could not be otherwise succinctly expressed. The correspondences so symbolized, moreover, aid us in shaping our Primitive Germanic formula: thus they assure us of an *e* rather than an *a* in the second syllable of this word. In the word for 'dead' the Gemanic forms alone would lead us to set up a formula of one syllable; it is the Indo-European relationship of the word which shows us that in Primitive Germanic and in Primitive West Germanic it must have had two syllables (cf. the formula above, p. 275). Beginning with the Primitive Indo-European formula, then, with its rather relative value, the history of the word 'father' can be traced, with more and more certainty as we go on, to the present time; and the same is true of all the lexical, phonetic, morphologic, and syntactic features of the language.

The method of thus tracing the history of languages wherever a number of related languages are given, is known as the *comparative method*. The vista which it opens to us for English presents the development from a primitive to the modern state. For, by any criteria we have of such things, 'Primitive' Indo-European was really a language of decidedly primitive aspect. It had three genders, three numbers, and eight cases of nouns, adjectives, and pronouns, and several voices, modes, manners, and tenses of verbs, each in three persons and three numbers, according to the person and number of the actor. All these were inflected with great complication and irregularity, by means of suffixes and intricate sound-variation, especially of vowels, together with some infixation and prefixation, including highly irregular reduplicated forms. The derivation, also, was complex, different suffixes, as also in inflection, demanding shifts of accent and sound-variation in the kernel of the word. Composition was frequent and was accompanied by changes of form in the members of the compound as opposed to their independent form as simple words. The syntax identified, as today, actor and subject, but in the predication of a quality the abstract verb could be omitted, as in Latin (p. 111). As the verb included pronominal mention of the actor, cross-reference as well as government related actor to action. The cases of nouns were used in government, — that is, the different case-forms expressed relations in which the noun stood to the verb or to other nouns. The adjective varied in congruence with the noun which it modified. The development from that time to this can be traced with increasing certainty as one approaches the testimony of narrower and narrower ranges of comparison.

7. Interaction of dialects and languages. The results of the comparative method do not extend to a set of phenomena which, accordingly, must be set aside wherever this method is used. As the comparative method is based upon the unity of sound-change with regard to different words within any dialect, it cannot be applied to words and forms which have come into one dialect from another dialect. Such words and forms, however, are very common. Wherever there is communication between different speech-groups, one or both come to use words heard in the language of the other, — words, usually, which have been associated with the appearance of some hitherto unknown object or idea introduced by the foreign people: as when we speak of *chiffons* and *ruches* by their French names, or of *Sprachgefühl, Ablaut, Umlaut, Zeitgeist, Wanderlust, Pretzels* by their German. If the two speech-groups that are in contact are mutually intelligible dialects, the borrowing may be quite general; if they are unintelligible, the mediators are those who, more or less perfectly, have learned the foreign speech.

The disturbance of usual phonetic conditions appears in such a word as *street*, High German *Straße*, which, normally, would point to a Primitive West Germanic *strǣtu*. This should then correspond, by Grimm's law, to a Latin word with *d* for the second *t* (the first, standing after spirant, is unaffected); but the Latin word we find is *strāta (via)* 'paved road'. The explanation is, of course, that the West Germanic people received the word and the knowledge of paved roads from the Romans, — at a time, needless to say, long after the sound-change known as Grimm's law had ceased to act.

Language-mixture, where the historical conditions are known, often determines the absolute date of a change, which the comparative method alone can, naturally, never fix. Thus the German *Straße* shows that the change of postvocalic *t* to a sibilant in High German (cf. p. 208) occurred after the Romans had made their appearance in Germanic territory.

As loan-words are usually of cultural significance, the study of etymology (p. 244) receives from them an added interest. The well-known contrast between the Old English ('Anglo-Saxon') stock and the French-Latin borrowings of English need hardly be mentioned; though many of the French words are today as common as those of older currency in the language, e. g. *beef, change, place, chair, table,* their adoption by the English can always be reduced to a cultural cause. Similarly, if to a smaller extent, we have words from every nation with which speakers of English have come into contact; from American Indian languages, for instance, the vegetable *squash, succotash, tobacco,* not to speak of *totem, papoose, squaw, wampum, wigwam, tomahawk, pow-wow,* which are still felt as foreign. Many other loan-words have come to us through a series of languages, as *banana, hammock* (originally from Caribbean languages, through Spanish or Portuguese), *candy, sugar, pepper, ginger, cinnamon* (originally from oriental languages, whence they came through Arabic, Hebrew, Greek, Latin, etc.).

Culturally significant words are not only thus bodily taken over, but are often imitated. Thus the Latin word *conscientia* 'conscience', a compound of *con-* 'with' and *scientia* 'knowledge', was imitated in the Germanic languages; thus German says *Ge-wissen,* Swedish *sam-vete,* Danish and Norwegian *sam-vittig-hed;* English has directly taken the Latin word in French form. The same is true of, such Latin words as *con-cipere* 'to conceive', from *capere* 'to grasp', German *be-greifen;* Latin *ob-jectum* 'object', literally 'thing thrown before one', older German *Vor-wurf,* and so on. The Slavic languages similarly imitate abstract words from German, Latin, and Greek; thus Russian ['soˑvʹisʹtʹ] 'conscience', [penʹi 'maˑtʹ] 'conceive, understand' are modelled on the German compounds, [prʹid 'mʹɛt] 'object', also, is literally 'thing thrown before one'.

When the foreign word is taken bodily into the language, it is subjected to assimilative influences. Its sounds are replaced by those of the borrowing speech, and its structure is often assimilated to that of the native words. This may not happen while the word is still used by those who know the foreign language and know that the word is foreign; as soon as it becomes genuinely popular, — that is, part of the universal usage, — it is sure to be assimilated. Most examples of sudden sound-change (p. 216) really belong here. Latin *peregrinus* 'pilgrim' became *pelegrinus* and *pilgrim* in the mouths of people whose native language was not Latin. The Latin *acētum* 'vinegar' became *atīko* in the mouth of Germans, whose language had at that time no closed $\bar{e}$, but, as the nearest sound, only $\bar{\imath}$, and no suffix *-īto* but a common one *-īko*. Hence the modern High German form *Essig* ['ɛsik] or ['ɛsiç]. This form shows us, moreover, that the German change of *a* to *e* before *i* ('umlaut', see p. 215) and of *t* after vowel to *s* (cf. *Straße* above and p. 208) and of *k* after vowel to [x, ç] (the form with *-k* in modern German is analogic) occurred since the first contact with the Romans.

So the Old French *sillabe* has become in English *syllable* in approximation to our suffix *-able*. *Hammock* was introduced into English from the Spanish *hamaca*, itself a no doubt assimilated form of a Carib word. In English it was little changed, because it happened to resemble the native words in *-ock*, such as *hassock*, *hummock*. In German, however, where it resembled nothing in the native stock, it was assimilated into the form of a compound *Hängematte* 'hang-mat'. Such complete change of an obscure word into a semantically organized form is called 'popular etymology'. It changed in German the Graeco-Latin *arcuballista* 'cross-bow' into *Armbrust*, literally 'arm-breast', in English the Graeco-Latin *asparagus* into *sparrow-grass* (*asparagus* being meanwhile constantly restored by those who know Latin). Old French *crevice* (itself a loan-word from Germanic) has become *crayfish* and *crawfish*.

When words pass from one dialect to another, mutual intelligibility modifies the assimilating process, in the sense that the phonetic differences are often correctly compensated. Thus we should naturally and unconsciously put into the equivalent American sounds a new word we heard from a Londoner. Nor need the words so borrowed necessarily be of cultural significance. Dialect-mixtures are as a rule recognizable only if some phonetic inconsistency is retained. Thus in the speech of the northern central part of the United States the vowel of such words as *bath, glass, laugh, path* is [æ], but many speakers who have grown up in this pronunciation will, when on their dignity, use the British [ɑ], — often inconsistently. In this way arise 'hyper' forms, where the affectation of a foreign pronunciation is carried beyond its scope in the imitated dialect itself; as when one speaks also [mɑn], where the English pronunciation itself has [æ]. The same phenomenon appears in German: speakers whose dialect has [i] for Standard German [y] will affectedly substitute [y]'s for their natural [i]'s even where the standard language has [i], saying [ty:r] not only for *Tür* 'door' but also for *Tier* 'animal', Standard German [ti:r].

Where words are permanently borrowed from one dialect by another, they may betray themselves, like loan-words from foreign languages, by their phonetic habit. London English, for instance, has no native words with initial *v-*; such as are not Latin-French are borrowings from a dialect south of the Thames, which regularly has initial *v-* for *f-*, e. g. *vat, vixen*. High German has no words with *b, d, g* after short vowel, except those like *Krabbe* 'crab', *Dogge* 'mastiff', which are loans from Low German. Phonetic investigation has shown that certain Latin words, such as *lupus* 'wolf', *bōs* 'head of cattle', *popīna* 'cook-shop' are borrowings from neighboring dialects, such as, perhaps, the Sabine.

It is a phenomenon of dialect-mixture when we find in English a number of the commonest words bearing unmistakable North Germanic character. The northern and central English dialects of Alfredian times and the Scandinavian speech of the Norse invaders of that period were not only mutually intelligible, but so much alike as to seem only different forms of one language. When the invaders settled by the side of the English, each dialect came to be interspersed with words of the other. Ultimately the English, spoken by greater numbers and also in the south, where there were no Scandinavians, carried off the victory but retained, for ever after, a number of words in Scandinavian form. Such words are *egg, give, guest, kettle, oar, they, skirt, sky.* The word *egg*, for instance, is the Scandinavian correspondent of the German *Ei*, Primitive Germanic *ajjon*; North Germanic, but not West Germanic changed *jj* to *gg*. *Give* and *guest* would have been palatalized in pre-English, like *yield* (p. 214); *kettle* similarly, like *child*. The case of *skirt* is especially interesting. In Old English *sk* had become *sh* [ʃ], and the cognate of Norse *skirt* was in English *shirt*. People were led, as a result of such doublets, — *scrub* and *shrub, skirt* and *shirt*, and the like, — where *sh* was spoken, to speak *sk* also: consequently *sk* occurs by the side of *sh* in many words that were not Scandinavian at all, — as in *scatter* by the side of *shatter*. Since that time words with *sk* have been multiplied, until those actually brought in by the Scandinavians are in the minority.

The transition from dialect-mixture to the unevenness of individual speech is, of course, a gradual one. It may be illustrated by several intermediate phenomena. Forms from slower and from more rapid speech exist side by side, e. g. *cannot: can't, does not: doesn't*. The same is true of morphologic doublets: a speaker who ordinarily says *If he were here, he would help us* may, after speaking with members of less conservative strata, occasionally say *If he was here*....

Another such phenomenon is the mixture of older with younger forms of speech. In most instances the older form has been preserved in some set phrase, subject to phonetic change, of course, but growing lexically or morphologically antiquated. Thus the Old English *sam-blind* 'half-blind' remained in use after the prefix *sam-* 'half' had ceased to be mobile or even to occur in any words but this; the word consequently, became assimilated into *sand-blind* and associated with a meaning 'totally blind'. Another striking instance is the German expression *mit Kind und Kegel* in the sense of 'bag and baggage', which today means, word for word, 'with child and ninepin'; — *Kegel* is really here an otherwise lost word meaning 'bastard'. The English *You had better go* preserves an otherwise lost use of *had* which troubles some speakers. Ultimately, of course, the syntactic development which crystallizes certain forms of discursively joined words into the various set forms of materially specialized constructions (such as preposition plus noun in English) is a process of preserving in set use what was formerly a flexible manner of speech. Thus, to add an example to those already given (pp. 114, ff., 171, ff.), our perfectic expression with *have* originated in such sentences as *I have written a letter*, which meant originally 'I have a letter written, in written condition' (literally or in the sense of 'have to my credit'). This turn of speech has been preserved as an expression of perfectic action, and, as its original meaning lost dominance, has been extended to such forms as *I have slept, I have lost a book*, where it could not at first have been used. This mixture of linguistic strata is thus a factor in the regular linguistic development.

Where alphabetic writing exists, older phonetic stages may be preserved and borrowed by later times. This has occurred most universally in the Romance languages, spoken in communities extensively familiar with written records of the older stage of their language, Latin. Thus the Latin *causa* 'cause, affair' has become the French *chose* 'affair, thing', but is preserved through writing in the French *cause* 'cause, lawsuit'; the Latin *sēcūritātem* (accusative of *sēcūritās*) 'security' has become *sûreté* 'safety, security' (whence the English loan *surety*), but has had written existence, whence the French took *sécurité* 'assurance, unconcernedness' and the English, through the French, *security*. The Latin *sēparāre* became French *sevrer* 'to wean, deprive' (from the French English borrowed *sever*), but was preserved in writing and borrowed as French *séparer* and English *separate*. These examples could be multiplied in great numbers. They are not essentially different from the 'spelling-pronunciations', in which an archaic spelling leads to the revival of phonetically divergent ancient forms. Thus the old *t* of *often, soften* has been long lost by phonetic change, but the influence of the orthography leads many speakers, some consciously, some unconsciously, to pronounce it. Indeed, there may arise in this way forms that were never spoken at all, such as *ye* for *the*, due to misreading of the old character þ (for *th*), and *author*, where learned orthographic pedantry alone is responsible for the *h*,[1] which, however, long ago has led to the substitution of [ϴ] for the older [t].

There can be no doubt, in fact, that the existence of written tradition has, by constantly demanding the association of fixed and conservative forms, impeded phonetic change. If we had no alphabetic writing, or if only a few of us could read, such forms as [juni'vɪsiti] would long ago have given way entirely to such as [jū'vɪsti] or even to such assimilative reformations as ['vɪsti] or ['vɑɪsti]. The written form thus tends to preserve the phonetic form of the language; though of course, it can do so only to a comparatively small extent. Our conscious control over the forms of writing is not yet extensive: the obstacles which the various attempts at improving English spelling have met are an example; nevertheless, as these attempts themselves show, not to speak of the successful governmental regulation of orthography in European countries, consciousness and systematic reasoning in this sphere are gaining ground. When the community will consciously and deliberately shape its orthography a great step toward the conscious influencing of language will thus have been taken. It is possible, in fact, that, very gradually, language, like religion, government, and other once purely communal processes, is developing into a conscious activity.

8. Standard languages. How fast and ultimately how far this development will progress it is, of course, impossible to say. To it belong, however, a number of characteristic features in the rise of the so-called *standard languages*. These are favored dialects which, either in written form alone or also in oral, are used all over a dialectally differentiated territory. At first they are used for communication between members of different dialects, the speaker whose dialect represents the less cultured community using, as well as may be, that of the more civilized neighbor. Gradually it comes that members of two dialects that are perhaps with difficulty intelligible to each other, will use, in speaking together, the same favored dialect, though it is native to neither of them, until at last it may become a second language for formal and non-local discourse all over the area. Soon there will be speakers in many parts of the country who can speak only the favored dialect, — such, for instance, as the upper classes of English, German, or French society, who rarely can speak the 'patois' of their native locality, but know only the 'national' or 'standard' language. The latter may ultimately crowd out the local dialects; this happened in ancient Greece and in the Roman Empire (where both related dialects and foreign languages gave way to Latin) and is rapidly happening in modern England.

Meanwhile the favored dialect is used as the language of literature and is learned by many out of books: the individual writer has considerable power to influence it. Cicero, Dante, Chaucer, the translators of the King James Bible, Goethe, and other writers of great and enduring renown have permanently moulded their language: in Shakspere we see the origin not only of many quotations, but also of some set forms of speech, which have come to us by virtue of his having used them. As the language of books, the standard language is subject to fixed canons of correctness: what good authors do not use is wrong. This consideration, as well as the necessity of teaching the standard speech to people who first learned a local dialect, leads to the compilation of grammatical descriptions of the language and to lexical summaries, dictionaries. Thus we arrive finally at a conscious standard of correctness, which modifies linguistic growth, especially in checking the spread of the easily recognizable morphologic innovations of the *was* for *were* type. New forms or words are usually recognized as such, — as dialectal, vulgar, incorrect, etc. — and consequently associated with a peculiar emotional tone. If a good author uses them, they may become part of the standard language, although they will long be felt as lacking in dignity. Such words are in English *slob, slobber, whang, thump, thwack, squunch, piffle*, and the like. Sometimes they gain ground rapidly; thus *mob*, the assimilatively shortened form of *mobile vulgus* was fifty years ago frowned upon as a barbarism. Entirely unchangeable are of course the literary languages which exist only in written form, such as Latin in the Middle Ages, Sanskrit, Classical Arabic, Hebrew. Although these may be occasionally spoken, the great preponderance of use is in careful writing according to the rules of the grammar and lexicon and on the model of classical authors.

The standard language may be the dialect of the capital in conservative form, as in France, England, and Russia (Moscow), or a mixed dialect as in ancient Greece, where the Koiné was composed of Athenian and Ionic (Asiatic Greek) elements. It has happened in a number of cases, now, that in the determination of the forms of such a language, individuals have been of influence. Modern Standard German, of complex origin, was, after all, brought into shape more by the careful work of Luther in his Bible-translation than by any other one factor. Modern Servian was molded by Karadjič upon older forms of the language, and the 'Landsmaal', one of the two competing standard languages of Norway, is in great part the creation of a nineteenth-century linguistic student, Ivar Aasen, who founded his work on the southwestern dialects of his country.

Thus it may fairly be said that language also, even if in smaller measure than any other social activity, has shared in the human progress from unconscious evolution into conscious shaping of conditions. In this phase of linguistic development two features are of special importance: the conscious teaching of languages, for the purpose, of course, of establishing communicative bonds, and the conscious observation of language, linguistic science.

CHAPTER IX.
THE TEACHING OF LANGUAGES.

1. The purpose of foreign-language instruction. In communities whose culture is undeveloped no languages are taught. The beginning of language-instruction comes always when ancient writings of artistic or, especially, ethical and religious importance are to be handed on to suceeding generations. Thus the Hindus study the Vedas and the Sanskrit epic and classical literature, the Mohammedans classical Arabic and the Koran, the Parsis Avestan, the Jews Hebrew, the Chinese the old literature of their country. In Europe the ancient Greeks of historical time studied Homer, whose language was even for them highly antiquated, the Romans Greek, the medieval and modern nations Ancient Greek and Latin.

To these studies are added, as the consciousness of nations increases, the languages of important fellow-nations. This is a deliberate widening of the bonds of communication (p. 291): it is desired that a large element of the nation understand the writing and speech of foreign contemporaries. Just as the study of ancient languages is to preserve the cultural tradition, so that of modern is to keep the community abreast of modern progress. The latter study is prompted also by material motives, such as the need of foreign languages in commerce and the desirability of promptly utilizing foreign inventions in science and industry. One may say that today the nation which contains no large class of people who understand foreign languages dwells in pitiable seclusion.

Finally, as the idea of humanity takes form, there comes the wish not only to be acquainted with the character and history of one's own nation, but also, in part as an elucidation of these, to understand the motives, achievements, and ideals of the sister-communities. At this stage, which the European nations more fully than America have reached, the school studies include not only instruction in foreign languages, but also a suitable introduction to the life, culture, and ideals of the foreign nations.

2. Character of the instruction. It is only in the last twenty-five years and in the European countries that success in modern-language teaching has ever been attained. Of ancient languages this cannot be said: it is true, however, that where here also success has been won, it has been by the same general methods as are today used for modern-language instruction in Europe: by a conscious or unconscious accordance with the fundamental processes of language-learning and, for that matter, of speech in general. Where, as in our own practice, this accordance is wanting, failure is inevitable. Of the students who take up the study of foreign languages in our schools and colleges, not one in a hundred attains even a fair reading knowledge, and not one in a thousand ever learns to carry on a conversation in the foreign language. This is due to the fact that almost every feature of our instruction runs counter to the universal conditions under which language exists. While a growing number of our teachers have acquainted themselves with the modern methods, their efforts are largely checked by the antiquated outer circumstances, such as the late age at which pupils begin the study and the small number of class hours, coupled with the reliance on home assignments, which are of little use in language-instruction.

Our fundamental mistake has been to regard language-teaching as the imparting of a set of facts. The facts of a language, however, are, as we have seen, exceedingly complex. To explain to the student the morphology and syntax of a language, be it his own or a foreign one, would require a long time, and, — even if it were done correctly by linguistically trained teachers, — would be of little or no value. To set forth the lexical facts would be an endless task, for not only does each word of the foreign language differ in content from any word of the native language, but this content itself is very difficult of definition. The greatest objection of all, however, is that, even if the pupil managed somehow to remember this immense mass of facts, he would scarcely be the more able, what with it all, to understand the foreign language in its written or spoken phase. Minutes or hours would often elapse before he could labor out the value of a sentence by recalling the facts concerned. Language is not a process of logical reference to a conscious set of rules; the process of understanding, speaking, and writing is everywhere an associative one. Real language-teaching consists, therefore, of building up in the pupil those associative habits which constitute the language to be learned. Instead of this we try to expound to students the structure and vocabulary of the foreign language and, on the basis of this, let them translate foreign texts into English. Such translation is a performance of which only people equipped with a complete knowledge of both languages and with considerable literary ability are ever capable. As a method of study, moreover, it is worthless, for it establishes associations in which the foreign words play but a small part as symbols (inexact symbols, of course) of English words.

The excuse usually given for this practice is that American conditions make only a 'reading knowledge' of the foreign language, — especially, if ancient, — of importance, — that it is not our purpose to enable pupils to order a meal in the foreign language. Reading, however, is no different from the other phases of using a language: the expressions of the language are not the given members of mathematical equations or puzzles, but must enter into a set of rapidly and easily functioning associative habits. Correct methods of language-teaching differ from those which we are at present unsuccessfully using not in aim, — any aim can here be attained by good as surely as it missed by bad teaching, — but in adaptation to the mental conditions underlying the activities of speech. In what follows I shall naturally speak of American conditions and assume that the ability to read rather than to speak is aimed at: needless to say that even here the desired associations cannot be formed without much oral and auditory practice. I believe, moreover, that American conditions are coming to make a 'speaking knowledge' more and more desirable and that the time is not far off when here as well as abroad the ability to converse in one or two foreign languages will be looked upon as one of the ordinary marks of education.

3. Age of the pupil. The best age at which to begin a foreign language is that between the tenth and twelfth years. If the study is begun earlier, the progress is usually so slow that nothing is gained, the pupil who begins later soon overtaking him who began younger. If the study is begun at the age indicated, further languages may be taken up at intervals of a few years; as the student accumulates experience, the later languages will be learned more rapidly and with less effort than the earlier, until a facility may be acquired which astonishes those who have had less practice. It is worth while to say this, because there exists a superstition to the effect that languages are acquired by some special power of the intellect which wanes in maturity.[1] If the first foreign language is begun later than the twelfth year or so, — and here we see, perhaps, the source of the bit of popular psychologizing just mentioned, — we find a growing disinclination on the part of the pupil to go through the constant practice by which alone success is attainable. Older students who have never before studied a language are too exclusively practised in conscious, logical grouping of facts to accept the repetition of what is already understood but not yet assimilated; when they have grasped the 'meaning' of a text in terms of the native language, they are disinclined to go on using the text with attention to the foreign expression. The necessary simplicity as to content of the elementary texts also bores them. At the age of ten or twelve, on the other hand, the pupil is attracted by the novelty of what he learns, enjoys the growing power of expression and understanding in a new medium, and the playing at being something strange (e. g. an ancient Roman, a German, or a Frenchman), nor is he intellectually too superior to the simple content of the earlier lessons. Once the habit of foreign-language-study has been at this age set up,

---

[1] It actually happens that students in our universities are excused from language requirements on the plea that they are 'too old' to learn languages.

the student finds no difficulty in going on to other languages even when he is more mature, for he knows from experience the necessity of the processes involved and the fruits which they so soon bear.

4. Equipment of the teacher. As to the preparation of the teacher, a prime requisite is, of course, mastery of the language to be taught, — in modern languages a knowledge comparable to that of an educated native speaker and in ancient a fluent reading ability and some facility in writing. This is so obvious that it needs no elaboration, yet we constantly find in our schools and colleges teachers whose knowledge falls far short of this demand. Such teachers are from the beginning incapable of successful instruction, for, though they may vociferously explain (in English) the abstract grammatical facts of the foreign language, they cannot give the pupil practice which will form and strengthen in him the associative habits which constitute the language. If the services of a teacher approximately possessing these qualifications cannot be obtained, the instruction should be given up, as it is only a waste of time.

The same may be said, though not so universally, of teachers possessing this but lacking another qualification; namely, the knowledge and experience of how a language must be taught. Next in uselessness to a teacher who does not know the language is the teacher who, to be sure, does know it, — he may be a native speaker of it, — but has not the linguistic and pedagogic knowledge of how to impart it. In English, — and, if he is a foreigner, often in broken English, — he indulges in descriptions of the beauty, conformity to logic, etc. of the language, and when the pupils, on the strength of this, fail to learn anything, he attributes the failure to their sloth, stupidity, or narrow-minded dislike of what is foreign. Ultimately such teachers become either indifferent easy-goers or irascible cranks.

School language-teaching has been successful only where thorough knowledge of the foreign language and training in the necessary linguistic and pedagogical principles, supplemented by experience in practice-classes under supervision, are demanded of all candidates for teaching positions. Even then centralized control, for instance by a government bureau, has been found desirable, as every one will understand who has heard at our teachers' meetings the grotesque 'methods' which uncontrolled and isolated teachers, innocent of the most fundamental principles of the subject or of any accepted writings about it, have developed during winters of teaching. While all instruction, to be worth anything, must be moulded by the teacher's personality, his whim, conceit, or lack of information must not be allowed to ignore the results of generations of labor and experience.

In short, the language-teacher must be a trained professional, not an amateur. The postponement of much elementary language-teaching to our colleges brings, aside from the unfortunate age of the students, the great disadvantage that it practically excludes such teachers. In accord with the true purpose of college and university, the instructors there employed are not pedagogues but people who have found their calling in the handing on of culture or in scientific teaching and research. The professional language-teacher who occasionally finds his way into these institutions soon learns that he can expect neither honor nor advancement for excellence in his vocation: he must exchange it for more purely cultural or scientific studies or be content with a minor position. Nearly all of the elementary language-teaching in our colleges is done, accordingly, by doctors of philosophy who have no training and no ambition in this direction, but find their interest and seek their advancement in linguistic or literary teaching and research. Their instruction is directed, with ulterior evil effect on that of the secondary schools also, by men who have come to the front in some special branch of linguistics or in literature and have often no understanding of the problems and conditions of foreign-language teaching. As long as this work is inappropriately left to colleges, these institutions should give employment and promotion to teachers who make it their business, and allow literary and linguistic scholars to stick to their last, for they are no more capable of this work than are grammar-school and high-school teachers of conducting graduate seminars.

5. Drill in pronunciation. Instruction in a foreign language must begin by training the pupil to articulate the foreign sounds correctly and without difficulty or hesitation. We have seen in Chapter II that the teacher's ability to pronounce these sounds does not involve ability to tell others how they are pronounced. This information must be given in terms of movement of the articulatory organs. The instruction must begin, therefore, with the elements of phonetics as applied to the pupil's native language and, by contrast, to the foreign one. Description alone is, of course, of no avail: the pupils must be brought to practise the foreign articulations until they have become automatic. This practice should be enlivened by the subject-matter, but it must remain practice in articulation, an unidiomatic articulation being in no case allowed to pass muster. Overgrown pupils, especially if unused to accurate and painstaking study, will content themselves with noting certain general resemblances to native sounds and interpreting the examples into the nearest corresponding native articulation. The phonetic drill must be based, in the case of languages that are unphonetically written, such as French, on a transcription into a phonetic alphabet. After pronunciation has been mastered, the irregularities of the standard orthography will cause much less difficulty than if they were at the beginning presented in inextricable confusion with the foreign pronunciation.

6. Method of presenting semantic material. As time goes on, the pronunciation will require less and less of conscious attention on the part of the learner. From the very beginning, however, the significance of the expressions that are practised should be made use of. The very first phonetic examples should be characteristic words and phrases. The signification of these cannot, as we have seen in Chapter IV (p. 85, ff.) be taught in terms of the pupil's native language. This would involve either false statements or, if these were to be avoided, lengthy, complicated, and easily forgotten explanantions. The foreign utterance must, instead, be associated from the very first, with its actual content. The beginning should be made, therefore, with expressions concretely intelligible: formulas of greeting, short sentences about objects in the classroom, and actions that can be performed while naming them.

As the work goes on to connected narrative and descriptive texts, this method must be continued. The texts, therefore, must at first be confined to very simple discourse about concretely illustrable matters. Pictures are here of great use. Any new text must be explained in terms of what has already been learned, not in English. Translation into the pupil's native language or other explicatory use of it must be avoided, for two reasons. The terms of the native language are misleading, because the

METHOD OF PRESENTING SEMANTIC MATERIAL 301

content of any word or sentence of the foreign language is always different from any approximate correspondent in the native language. A pupil taught that the German *lesen* means 'read' will say *ich lesen* instead of *ich lese*. If he is taught that *wenn* means 'when', he will confuse it with *als*, and if he is taught that *ob* means 'if', he will confuse it with *wenn*. Once such associations are formed, — and their fictitious simplicity makes them comparatively easy to fix, — no amount of explanation or insistence on the part of the teacher will overcome them. The second reason for the avoidance of translation is that, in the association of the foreign word with the native one, the latter will always remain the dominant feature, and the former will be forgotten. The learner will know that he has met the foreign word for 'pencil', but the sound and spelling of the foreign word will be very hazy in his mind. Where continued translation has given facility in these associations, the pupils scarcely look at the foreign text before the English word, right or wrong, becomes conscious. The result is that their foreign vocabulary remains small; they are forced to look up in the glossary over and over again the same common word, and, whenever they look it up, their habit leads them to fix only the native interpretation and to go on with the text. Every teacher has known students who have read hundreds of pages in a foreign language and yet have to look up dozens of the commonest words in any page of a new text — or even of the old, if they are asked to re-read.

Instead of translation the work with a text should consist of repeated use of its contents in hearing, reading, speaking, and writing. The beginning is best made before the pupil has even seen the text. The teacher explains in the foreign language the new expressions which are to occur and leads the pupils to use them in speech over and over again. Then the pupils are required, first, to read the new selection correctly after the teacher, later, to answer, with the book, then without it, simple questions about it, to converse about its subject-matter, and to retell it in speech and in writing. The text should not be left until every phase of it has been thoroughly assimilated: no text should in the beginning be used whose linguistic contents are not important and common enough to deserve such assimilation.

The range of work that the pupil can do outside the classroom is here very small. The danger that he will practise false pronunciation or usage must make the teacher very cautious in the assignment of outside lessons. Copying the text and preparation of lists of words and sentences taken directly from it are least dangerous. As the work must thus be done almost entirely in the classroom, eight hours a week of class-work are not too much in the first year or two.

It is only after the pupil has mastered for speaking and writing as well as reading a good central stock of words, forms, and constructions, that more rapid reading should be undertaken. Without a nucleus of expressive material over which the pupil has full and accurate control, the necessary analogies even for that degree of understanding which we call a reading-knowledge are lacking.

7. Grammatical information. The amount of text covered in the first year or two cannot be large. It is to be measured not by the page, but by the amount of new material introduced. Beginners will do well, if they learn a thousand words in the first year of the first foreign language. A hundred pages of carefully prepared easy text will contain this amount of material.

The texts need not be arranged in terror of introducing new grammatical features before they have been systematically — i. e. theoretically, — explained. Grammar, as such, is not necessary for the use or understanding of a language: the normal speaker or reader is not conscious of the grammatical abstractions. In foreign-language teaching grammar is of use only where it definitely contributes to the ease of learning. When a new text appears the learner should be able to tell where he has met the words and phrases it contains and others like them. Now, when he meets, let us say, a new inflectional form of a known word, the differences in the use of the two forms should be carefully illustrated and practised. After a time, when a considerable number of such collocations has been made, — when a number of singulars and plurals, for instance, have been compared as to use and form, — the grammatical statement, if simple enough to be of help, may be given. In fact, it will be unnecessary, for the pupil will with considerable interest, have formulated it for himself. On the other hand, the grammatical statement must often be kept temporarily incomplete. The German dative case, for instance, is of so heterogeneous use that a statement of its value would take a long time and would be unintelligible to any but a linguistically trained learner. Instead, we may collect our accumulated examples of datives, observe the forms, and their occurrence after certain verbs and certain prepositions and independently in the sentence. All this need not be done at once: the dative with prepositions, especially, in its contrast with the accusative, may, as the most definitely recognizable use, be collected and observed long before the other types. In every instance the forms themselves in their natural connection should be practised to the point of thorough habituation before the abstract statement is given. Consequently the grammatical features of a new text are of secondary importance, provided that it is easily explained and understood. Grammar should be used only as a summary and mnemonic aid for the retention of what has been already learned. Where it cannot be so used, it should be omitted.

8. **Texts.** While the matter read should, of course, be characteristic of the foreign nation's life and culture, the selections should not hasten to tell too much at the cost of simplicity. Selections of literary value should not be introduced before the pupil can understand them: if he cannot, their literary qualities are lost to him. The transition from the mere learning of the foreign language to the study of its literature and culture must be gradual, especially in the case of the first language studied. This language, however, should by the end of the secondary-school period, have become so familiar that the last years are spent entirely in the study of works of ethical, artistic, and generally cultural interest. In the languages later begun the practice in acquiring languages will make up for the shorter time of study. All reading, no matter of what nature, should be within the pupil's immediate range of understanding of the foreign language. The great bulk of the time must be taken up in fixing in the pupil's mind the value of the foreign expressions, until these, when seen or heard, are automatically understood. It is only on the basis of such knowledge as this that reading can go on at a rate which makes an ideal effect upon the pupil possible. The premature reading, or rather pottering through foreign literature in our schools (e. g. *Wilhelm Tell* in the second year of ill-taught German) is a mere working-out of senseless puzzles.

The interpretation of what is read must always be pedagogic rather than scientific in purpose. The aim of foreign-language instruction is to acquaint the pupil with the foreign language, through it with the foreign culture, and generally, as in all other school studies, to train him to a higher mentality, in every sense of the word. The scientific study of the foreign-language or literature is entirely inappropriate for a school foreign-language course. By postponing this course to the high-school and college we have brought about confusion of elementary foreign-language learning with the aims of scientific linguistics and scientific literary history. These studies belong to a later stage of education, in which, to be sure, both should be represented; but an exposition of Grimm's law in the elementary German classroom, or of the motives of romanticism in that of second-year French is a deplorable farce.

The texts, then, as the pupil grows familiar with the language and at the same time progresses towards maturity, should be selected more and more for their inner content. From the simplest elementary selections we may proceed to easy short stories, then to more serious historic, descriptive, and narrative prose and to drama and poetry. Toward the end of the course summaries of the literary, cultural, and political history, — preparing for possible college courses in these subjects, — should be read.

9. References. The English reader will find details about the methods of language-teaching in the two following books and in the bibliographies which they contain:

Otto Jespersen, *How to Teach a Foreign Language*, London and New York (Macmillan) 1904 and 1908.

Leopold Bahlsen, *The Teaching of Modern Languages*, Boston (Ginn) 1905.

The latter book contains a brief review of the history of language-teaching in Europe, which shows plainly that our language-teaching differs from that of the European countries not as a mere difference in choice of methods (e. g. that they use the 'direct' and we some other 'method'), but that most of our practice is half a century or so behind that of the European schools, which has kept better pace with scientific insight into language.

CHAPTER X.
THE STUDY OF LANGUAGE.

1. The origin of linguistic science. *Linguistics* (German *Sprachwissenschaft*, French *linguistique*) took its beginning, historically, in the study of writings which were preserved for their religious or esthetic value. As these texts antiquated, interpretation of their language became necessary and led finally to a grammatical codification of their forms. In this way the study of philology German *Philologie*, French *philologie*), — that is, of national cultural tradition, — came to include a linguistic discipline whose aim was the practical one of making intelligible and preserving certain writings. Thus originated the treatises of the Indian grammarians (chief among them Pāṇini, fourth century B. C.), the Ancient Greek grammar (especially Dionysios Thrax, second century B. C., and Apollonios Dyskolos, second century of our era), the Latin grammars (Donatus, fourth century, Priscian, sixth century), the Hebrew grammar, and so on.

The linguistic study at this stage was properly a means to an end, a prodrome to philology. Nevertheless, there were always scholars, who, be it from a genuine but misguided interest in language or from sheer pedantry, confined themselves to this grammatical study. Thus there developed a pseudo-linguistics, which occupied itself with grammatical dissection of texts, with haphazard etymologies, and with vague theorizing as to origins.[1]) A further impulse to this grammatical study was felt when the popular language deviated from that of the texts to the point where the latter became unintelligible, or when people of alien speech adopted the culture and with it the philologic studies of a more advanced nation. Both of these conditions were given in medieval Europe, where classical Latin had become unintelligible to the people of Romance tongue and was foreign to the northern nations. At first the teaching of Latin (and, when it was revived, that of Greek) was conducted on a sensible basis: the language was spoken, written, and read until the student had firm command of it and easy access to the classical literature. Later, however, pedantry prevailed: in spite of such great educators as (in the sixteenth century) Ascham and (in the seventeenth century) Ratichius and Comenius, theoretical grammar came more and more to be looked upon as a means of learning the ancient languages. This went so far that, for example, up to very recent times English schoolboys had to memorize the entire contents of a Latin grammar before they were allowed any real contact with the language. It was only a slight alleviation of this barbarity when the rules of grammar were at least illustrated by disconnected sentences. This latter method prevailed when, early in the nineteenth century, modern languages came to be studied in Europe for practi-

---

1) Owing to this occupation the term 'philology' has come to be misused in English first as meaning linguistics and then even in reference to misplaced and piddling grammatical study. The best usage, however, — that, for instance, of the greatest of English-speaking linguistic scholars, the American William Dwight Whitney, — does not sanction this; philology is the study of national cultural values, especially as preserved in the writings of a people, linguistics the study of man's function of language.

cal purposes; accordingly, the grammatical facts of these were codified in imitation of Latin and Greek and became the basis of instruction. This sentence-method, used in the books of Ahn, Ollendorff, and many successors, is still, in various modifications, supreme in American schools.

In this way pseudo-linguistics, supported by a false pedagogic idea, held the field until the nineteenth century. There had, to be sure, been attempts in the preceding centuries to attain a genuine understanding of language, but these were frustrated chiefly by the aprioristic, purely logical — unhistorical and unpsychologic — manner of consideration and also, in spite of the comparison of Arabic, Hebrew, and the writers' own modern languages, by the confinement of the study to a narrow and accidental group of idioms. The work of such men as Schottelius, de Brosses, Fulda, and even, early in the nineteenth century, Bernhardi, remained, therefore, without direct results.

It was the opening to Europe of India and the widening of cultural and scientific interests which we call the romantic movement, that led to a more fruitful study of language.

The romantic interest in things ancient and distant made European thinkers ready to receive the Indian culture which such men as William Jones and Colebrooke brought from the East. This culture included, in the manner above described, grammatical treatises dealing with Sanskrit, the sacred and literary language of India, — treatises in which European scholarship found a linguistic achievement beyond any it had known. For, while the Sanskrit grammar had not attained to the idea of a science of language and served in India the same purpose of mis-instruction of the young that Latin grammar had fulfilled in Europe, its original task of preserving through millenia the norm of classical usage was satisfied by a highly exact description of Sanskrit pronunciation and word-formation. The former of these, especially, was a revelation to European students, who had never given attention to the articulations of speech. Medical investigators, meanwhile, — owing, again, to the romantic impetus, — came to study the physiology of language, until we find the two tendencies, represented, for example, by the physiologist Brücke and the linguist and philologian Scherer, culminating in the modern discipline of phonetics. In respect to word-formation also, the transparency of the Sanskrit language and the excellent treatment it had received from the Hindu grammarians, afforded a new insight into the development of linguistic forms. Modern linguistics more than any other phase of our cultural life, is a heritage from India.

The romantic impulse led to a widening of the group of languages studied, which, with the insight afforded by Sanskrit, resulted in the recognition that a number of languages of Europe and Asia are related. This recognition, made by William Jones and Friedrich Schlegel, was shaped by Franz Bopp (1791—1867) into a scientific investigation, which showed definitively that these languages are divergent forms of an earlier uniform parent language. This investigation, brought into fuller and more accurate form and subjected to more careful method by the work of such men as August Friedrich Pott (1802—1887) and August Schleicher (1823—1868), has grown into the study of Indo-European linguistics, which to this day has remained the central and best-known field of linguistic science.

The progress of Indo-European linguistics gave new interest to the study of Latin, Greek, Sanskrit, and the modern European languages. The first three were directly involved in the origin of Indo-European study, and the groups of modern languages soon received their individual treatment. This has been fullest in the Germanic and the Romance languages. Jacob Grimm (1785—1863) laid the foundation of the former in his monumental *Deutsche Grammatik* ('German', — we should say today 'Germanic' — Grammar), the first great scientific linguistic work of the world, and perhaps even today the greatest. On Grimm's model C. F. Diez (1794—1876) founded the study of the Romance languages in his *Grammatik der romanischen Sprachen*. The scientific study of the Celtic group received its basis in the *Grammatica Celtica* of J. K. Zeuss (1806—1856) and that of the Slavic languages in the *Vergleichende Grammatik der slawischen Sprachen* of Franz von Miklosich (1813—1891).

The new interest in linguistics did not, of course, confine itself to the Indo-European languages: it led also to the study of language in general. This study received its foundation at the hands of the Prussian statesman and scholar Wilhelm von Humboldt (1767—1835), especially in the first volume of his work on Kavi, the literary language of Java, entitled *Über die Verschiedenheit des menschlichen Sprachbaues und ihren Einfluß auf die geistige Entwickelung des Menschengeschlechts* ('On the Variety of the Structure of Language and its Influence upon the Mental Development of the Human Race'). Humboldt's work has been followed in two directions. The study of the languages of the world has resulted in a series of disciplines parallel to Indo-European linguistics, each studying a set of related idioms. The chief families today so recognized are the Semitic, the Hamitic (these two are thought to be in turn descended from a common earlier speech), the Uralic (Hungarian, Finnish, and other languages), the Altaic (Turkish, Tartar, etc.; these two groups also are thought by many to be related), the Caucasian (in the Caucasus; the most important language is Georgian), the Malayo-Polynesian, the Indo-Chinese (Tibetan, Burmese, Siamese, Chinese), the Dravidian, the Bantu, and the various American families, such as the Athapascan and the Algonquian. These have progressed in various degrees toward a scientific comprehension like that which we have of the Indo-European languages. The study of the American languages, though supported in praiseworthy manner by our government, is hampered by many external conditions, including the lack of investigators with linguistic and especially phonetic training.

The other direction in which Humboldt may be said to have led the way, — although here the older grammarians have been not without influence, — is the study of the conditions and laws of language: its psychic and social character and its historical development. This study was furthered by the growth of psychologic insight and of the historical point of view and method, — both of which are from the beginning related to the linguistic studies by the common origin in the romantic movement. Especially active in the psychologic interpretation of language was H. Steinthal (1823—1899); the American scholar W. D. Whitney (1827—1894) applied to the historic phase a remarkable clearness and truth of comprehension, to be appreciated in a field from which mystic vagueness and haphazard theory have been slow to recede. Both of these men have been followed by numerous investigators who have contributed to our understanding of the mental processes of speech and of its change and development in time; the great advance of psychology in recent decades and the rise of social and ethnologic studies have been, of course, of the highest benefit to this phase of the science of language

2. How to study linguistics. a) The student who wishes to devote all or any considerable part of his time to the study of language should begin with that language whose facts are immediately accessible to him, — of course, his own. He should diligently watch his articulations, practise their phonetic notation, and observe individual and local variations from his own usage. This observation must be accompanied by an elementary study of phonetics, for which one of the following books, in the beginning preferably the last-named (which contains a brief phonetic text in three varieties of English, including American), should be used:

Henry Sweet, *A Primer of Phonetics*, third edition, Oxford 1906.

Otto Jespersen, *Lehrbuch der Phonetik*, second edition, Leipzig and Berlin 1913.

Paul Passy, *Petite phonétique comparée*, second edition, Leipzig and Berlin 1913.

A fuller and by far the best treatise on phonetics, which the student should later use, is:

Eduard Sievers, *Grundzüge der Phonetik*, fifth edition, Leipzig 1901.

The learner should then go on to the morphology and syntax and finally the phraseologic and stylistic features of the language he hears and speaks every day. There are, unfortunately, few descriptions of modern English which can be consulted in this connection. The southern British usage is given in:

Henry Sweet, *A Primer of Spoken English*, fourth edition, Oxford 1906.

The northern British usage, more conservative and more like the American, is given in:

R. J. Lloyd, *Northern English: Phonetics, Grammar, Texts*, Leipzig 1899.

b) The approach to the historic development of language should then be made through the medium of English. For this the aids are copious. One may first read:

Otto Jespersen, *Growth and Structure of the English Language*, Leipzig 1905.

J. B. Greenough and G. L. Kittredge, *Words and their Ways in English Speech*, New York (Macmillan) 1901, and then the various 'readers' and 'primers', true models of their kind, of the late Henry Sweet, published by the Oxford University Press, viz., for Old English:

Henry Sweet, *Anglo-Saxon Primer*, eighth edition;

Henry Sweet, *Anglo-Saxon Reader*, eighth edition;

Henry Sweet, *A Second Anglo-Saxon Reader: Archaic and Dialectal*,

and for Middle English:

Henry Sweet, *First Middle English Primer*, second edition;

Henry Sweet, *Second Middle English Primer: Extracts from Chaucer*, second edition.

These should be supplemented by the historical accounts of the development of English in:

Heny Sweet, *Primer of Historical English Grammar*, which is a condensed version of:

Henry Sweet, *Short Historical English Grammar*, which, in turn, is a separate publication of part of the historical material of:

Henry Sweet, *New English Grammar* (two volumes).

Especially important is the last of these, which contains a readable and fairly complete account of the phonetic, morphologic, and syntactic development of English from Old English to the present time.[1]) This historical

---

1) The general linguistic and grammatical disquisitions at the beginning of the book are not, however, to be recommended

study of English should be rapid and extensive rather than intensive, — unless, indeed, one intends to take English for one's special field, — for it is more important at this stage to get a general idea of linguistic development than to learn the particular historic facts of English.

c) Simultaneously with the preceding study the general facts and principles of linguistics should be the subject of a course of somewhat more intensive reading. If one has not studied psychology, some modern text of it should be read. The beginning of linguistics is best made with one of Whitney's books:

W. D. Whitney, *Language and the Study of Language*, New York (Scribner) 1867 (and successive reprints),

W. D. Whitney, *The Life and Growth of Language*, New York (Appleton) 1875 (and successive reprints).

These books, though today incomplete, are fundamental works of our science and are, moreover, written in a style of remarkable clearness and dignity. After this, one should read, for the principles and methods of modern linguistics:

B. Delbrück, *Einleitung in das Studium der indogermanischen Sprachen*, fifth edition, Leipzig 1908,

H. Paul, *Prinzipien der Sprachgeschichte*, fourth edition, Halle 1909. (An English adaptation of the second, 1886, edition is Strong, Logeman, and Wheeler, *Introduction to the Study of the History of Language*, London 1891),

H. Oertel, *Lectures on the Study of Language*, New York (Scribner) 1902.

The semantic phase of linguistic development is cleverly and interestingly, though, unfortunately, from the standpoint of 'popular' psychology, discussed in

M. Bréal, *Essai de Sémantique*, fourth edition, Paris 1908. (An English translation of the third, 1897, edition by Mrs. H. Cust appeared in London in 1900).

Later it is advisable, because the books so far named are for the most part not fully modern as to psychologic interpretation, to study carefully the great linguistic work of the philosopher and psychologist Wundt:

W. Wundt, *Völkerpsychologie*, 1. und 2. Band, *Die Sprache*, third edition, Leipzig 1911.

It is convenient to supplement this with the Indo-European linguist Delbrück's critique and valuation, which appeared in answer to the first edition (1900) of Wundt's book:

B. Delbrück, *Grundfragen der Sprachforschung*, Straßburg 1901,

and with Wundt's answering statement, important as to the relation of psychology, descriptive linguistics, and historical linguistics:

W. Wundt, *Sprachgeschichte und Sprachpsychologie*, Leipzig 1901.

A highly suggestive book on the history of language is

Otto Jespersen, *Progress in Language, with Special Reference to English*, London 1894 (and reprints).

d) The general aspects of language cannot be understood without at least some acquaintance with divergent forms of speech. The best aid for this is the clear little description of eight languages of widely different types (with an illustrative text of each),

F. N. Finck, *Die Haupttypen des Sprachbaues*, Leipzig 1910.

A very useful list of the languages of the earth, arranged in families, — though perhaps too optimistic in the assumption of relationships, — is another booklet by the same author:

F. N. Finck, *Die Sprachstämme des Erdkreises*, Leipzig 1909.

Brief summaries, valuable for reference, of the grammatical facts of a large part of the languages of the world are given in

F. Müller, *Grundriss der Sprachwissenschaft*, four volumes, Vienna 1876, ff.

The more general, in part the practical aspects of linguistics, are treated in the lively, if not always fully modern book,

G. von der Gabelentz, *Die Sprachwissenschaft*, second edition, Leipzig 1901.

The relation of linguistics to ethnology, strangely neglected in all these books, is briefly discussed by Professor Boas in the Introduction of the Fortieth Bulletin of the Bureau of Ethnology of the Smithsonian Institution, namely:

F. Boas, *Handbook of the American Indian Languages*, Part I, Washington 1911.

A good introduction to ethnology, containing an excellent chapter on language, is:

R. R. Marrett, *Anthropology*, New York (Holt) and London [1911].

e) Meanwhile the student will have chosen some language or group of languages as his special field of study, — as, for example, English, German, French, Latin, Greek, or Sanskrit, or, of groups, the Germanic, the Romance, or the Slavic languages. If, as is usually with us the case, some Indo-European language or group is chosen, the study should be accompanied by that of the Indo-European family in general. There are two excellent brief compendia of what is known about this group; the first fuller and more exact, the second better suited to continuous reading:

K. Brugmann, *Kurze vergleichende Grammatik der indogermanischen Sprachen*, Straßburg 1904.

A. Meillet, *Introduction à l'Étude Comparative des Langues Indo-Européennes*, third edition, Paris 1913.

These books contain ample bibliography, not only of Indo-European publications, but also of those on the various groups constituting the family. A fuller account, with complete bibliography, is

K. Brugmann and B. Delbrück, *Grundriß der vergleichenden Grammatik der indogermanischen Sprachen*, first edition, five volumes, Straßburg, 1886—1900, second edition, first three volumes, ibid. 1897—1911. (For those parts which have not yet appeared in the second edition the first must be used; the first two volumes of this have appeared in an English translation in four volumes: J. Wright, R. S. Conway, and W. A. Rouse, *Elements of the Comparative Grammar of the Indo-Germanic Languages*, New York, Westermann, 1888—1895).

If the student's chosen language belongs to any one of the large branches of Indo-European, he should make also a study of this branch and of the other languages in it; — thus, if he is specializing in English, he should not neglect Germanic linguistics and the study of Frisian, German (High and Low, including Dutch), Scandinavian, and Gothic. The nucleus of one's work should be, however, the intensive study of some one language or group, based, if possible, on the present speech as heard, as well as on texts, — for comparative purposes of course on the oldest, — and on the standard books and articles about the subject. In this work the student will learn to understand also the general principles more thoroughly than is possible at second hand. In time he will find gaps in our knowledge or errors in our interpretation which he will be able to fill out or to correct, if he is willing to devote himself to a strict adherence to historic fact in all its details and to an inflexible discrimination between mere surmise and scientific certainty.

3. Relation of linguistics to other sciences. a) *To philology.* Linguistics, we have seen, took its origin in philology, — in the study of national culture. The relations between the two sciences are still manifold. The most original of these relations, the practical one, is obvious: for philologic study thorough knowledge of the language of the community and of its writings is a necessary instrument. If the community has a long cultural history, as in the case of France, Germany, or England, this knowledge must extend to the various historic forms of the language and will naturally shape itself into a study of the linguistic history of the nation. The philologist must not, however, mistaking the means for the end, confine himself to this linguistic study: if he wishes to remain philologist, his aim must be the understanding of the more conscious cultural activities of the nation; if he wishes to go over to linguistics, it will be his duty to study also the elements and principles of this science and, to some extent, the linguistics of other nations. The few scholars who have been successfully active in both philology and linguistics made a study of both sciences, — a twofold task exceeding the abilities of most men; there has been on the other hand some confusion, beyond that in name, of the two sciences, usually in the shape of philologists who neglected the genuine values of their own science for amateurish but pedantic pseudo-linguistics.

Aside from the practical relation of linguistics to philology, there is an intrinsic connection between them, which, however, has been overestimated rather than neglected. This connection inheres in the fact that language is the most elementary cultural activity and bears traces, always, of the more deliberate cultural achievements of a nation, both in the clearness and flexibility of its syntactic and stylistic forms and in the vocabulary. The cultural features of the latter are revealed, of course, by etymology, in the study of semantic changes and word-borrowings.

b) *To literary history and criticism* (German *Literaturwissenschaft*). The science of literary history, recently also named (in my opinion, misnamed) 'comparative literature', has like linguistics, grown out of philology, with the aim of studying not the cultural achievements of this or that nation, but the development of literature (storytelling, poetry, drama, and so on) among nations, groups of nations (such as western Europe), and among mankind universally. As the instrument of literature is language, the student of literature needs a general, if elementary knowledge of the nature and development of language; as, on the other hand, the use of language in literature is a powerful factor in the history of the former, the linguist must often consult the student of letters.[1])

c) *To history*. Since language changes in time, its history is part of that of the speaking community. This is true most evidently of the external history of language, — of its differentiation into dialects, its uniformization by a standard form of speech, its spread over tributary peoples, or of a nation's adoption of an alien language

---

1) Utterly unscientific is the notion that linguistics is in some way an illegitimate rival of the study of literature, and that any and all linguistic students ought properly to transfer their activity to the latter field. This notion is an offshoot of the idea that only professional study of literature enables one to love or understand it. As a matter of fact, linguistic scholars, owing to their contact with texts of various languages, are often fair connoisseurs of literature

under conquest. It is no less true, however, of the internal history, where every change of language is of course really a historic event.

Nevertheless, historians have not, as a rule, included linguistic history in their studies or treatises. The exceptions are twofold. Wherever there has been a conscious linguistic activity, especially in the formation or spread of a standard or literary language, history has taken notice. Thus, of the history of the English language, the rise of London English during the Chaucerian period, of the history of German, the origin of Standard German in the imperial offices and in Luther's Bible-translation, have alone been included in the histories of these nations. While this exclusion of most linguistic history has been tacitly made, it can be justified, if one limits history to those events in which deliberate individual action has demonstrably or presumably played a part. The second phase of linguistic development which has been included in history is the testimony of vocabulary to material surroundings and events; thus the stratum of Romance loan-words introduced into English after the Norman conquest finds mention in histories of the English people. In so far as the data so furnished by language come directly from historic periods, they are useful in cultural history (German *Kulturgeschichte*); in so far as they are derived, by the comparative method, from prehistoric times, they are of moment, — though the methods of interpretation are not yet certain, — in pre-history (German *Urgeschichte*).

d) *To ethnology.* Language is the most purely communal of human activities, — the one least amenable to modification by individuals and least obscured by the secondary rationalizing explanations familiar to ethnologists. The unconscious communal grouping of ideas (formation of categories) takes place nowhere so freely as in language. This is true not only of the grammatical groupings and those implied in the vocabulary, — for every word involves a classification of experiences (p. 63), — but even of the sound-system, which represents a communal selection of a limited number of places of articulation and manners of articulation from among a possible infinite variety (p. 53).

Thus the language of any single community at a given time is an important part of the ethnologic data concerning it. This does not mean, however, that linguistics is part of ethnology, for it is only the descriptive data which the two sciences have in common. The linguist can collect these data and proceed to the interpretation of their origin and relation to other forms of speech, or at least to their insertion into a general scheme of linguistic development and distribution; their comparison with the other ethnic data, such as those of religion, myth, and custom, with view to a characterization of the community, must be left to the ethnologist.

e) *To psychology.* The relation of linguistics to psychology is, on the one hand, implied in the basic position of the latter among the mental sciences. These sciences, studying the various activities of man, demand in differing degrees but none the less universally, a constant psychologic interpretation. Perhaps this is but negatively true: perhaps the student of a mental science could and ideally should refrain from any running psychologic interpretation; in practice, however, such interpretation is unavoidable. In describing an analogic or semantic change, for instance, linguists most usually outline the conditions of mental predisposition which brought it about. If they do not do this in terms of scientific psychology, they will resort to rationalizing 'popular psychology', — to such explanations as that the new form was desired for greater 'clearness' or 'convenience'. As language is in its forms the least deliberate of human activities, the one in which rationalizing explanations are most grossly out of place, linguistics is, of all the mental sciences, most in need of guidance at every step by the best psychologic insight available.

On the other hand, psychology makes a wide use of the results of linguistics. Modern psychology recognizes two sources of information. The one is introspective analysis under the control of mechanical (experimental) devices which record the physical correlates of the mental process. The information so obtained applies to the activity of the individual human mind. This activity is always conditioned, however, in varying degrees, on past experiences which in themselves are products of mental action of other individuals. Thus, when one speaks a sentence, the form it takes is due to the utterances which the speaker, since infancy, has heard from the other members of his community. It is due, in other words, to a series of connected mental processes extending indefinitely back into time and occurring in an indefinite number of individuals. Such mental processes, then, as those involved in the utterance of speech cannot find their explanation in the individual, — he receives his speech-habits from others, — but must be traced for explanation from individual to individual ad infinitum. They are products of the mental action not of a single person, but of a community of individuals. These products, — not only language but also myth, art, and custom, — are the data which make possible the second phase of psychology, social psychology, (German *Völkerpsychologie*). As language, moreover, is less subject than these other activities to individual deliberate actions which interfere with the communal nexus, it is the **most** important domain in the study of social psychology.

f) *To philosophy.* I shall not presume to enter here upon the epistemologic problems in which linguistic considerations must play a part. Far more of our experience than one generally assumes is shaped by the linguistic habits in which we live. The apparatus of logic, more especially, depends upon the language we speak: the logical forms, in other words, must develop historically with the language. Not only our more abstract concepts, but also those of qualities and actions are due to linguistic forms, or rather, are the subjective phase of linguistic forms, which have been evolved in the course of time. Much of our philosophy, in consequence, moves captive in the plane of its authors' language, which it should, for freedom, transcend, — as it can only through the study of language.

To come to a simpler matter, the development of language occupies a peculiar and interesting position in the universal growth of things which philosophy essays to study. Faster than biologic evolution, so fast indeed that a change like the one from the Indo-European parent-language to modern English takes place, as it were, under our very eyes, yet incomparably slower and more unifiable, to our comprehension, than the historic change in other human activities, linguistic development may represent to us a type of progress intermediate between these.

The unfolding of the unconscious into consciousness takes place nowhere to our direct knowledge so clearly as in the activity of speech. In the spread of single languages over whole continents, and in the more conscious shaping of these languages, lies the beginning of a growing rationalization of speech. If movements such as that for an artificial world-language, which would seem to be here in the current of natural progress, have met with failure, this is because they have been but superficially rational and for the most part mere distortions of the languages we have unconsciously developed. Linguistic science has not come to a point where the artificial creation or preservation of a language is possible or even conceivable. Nevertheless, such misplaced attempts throw light upon the growing consciousness in the domain of communicative activity. One need think only of international signals, numerals, the division of time, the metric system, and the like, to see the increasing amenability of this domain to purposeful modification. It is in this development, — in such phases of it as the teaching of reading and writing and of standard languages and foreign languages in schools, in the treatment of the deaf and dumb, in stenography, in the preparation of international means of communication, — that linguistic science finds more and more its active part in human progress. In short, linguistic science is a step in the self-realization of man.

INDICES.

The numbers refer to pages.
Words in brackets are to be taken as cross-references.

1. AUTHORS, etc.

Aasen 290
Ahn 309
Apollonios Dyskolos 307
Ascham 308.

Bahlsen 306
Bernhardi 309
Bible, King James translation 289; Luther's translation 290, 321
Boas 317
Bopp 310
Bréal 172, 315
de Brosses 309
Brücke 310
Brugmann 317, 318.

Carroll 237
Chaucer 59, 195, 289, 321
Cicero 289
Colebrooke 309
Comenius 308.

Dante 289
Delbrück 315, 316, 318
Diez 311
Dionysios Thrax 307
Donatus 307.

Edkins 19
Epicureans 14.

Finck 316
Fulda 309.

von der Gabelentz 317
Goethe 289
Greenough 314
Grimm 208, 311.

Van Helmont 237
Herder 14
Herodotus 13
Homer 292
Horace 181
von Humboldt 311, 312.

International Phonetic Association 23.

Jespersen 305, 313, 314, 316
Jones 309, 310.

Karadjić 290
Kittredge 314
Koran 292.

Lloyd 313
Luther 296, 321.

Marrett 317
Meillet 318
von Miklosich 311
Müller 317.

Oertel 315
Ollendorf 309.

Pāṇini 307
Passy 99, 313

Paul 315
Pott 310
Priscian 307.

Ratichius 308
Rousseau 14.

Scherer 310
von Schlegel 310
Schleicher 310
Schottelius 309
Shakspere 195, 249, 289
Sievers 313

Steinthal 312
Sterne 249
Stoics 14
Sweet 313, 314.

Vedas 292
Verner 278.

Whitney V, 308, 312, 315
Wordsworth 247
Wundt VI, 316.

Zeuß 311.

2. LANGUAGES.

English, mentioned on almost every page, is not here included; see Table of Contents and cf. also West-Germanic, Germanic, and Indo-European.

Albanese: relationship 270, 272 (Indo-European)
Algonquian languages (Mesquaki) 171, 312
Altaic languages (Tartar, Turkish) 311
American Indians: gesture-language 4, 6; languages of (Algonquian, Athapascan, Caribbean, Chinook jargon, Greenlandish, Lule, Nahwatl, Tsimshian): objectivity 63, f., genders 109, diversity 262, decrease 262, 264, loan-words in English 282, study 19, 312; picture-writing 7
Arabic: sounds 24, 33, 54, possessor with object 107, 149, loan-words through A. into English 282, literary language 290, study 293, 309, (Semitic)
Armenian: sounds 36, 40, relationship 270, 272, history 276, 277 (Indo-European)
Arowak: numbers 89 (Caribbean)
Aryan = Indo-Iranian
Athapascan languages 312: distribution 266, f.

Avestan: relationship 272, history 272, 276, 277, 278, study 292 (Iranian)
Aztec = Nahwatl.

Baltic languages (Lettish, Lithuanian, Prussian): qualities with object 106, relationship 270, 272, f., decrease 265 (Indo-European)
Bantu languages (Kafir, Subiya) 312; genders 109, 143, number and person as gender 143, congruence 153, 182
Basque: numbers 90
Bohemian = Čechish
Bulgarian: relationship 270, history 225, 278 (Slavic)
Burmese: relationship 312 (Indo-Chinese)
Bushman (Kham) 90: sounds 27.

Canarese: sounds 54 (Dravidian)
Caribbean languages (Arowak) 89: loan-words in English 282, 283
Caucasian languages (Georgian) 312

INDICES

Čechish: sounds 26, 29, word-stress 49, 101, relationship 270, history 215 (Slavic)
Celtic languages (Irish): emotional relations 171, relationship 270, 272, decrease 265, study 311 (Indo-European)
Chinese: sounds 24, 51, 54, 55, writing 22, words 85, f., 98, word-form 93, 101, derivation 152, 168, homonymy 207, compounds 97, 161, 189, parts of speech 126, f., 128 — not as in English 112, f., 126, sentence-stress 53, sentence-pitch 177, word-order 113, 115—7, 119, 188, congruence 130, f., tense 68, f., 144, number 108, 142, interrogation 92, dialects 22, relationship 312, literary language 22, 292, study 19, 292 (Indo-Chinese)
Chinook jargon 262
Cistercian monks' gesture-language 5.

Danish: sounds 29, f., 33, 40, genders 109, relationship 268, influence of Latin 282 (Scandinavian)
Dayak: 157 (Malayan)
Dravidian languages (Canarese) 312: influence upon Indic 220 (cf. 192)
Dutch 237: sounds 28, relationship 266, f., 269, history 230, standard language 265, study 318 (West Germanic).

Finnish: cases 107, f., 144, relationship 311 (Uralic)
French: sounds 27—40, 44, f., writing 22, 300, words 87—90, 163, liaison 99—102, 257, genders 109, sentence 48, 53, 99, 171, 173, 175, 257, f., history 90, 214, 225, 232, 235, 241, f., 244, 248, 255—8, 274, 287, spread 262, 264, standard language 264, 289, f., relationship 266, loan-words in English 212, 225, 281—4, 287 study VI, 300, 305, 317, 319 (Romance)
Frisian: history 267, 274, f., relationship 266—9, study 318 (West-Germanic).

Georgian: sounds 40, sentence 110, 173, f., relationship 312. (Caucasian)
German: sounds 19, 24, 28—40, 51—3, 55, 195, 210, 219, writing 22, words 49, 75, 81, f., 86—9, 162, 164, derivation 106, 207, genders 109, 129, f., 142, f., 151, inflection 87, 93, 129, f., 143, f., 147, f., 153, f., 156, 180, 184, 186, sentence 48, 93, 173, 191, 193, f., history 208, f., 213, f., 216, f., 230, 232—5, 242, 244, f., 249, f., 274, f., 277, f., 281—6, loans from Latin 216, f., 281, 283, loan-words in English 70, 281, relationship 264—7, 269, standard language 265, 289, f., 321, study 301, 303—5, 317, 319 (West-Germanic)
Germanic languages (Gothic, Scandinavian, West-Germanic) 269; history 201, 206, 208, 211, 214—6, 218, 221, 229 f., 234, 272, 276—9, 285, relationship 269, f., study 311, 317, f. (Indo-European)
Gothic: history 272, 275—9, relationship 269, study VI, 218. (Germanic)
Greek: sounds 32, 47, 51, 152, writing 20, derivation 152, composition 164, inflection 92, 109, 116, f., 142, 145—8, 156—7, 164, sentence 116, f., 184,

history 116, f., 217, f., 230, 243, 265 f., 272, 276—9, loan-words from G. 237, 282—4, relationship 261, f., 270, literary languages 263, 289, f., study 292, 307—10, 317 (Indo-European)
Greenlandish: sounds 33, 54, inflection 107, 110, f., 135, 149, f., 174, objectivity 104, f., sentence 110, f., 179, 190, f.

Hamitic languages 311
Hebrew: sounds 24, loan-words through H. into English 282, literary language 290, study 292, 307, 309 (Semitic)
Hindustani 262 (Indic)
Hottentot 27
Hungarian 31, 311 (Uralic).

Icelandic: word-stress 49, 101 relationship 268, history 275, 277, f. (Scandinavian)
India, languages of: sounds 28, 30, 54, 256, writing 20, sentence 192; see Dravidian and Indic
Indians see Americans Indians, Indic languages (Hindustani, Sanskrit) 219, f., 270 (Indo-Iranian)
Indo-Chinese languages (Chinese) 312
Indo-European languages (Albanese, Armenian, Baltic, Celtic, Germanic, Greek, Indo-Iranian, Italic, Slavic, Tocharic) 269—73, 276—80, sentence 172, Primitive I.-E. 106, 201, 225, 229, 234, 254, 256, f., study 310—2, 317, f.
Indo-Iranian languages (Indic, Iranian) 270, 277, f. (Indo-European)
Iranian languages (Avestan) 270, 272 (Indo-Iranian).
Irish: sound-variation 102, f., 128, f., 131, 151, 257, sentence 175, 256, f., history 272, 276—8 Celtic)
Italian: sounds 29, 31, f., 45, 53, 92, derivation 105, 165, verb 107, pronoun 88, genders 132, history 214, f., 225, 227, 274, relationship 266, literary language 289 (Romance)
Italic languages (Latin) 270, 272, 285 (Indo-European).

Japanese 20, 48, 70, 88, 157
Javanese, see Kavi.

Kafir 153—5, 182 (Bantu)
Kavi 311 (Malayan)
Kham 90 (Bushman).

Latin (for modern development see Romance): writing 20, f., inflection 135, 154—7, tenses 68, 144, voice 115, 145, 173, genders 103, cases 92, 108, 115, f., 144, f., 185—7, pronouns 88, f., 118, 176, adjective 106, sentence 68, f., 98, f., 107, 111, f., 118, 148, 162, 168, f., 172, 176, 179, 192, 194, 258, congruence 181, word-order 171, 186, f., history 212—5, 217, f., 225, 230, 232, 241—4, 248, 255, f., 272, 274, 276—8, 283, 287, loans from other Italic languages 285, loans to English 106, 212, 281, 284, 287, to German 281, 283, influence on other languages 282, relationship 270, spread 257, 262—4, 266, f., 289, literary language 289, f., study 292, 307—10, 317 (Italic)
Lettish 24, 270 (Baltic)
Lithuanian: sounds 31, 47, 51, derivation 106, relationship 270, history 272, f., 277, f. (Baltic)
Lule 150, 174.

INDICES

Malay 85, f., 86, 88, 93, 98, 156, f., 261, f. (Malayan)
Malayan languages (Dayak, Kavi, Malay) 132, 157. Malayo-Polynesian)
Malayo-Polynesian languages (Malayan, Polynesian) 312
Mesquaki 171 (Algonquian).

Nahwatl: inflection 135, 146, 149, 157, compounds 160, 164, f., 254, sentence 98, 167, 169, 179, 253
North Germanic — Scandinavian
Norwegian: sounds 31, 37, f., 51, 53, 92, 100, f., 152, 164, 177, pronouns 89, genders 109, derivation 152, composition 164, sentence 173, 177, relationship 261, 268, influence of Latin 282, literary languages 290 (Scandinavian).

Oscan 270 (Italic).

Polish: sounds 31, f., 49, 101, pronouns 88, history 215, relationship 270 (Slavic)
Polynesian languages 54, f. (Malayo-Polynesian)
Portuguese 264, 266, 282 (Romance).

Romance languages (French, Italian, Portuguese, Roumanian, Spanish): sounds 40, 44, f., 47, 53, f., derivation 106, 248, genders 143, relationship 262, f., 266, f., history 255, f., 274, spread 264, study 220, 311, 317, 321 (See Latin)
Roumanian 266 (Romance)
Russian: sounds 31, 36, 38, 40, f., 45, 48, f., 51, 65, 152, pronoun 65, 88, adjective 111, 135, manner 145, sentence 92, 111, 172—4, history 212, f., 215, influence of other languages 282, relationship 270, spread 262, literary language 290 (Slavic).

Sanskrit: sounds 26, 51, 54, sandhi 102, 128, inflection 155, numbers 142, cases 144, 167, 184, voices 145, f., conjugations 145, f., reduplication 156, f., compounds 106, 160, f., 164, sentence 192, 194, relationship 230, history 218, 220, 230, 272, 276—9, literary language 290, study 292, 307, 309, f., 317 (Indic)
Scandinavian languages (Danish, Icelandic, Norwegian, Swedish) 143, 173, 268, f., relationship 269, history 230, 275, loans to English 285, study 318 (Germanic)
Semitic languages (Arabic, Hebrew) 33, 107, 133, 311
Servian 270, 290 (Slavic)
Siamese 312 (Indo-Chinese)
Slavic languages (Bulgarian, Čech, Polish, Russian, Servian): sounds 29, f., 32, 40, f., 44, f., 47, 53, f., pronoun 89, genders 142, manner 145, derivation 106, sentence 92, history 215, 218, 225, 227, 265, 272, f., influence of other languages 282, relationship 270, study 220, 311, 317 (Indo-European)
Spanish: sounds 28, 31, f., history 248, 274, loans to English 282, f., relationship 266, spread 262, 264, standard language 264 (Romance)
Subiya 143, 182 (Bantu)
Swedish: sounds 30, 37, 51, 53, 100, f., 152, relationship 268, influence of Latin 282 (Scandinavian).

332 INDICES

Tartar 311 (Altaic)
Tibetan 312 (Indo-Chinese)
Tocharic 272 (Indo-European)
Tsimshian 151, 157, 253
Turkish: sounds 36, inflection 95, f., sentence 192, relationship 311 (Altaic).

Umbrian 270 (Italic)
Ural-Altaic languages (Altaic, Uralic) 311

Uralic languages (Finnish, Hungarian) 107, 144, 311 (Ural-Altaic).

West - Germanic languages (Dutch, English, Frisian, German) 200, 266, f., relationship 268, f., history 229, 274, f., 279, 281, 285 (Germanic)
Wolof 174.

2. SUBJECTS.

Ablaut 153, 229
abnormal sibilants 31
absolutive 178, f., 254
abstract words 65, f.
action-words 65, f.
actor and action categories 67, f., 112, 115, 121, 148, 172—5
adaptation 225, f.
adjective 122, f.
adverb 123, f.
affix 153—6
alphabet 20
alveolars 28
analogic change 59, f., 196, 221—37
analysis of experience 59—63, 85—90, 142, 237, f.
anaphoric words 89
animals 56, f.
aphasia 67
apperception 57, f., 60, f.
article 117, f., 175, f.
articulation 19—55, 195, f., 299, f.
arytenoids 24, 26
aspect, see manner
aspirate initial 26, 33, 40; a. stop 40, 53, f.
assimilation 59, f., 196, f., 219, 221—51, 283, f.
assimilation of articulations 214—6
association 57, f., 66, f., 69, f.,

82, 120, 133, f., 139—41, 197, 219, 221—51
attribute, attribution 61, 110, f., 122, 149, f.
attributive languages, see objective
automatic sound variation 23, 54, f., 151, 155, f., 220, f., 250.

Back vowels 34
bilabials 28
blade 30, f.
breath 9, 24, 26
breathed, see unvoiced.

Cartilage glottis 26
case 107, f., 122, 143, f., 183, f.
categories 67—9
cerebrals 30
change 15, f., 195—258
child 10—3, 228
choke 40; cf. glottal stop
close syllable stress 47
command 76, 121
comparative method 200, f., 274—80
compound syllable pitch 51, f.; c. s. stress 47, 52
compound words 96—8, 104, 106, 140, 159—66, 235, f., 254
concept 58, 63, 65, f., 85—7
condensation 241—3

congruence 127—31, 180—2
conjunction 124, 193, f.
consonants 28—33, 153
contamination 224, f.
coronals 28—30
cross-reference 178—80.

Deaf-mutes 5
declarative, see statement
definite and indefinite categories 117, f., 175, f.
deictic words 64, f., 88, f.
dentals 28—31
derivation 141, 150, f.
dialects 260, f.
diminutive 105, f.
diphthong 43
discursive relations 60—2, 110—4, 169—70
dissimiliation 216—8, 283
dominant element of experience 7, 58, 63, 83, f., 238—51; d. e. in sentence 50, f., 113, f., 170, f., 175.
dorsals 28, 30—3
doubled 45, 52, f.
duration 52, f.

Emotional relations in sentence 49, f., 113, 170, f.; cf. dominant element
enclitics 49, 100
ethnology 256, 317, 321, f.
etymology 244, f., 281, f.
evolution of language 252—6
exclamation 70, 73—7, 91, f., 121
exclusive 88
exocentric compounds 161
explosives, see stops
expressive movements 1—10.

Formational elements 62, f., 79, f., 93—6, 108—9, 221—37
fortes 39, 53, f.
fricatives, see spirants
front vowels 34.

Geminate, see doubled
gender 109, 129, f., 142, f., 182
gestures 4—7, 14, f.
glides 40, f.
glottal stop 24, f., 33, 40
glottis 24—6, 40
government 182—6
grammar 289, 302—4, 307—9
Grimm's law 208
group stress 48—50
gums 28—30.

Haplology 217
high vowels 34
homonymy 125, 157, f., 181, 185, 206, f.
hypotaxis 191, 193, f.

Imperative 92, 147, f.
inclusive 88
infinitive 118, f., 121
infix 155, f.
inflection 140—50
intensity, see stress
interdental 28
interjection 73—7, 124
interrogative, see question
invention of words 12, 236, f.

Kernel 153, f.

Labials 28
labialized 41
labiodentals 28
languages 261, f.
laryngeals 24, f., 33
larynx 24, 33
laterals 29, f., 43
lenes 39, 53, f.
length, see duration
liaison, see sandhi
lips 28, 31, 34, 41
literary languages 290, 292
loan-words 70, 106, 132, 280—5
local relations 107, f., 116, f.
logical, see discursive
loose, see wide

loudness, see stress
low vowels 34
lungs 9, 24.

Manner of action 144, f.
manner of articulation 54, 208
material relations in sentence 114—9, 171—4
meaning, see association, semantic change
metaphor 247—9
metathesis 216, f., 283
mid vowels 34
mixed vowels 34
mixture of articulations 41
mixture of dialects 284, f.
mode 146—8
morphologic categories 68—70, 103, 141—50
morphologic classes 108—10, 120—40, 221—37
morphologic sound-variation 151—8
morphology 110, 120—66, 221—87
murmur 25, f.
musical sound 27.

Names 247, f.
narrow vowels 84
nasals 27, f., 43
nasalized 27, f., 88
natural syllables 42—6
noise 27
nominal languages, see objective
non-syllabics 42, f.
noun 111, f., 121, f., 136—8
number 121, f., 141, f., 148, f.
numerals 89, f.
numeratives 130, f.
nursery words 11, f.

Object affected 115, f., 121, 127, 143, 148, f., 176, 187
objective languages 64, 104, f., 107, 111
object-words 63, f.

onomatopoeia 81
open syllable stress 47
oral articulation 27—38
origin of language 13—6
orthography, see writing
outcry 9, 73.

Palatals 31, f.
palatalization 214, f.
palatalized articulation 31, 41
palate 27—31
parallel forms 141
parataxis 191, 193, f.
participle, see verbal adjective
parts of speech 112, 120—7
person 121, 148, f.
philology 307, f., 319, f.
phonetic alphabet 23, 300
phonetic change, ph. law, see sound-change
phonetic-semantic parallelism 136, f.
phonetic-semantic word-classes 131—5
phonetics 19, 299, 313
picture-writing 7, 20
pitch 25, 51, f., 151, f., 177, f.
place of articulation 54, 208
plain stops, see pure
post-dentals 28—30
predicate, predication 61, 64, 110, f., 121
prefix 155—6
preposition 117, 124, 143
primitive creations 235
proclitics 49, 100
pronoun 64, f., 87—9, 123, 143
pronunciation, see articulation
proportional analogy 226, f.
psychology VI, 14, 222—4
pun 99, f.
pure initial 40
pure stop 40, 53, f.

Quality-words 65, f.
quantity, see duration
question 52, 71, 91, f.

INDICES 335

Reduplication 156, f.
relation 66, 105, 107, f.
relative pronoun 193, f.
root 154
rounded 31, 34, 41.

Sandhi 101, f.
semantic change 7, 16, 78, 237—51
semantic parallelism 139
semi-vowels 42
sentence 48—53, 60—3, 76, 110—9, 167—94
sentence-equivalents 170
sentence-pitch 51, f., 92, 176—8
sentence-word 64, 111, f., 253
serial relation 113, 124
set phrase 116, f., 122, 124, 188, f., 248, f., 286, f.
sibilants 30, f.
soft palate 32; cf. velum
song 10
sonority 42—5
sound 8, f., 14
sound-change 16, 77, 202—21
sound-symbolism 79, f., 93, 235, f.
sound-variation, see automatic, morphologic
spelling, see writing
spirants 27, f.
standard languages 288—90.
statement 71, 91, f.
stops 27, f., 39, f.
stress 25, 42—53, 152, 177, f.
stress-group 48—50
stress-syllable 44—8, 52, f.
subject 61, 110, f., 115, 121
subordinate clause 124, 190—4
substitution of sounds 219, f.
suction-sounds 27
suffix 154
suppletion 158, f.
syllabaries 20
syllabics 42—7
syllable 42—53
syllable-boundary 43—6

syllable-pitch 51, f.
syllable-stress 43—7
syntactic categories 68, f., 112, 115, 117, f., 121, 174—6
syntax 119, 167—94.

Teeth 29—32
tense 62, 68—70, 121, 144, 183
tense vowels, see narrow
tone-color 27—29, f.
tongue 27—33
total experience 56—63
transitive verbs 176; t. words 127
translation 300, f.
trills 29, 33, 43
triphthong 43.

Umlaut 152, 230, f.
unrounded 34
unvoiced 25
uvula 27, 33
uvulars 32, f.

Velars 32
velum 26, f.
verb 111, f., 121, 138, f.
verbal adjective 122, 191, f.
verbal noun 122
Verner's law 216, 229
vocal chords 9, f., 24—6, 33
vocative 92, 144
voice 9, 25
voiced 25
voices of verb 145, f.
vowels 27, 33—8, 152, f.

Whisper 26
wide vowels 34
word 48—51, 62—70, 82—90, 93—110, 120—66, 221—51
word-order 92, 114—8, 127, f., 185—8, 193, f.
word-pitch 51
word-stress 48—50
writing 7, f., 19—24, 287, f.

An Important Work by a Great Philologist

SWEET'S PRACTICAL STUDY OF LANGUAGES
By Dr. Henry Sweet, of Oxford, England. xiv—280 pp. 12mo. $1.50.

The body of this book is given to the discussion (reinforced by telling illustrations) of practical problems which daily confront the teacher of languages—the choice and proper use of grammar and dictionary, the solution of reading matter, the use of translation, composition, conversation, etc. An exposition of the photometric basis of language study occupies the first few chapters.

The Nation:—Few schoolmasters are so perfect in their art as to find no profit in the perusal of this rich offering of recorded experience, original suggestion, and independent criticism. . . . The teacher will discover an abundance of practical ideas and precepts that cannot fail to stimulate reflection. . . . The personal note lends additional interest to a work which from cover to cover contains not a page that is dull or commonplace.

J. W. Bright, Professor in Johns Hopkins University:—It is admirably done, and will be found instructive both to the scholar and to the general reader, and uniformly suggestive throughout a surprisingly wide range of topics.

The Outlook:—Represents the advanced line of the demand for reform of antiquated or unsound methods of language study. The author's comprehensive grasp both of general principles and minute details covers the field with a thoroughness worthy of all praise.

Journal of Pedagogy:—For the teacher who is eager to make the learning of foreign languages—ancient and modern—yield better educational results than is often the case there is no more suggestive and stimulating volume in English.

Chicago Evening Post:—Certainly the best work the presses have issued bearing upon this particular study.

The Dial:—A philosophical study of method in teaching the foreign languages, ancient and modern. . . . His book is of great value to teachers.

HENRY HOLT AND COMPANY
PUBLISHERS   NEW YORK

BELLOWS'S FRENCH AND ENGLISH DICTIONARY. *Revised Edition*

Thoroly revised and enlarged by WILLIAM BELLOWS, with the assistance of AUGUSTE MARROT and GUSTAVE FRITEAU. 690 pp. 12mo. $1.50.

Among the original features embodied in this work may be mentioned:

1. The arrangement of both language divisions (French-English, English-French) concurrently on the same page: words of a similar spelling and meaning in both languages being shown in the French division only.
2. The distinguishing of genders by the use of different types—all feminine words being shown in italic.
3. The indication, in French words, of the liaison or of its absence.
4. The conjugations of all the French irregular verbs, and the reference by number to such conjugations from the text of the dictionary.
5. The tables giving full details of comparison between the metric and the British systems of weights and measures.
6. The table giving the chief events in the history of France and England.
7. The rendering of many technical and other words and phrases not given in any other dictionary.

Its most notable feature is its unparalleled richness in idiomatic and colloquial renderings in both languages. Upon this point Oliver Wendell Holmes, in commenting on the *Pocket Edition,* said:

"I have been reading a recent French work which has a great number of slang words in it; indeed it was written partly to show up the new French vocabulary; but it has also a great number of familiar conversational phrases. Now I found that your little microscopic dictionary was equal to the hard task I put upon it; surprising me by the richness of its little columns, and the exceedingly knowing way in which common French colloquialisms were rendered into corresponding English ones. I was fairly astonished that such an atom of a book could be such a cyclopedia of phrases. I consider the little lexicon the very gem of my library."

HENRY HOLT AND COMPANY
PUBLISHERS NEW YORK

BELLOWS'S A NEW GERMAN-ENGLISH AND ENGLISH-GERMAN DICTIONARY

By MAX BELLOWS, proofs revised by CLARENCE SHERWOOD and WILHELM JOHANN EGGERS. 806 pp. 12mo. $1.75

On the same general plan as John Bellow's *French and English Pocket Dictionary:* both alphabets on one page, complete vocabulary of current speech, numerous devices for ready reference, invaluable reference tables, etc. Roman type is used thruout, a prime recommendation to a growing class of readers.

The subject matter has been brought thoroughly up to date, and in order to make it as useful as possible to a wide circle of readers, a great number of technical terms and expressions are included. Among special subjects thus dealt with may be mentioned nautical science, typography, and many branches of engineering, including such recent developments of the latter as automobilism and aviation. In the spelling of German words the most recent orthography has been followed, viz., that given in the "Rechtschreibung der Buchdruckereien deutscher Sprache," a work carried out by Dr. Konrad Duden by the direction and with the co-operation of the printers' societies of Germany, Austria, and Switzerland, and regarded in those countries as authoritative.

W. H. CARRUTH, *Stanford University:*—I find it quite as serviceable as the Bellows *French Dictionary.* I know of no better work within the same compass.

THE NATION:—A marvel of compactness. . . . The vocabulary includes the most recent technical terms in both languages. Examples seem at first, as is inevitable in a relatively small manual, somewhat few under the more common words; but they are really more abundant than they seem; they clearly reveal the meaning and the uses of the word in question, and they have the true idiomatic ring in both tongues. The page is unusually open and handsome.

WILLIAM LYON PHELPS, *Yale University:*—The Bellows are absolutely the most useful, most practical, most sensible dictionaries of German and French that I have ever seen. I am going to call the attention of my classes to them.

HENRY HOLT AND COMPANY
PUBLISHERS   **NEW YORK**

CPSIA information can be obtained
at www.ICGtesting.com
Printed in the USA
LVHW010814060221
678554LV00006B/55